EXCEL MADE EASY

The Complete Guide to Becoming an Excel Expert, Save Time and Accelerate Your Career (With Over 150 Illustrations)

ALEX MORRISON

TABLE OF CONTENTS

INTRODUCTION: FROM EXCEL FRUSTRATION TO MASTERY

Transform from Excel novice to confident data master, gaining the skills to complete in 30 minutes reports that now take you 2 hours

Your Journey to Excel Expertise

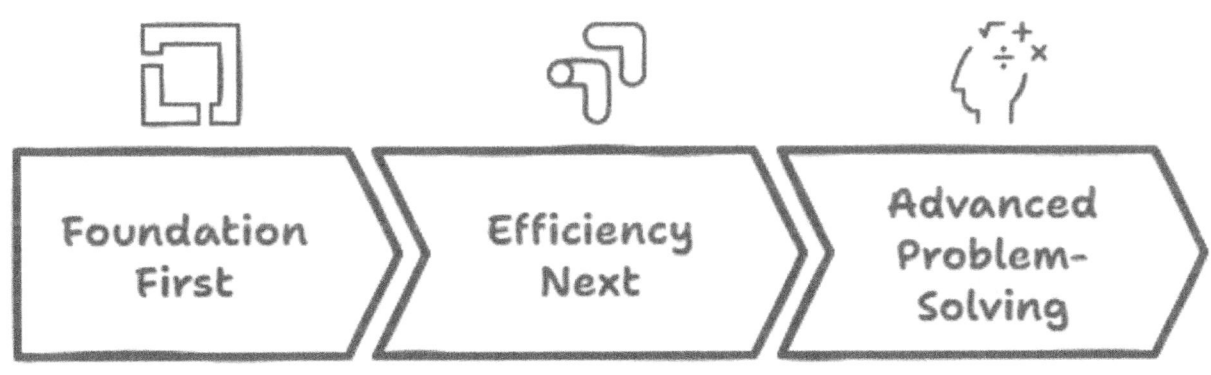

Strategic Excel Learning Path

Foundation First

Start with essential skills like data entry and basic formulas

Efficiency Next

Focus on shortcuts and automation for improved efficiency

Advanced Problem-Solving

Master PivotTables and macros to solve complex problems

Mastering Excel isn't about memorizing endless formulas or navigating through a maze of complex menus—it's about understanding how to harness its power to solve real-world problems. Whether you're creating reports, automating tasks, or analyzing data to drive business decisions, Excel is a tool that, once mastered, can elevate your career in ways you never imagined. But how do you go from struggling with spreadsheets to becoming the go-to Excel expert in your workplace? The answer lies in **building a structured approach, focusing on real-world applications, and continuously improving your efficiency**.

The Learning Curve: From Struggle to Mastery

If you've ever watched a colleague seemingly **work magic** in Excel—creating flawless reports, using complex formulas effortlessly, or analyzing large datasets in seconds—you might have thought, *"I'll never get there."* But here's the truth: **Excel mastery isn't about talent; it's about strategy and practice**.

Think of learning Excel as **learning a new language**. At first, the symbols and commands may seem like gibberish, but with time, repetition, and the right guidance, patterns start to emerge. Soon, you're not just copying formulas—you're **understanding their logic**, applying them to new scenarios, and solving problems efficiently.

Many professionals hit a plateau in their Excel skills because they rely on **trial and error** rather than structured learning. They learn just enough to get by—until they encounter a problem they don't know how to solve. That's where the right approach changes everything.

Adopting a Strategic Learning Method

The key to becoming proficient in Excel isn't cramming all its features at once—it's learning **the right skills in the right order**. Here's a simple but highly effective **three-stage approach** to Excel mastery:

1. **Foundation First:** Start with the essentials—data entry, formatting, and basic formulas like SUM, AVERAGE, and IF statements. These may seem simple, but mastering them early on **builds confidence** and prevents errors later.
2. **Efficiency Next:** Once comfortable with the basics, shift focus to **shortcuts, automation, and data management techniques**. This is where Excel stops feeling like manual labor and starts working for you.
3. **Advanced Problem-Solving:** Finally, dive into **PivotTables, complex formulas, Power Query, and automation with macros**. This is where you transition from being a user to being **an Excel expert who solves real business problems**.

By following this structured learning process, you **reduce frustration, speed up mastery, and retain skills better** than through random, unstructured learning.

Applying Excel to Real-World Challenges

Imagine this scenario: You've just been assigned the task of preparing **a monthly sales report**. You could manually enter numbers, apply basic formatting, and spend hours calculating totals—or, you could automate the entire process using **PivotTables, formulas, and conditional formatting** to highlight trends at a glance.

Now, consider this: If you could cut your reporting time in half while delivering **better insights**, how would that impact your productivity? More importantly, how would it position you in your company? This is the power of Excel expertise—it transforms you from someone who simply "manages data" into someone who **extracts value from data**.

Each Excel function you learn isn't just a **technical skill**, but a **career asset**. The ability to quickly analyze data, build dynamic reports, and create error-free calculations **makes you invaluable** in any organization. And as you grow more confident, you'll no longer see Excel as a frustrating necessity—but as a powerful ally in accelerating your career.

How This Book Will Transform Your Career

Business Analysis Components

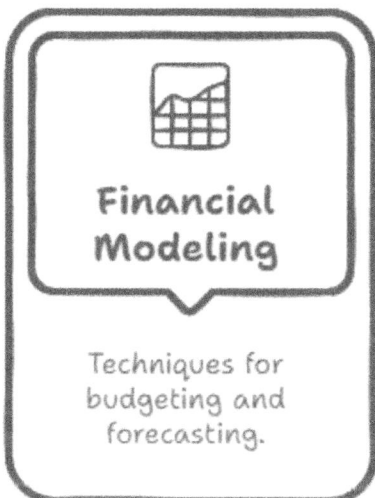

Financial Modeling

Techniques for budgeting and forecasting.

Marketing Analysis

Evaluating campaigns through data visualization tools.

Project Management

Tracking projects with automated reporting dashboards.

Mastering Excel isn't just about improving technical skills—it's about **unlocking new career opportunities, boosting productivity, and positioning yourself as an indispensable asset in your workplace**. Whether you're looking to earn a promotion, transition into a more analytical role, or simply get through your daily workload faster, this book will provide the structured, real-world approach you need to make Excel work for you—not the other way around.

From Task Executor to Decision Maker

Many professionals use Excel **reactively**—they perform tasks as assigned, input data, create reports, and follow established workflows. But the real game-changer is learning to use Excel **proactively**—to analyze data, spot trends, automate tasks, and provide insights that drive smarter business decisions.

Imagine your manager asks for a monthly performance report. You could manually compile data, calculate metrics, and format charts—a process that might take hours. Or, you could use **PivotTables, formulas, and automation tools** to generate the report in minutes, with dynamic filtering options that let stakeholders explore the data interactively. By shifting from **data entry to data analysis**, you not only **save time** but also **become a strategic thinker who adds value to discussions**.

Employers don't just want employees who can follow instructions—they want professionals who **identify inefficiencies, solve problems, and create solutions**. This book is designed to equip you with those skills, **making you the person people turn to when they need real answers from their data**.

Saving Hours Each Week With Smarter Workflows

One of the biggest workplace frustrations is spending hours on **repetitive, manual Excel tasks**. Whether it's copy-pasting data, reformatting reports, or recalculating figures, inefficient processes **drain productivity and increase the risk of costly errors**.

This book will show you how to:

- **Automate Repetitive Tasks** – Learn how to use **Excel Macros** and built-in automation tools to eliminate mundane tasks.
- **Leverage Time-Saving Shortcuts** – Master **keyboard shortcuts, formula hacks, and custom functions** to drastically speed up your workflow.
- **Build Dynamic Reports That Update Instantly** – Create **interactive dashboards** that refresh with new data, reducing manual adjustments.

By optimizing your Excel skills, you **free up time for higher-value work**, whether it's brainstorming new strategies, refining reports, or preparing for leadership roles.

Becoming the Go-To Excel Expert in Your Workplace

Every office has *that* person—the one colleagues turn to when they're stuck on an Excel problem. Maybe they need help fixing a formula, structuring a dataset, or designing an automated template. Becoming that **go-to Excel expert** doesn't just boost your reputation—it makes you an **indispensable asset to your team and company**.

This book provides **real-world case studies, practical exercises, and step-by-step tutorials** to help you gain confidence in handling complex Excel tasks. You'll learn how to **present data persuasively, build analytical tools for decision-making, and communicate insights clearly**, setting you apart from colleagues who rely on surface-level Excel skills.

A Competitive Edge in Any Industry

Regardless of your field—**finance, marketing, project management, HR, sales, or operations**—data-driven decision-making is becoming the norm. Employers increasingly seek professionals who can **interpret numbers, forecast trends, and support business strat-**

egies. With the skills from this book, you'll be better equipped to handle industry-specific Excel challenges, whether it's:

- **Financial modeling for budgeting and forecasting**
- **Marketing campaign analysis using data visualization tools**
- **Project management tracking with automated reporting dashboards**

Excel isn't just a technical tool—it's a **career accelerator**. By investing in your Excel expertise, you're investing in your **professional growth, job security, and long-term success**.

PART 1

EXCEL FOUNDATIONS – BUILDING A STRONG BASE

SETTING UP FOR SUCCESS: CUSTOMIZING YOUR EXCEL WORKSPACE

Create your personalized Excel command center with all essential tools just one click away, saving up to 45 minutes every day

Optimizing the Interface for Maximum Efficiency

When it comes to **working efficiently in Excel**, the difference between frustration and fluency often lies in how well you've customized your workspace. Most users **leave Excel's default settings untouched**, not realizing that a few simple tweaks can save **hours of work** each week. A well-optimized interface ensures that the tools you need are always **within reach**, reducing unnecessary clicks and making repetitive tasks **faster and smoother**.

Customizing the Quick Access Toolbar (QAT)

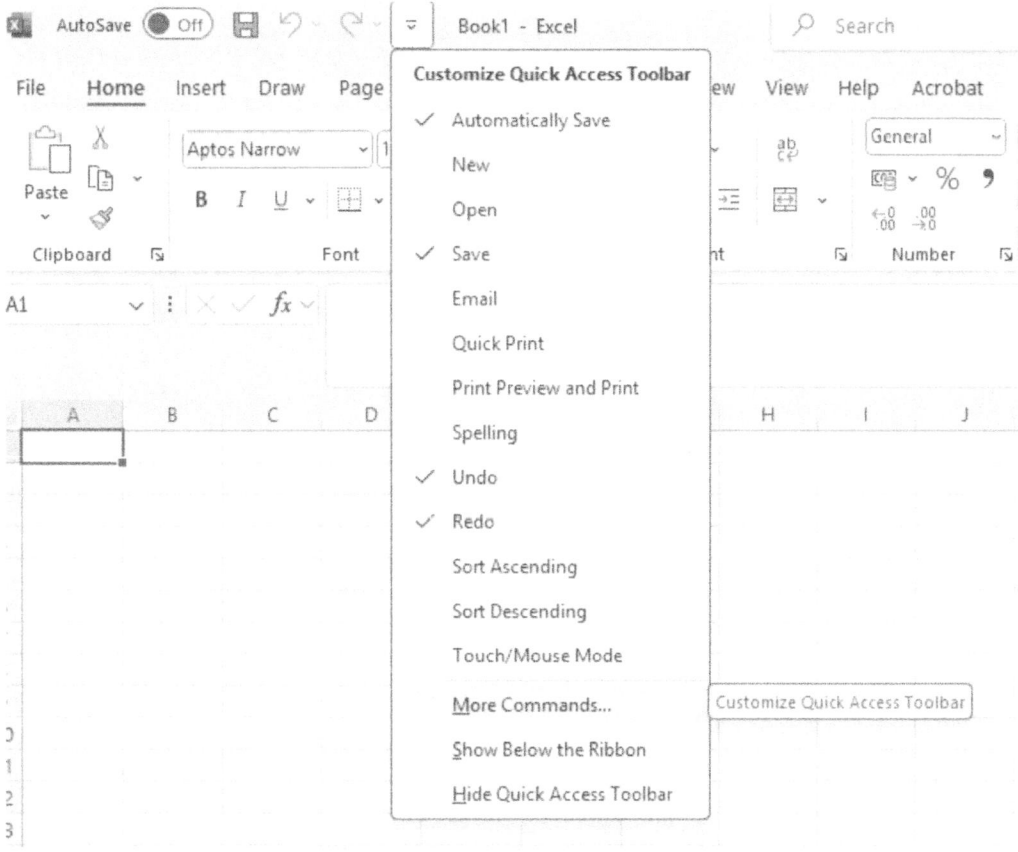

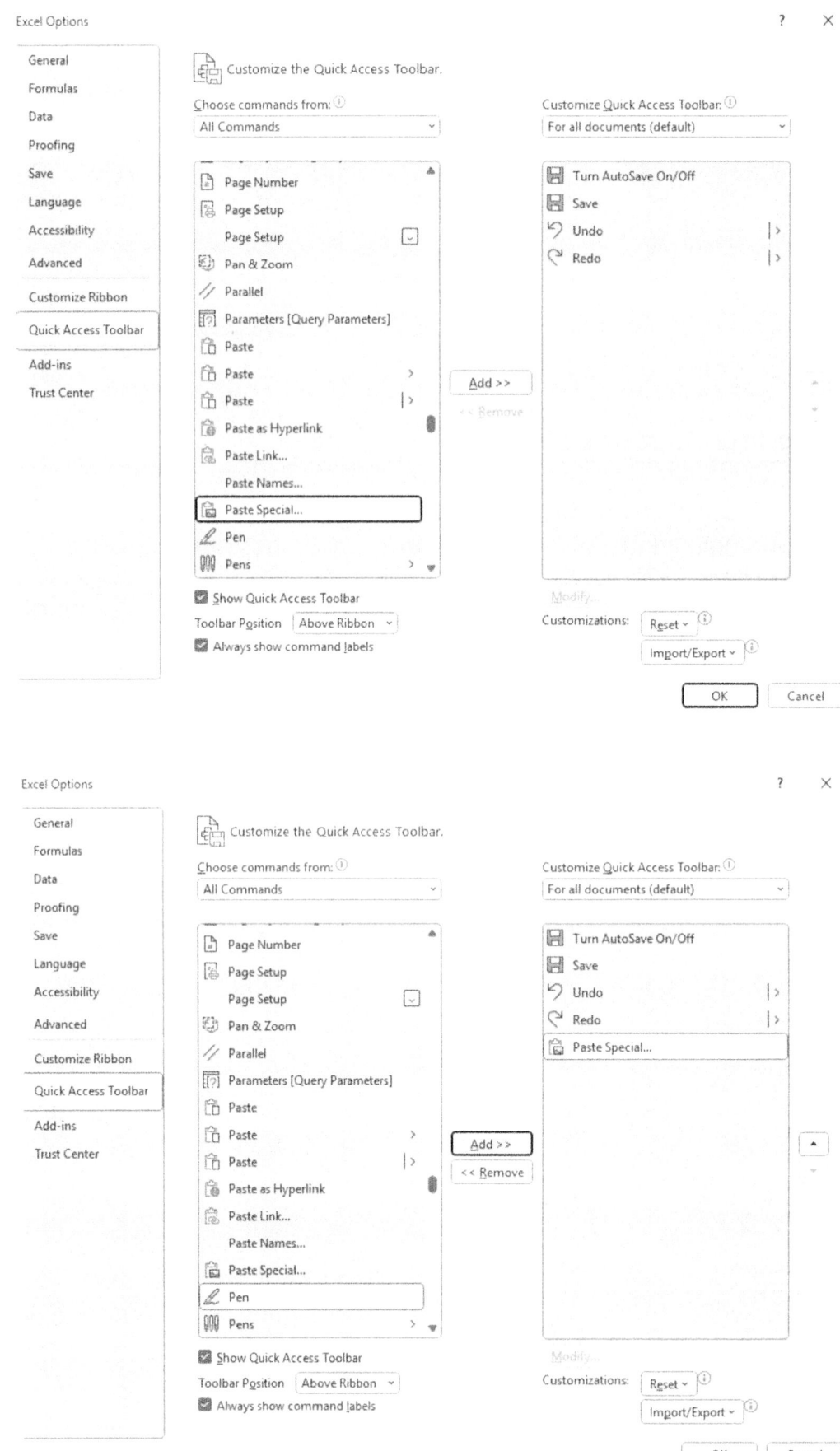

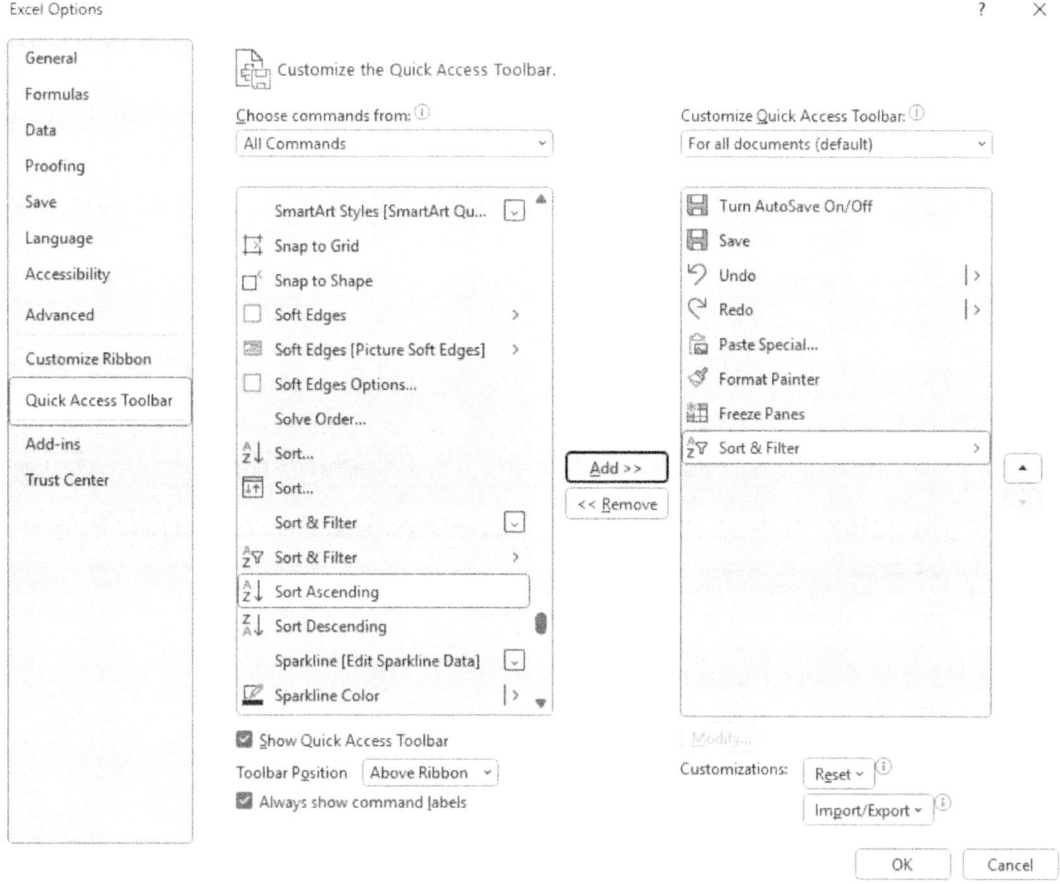

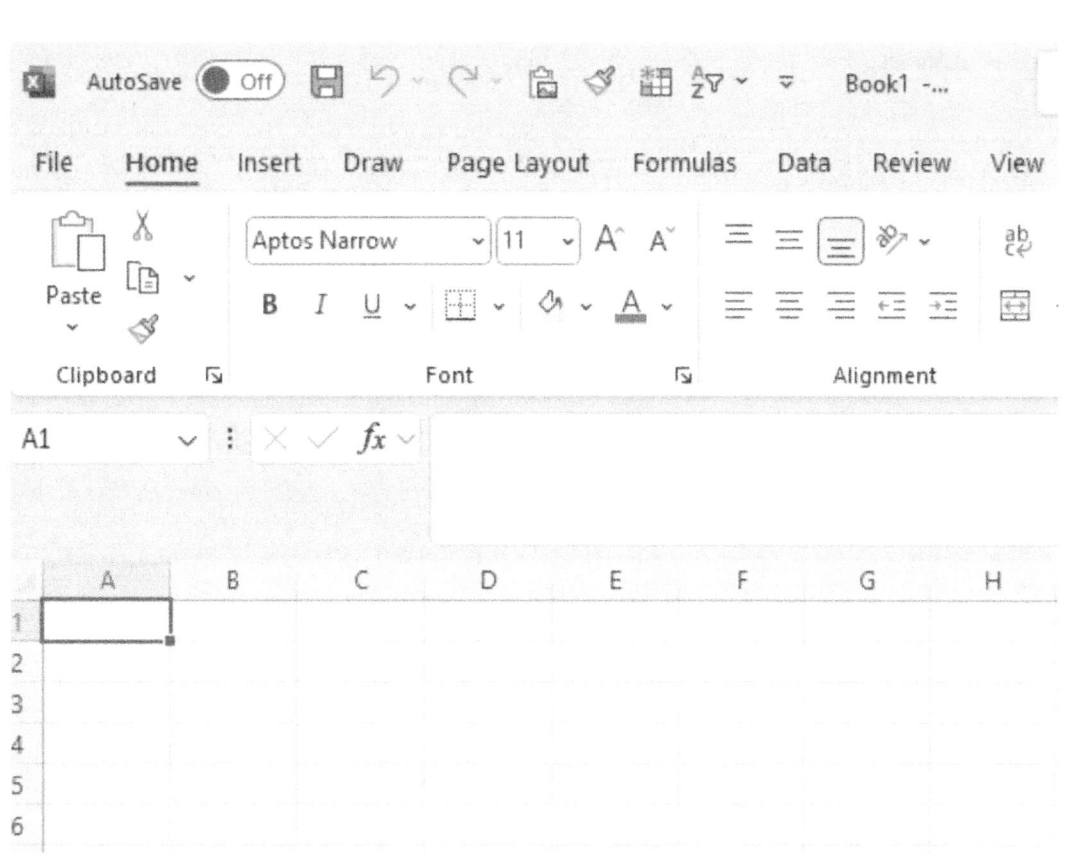

By default, Excel places commonly used commands—**Save, Undo, and Redo**—in the **Quick Access Toolbar (QAT)** at the top of the window. But did you know that you can **fully customize this toolbar** to include your most-used functions? Instead of **navigating through multiple ribbons** every time you need to insert a PivotTable, apply conditional formatting, or refresh data, you can place these functions **right at your fingertips**.

To customize the QAT:

1. Click the **dropdown arrow** next to the QAT.
2. Select **More Commands** to open the customization menu.
3. Add frequently used commands like **Paste Special, Format Painter, Freeze Panes, and Sort & Filter**.
4. Click **OK**, and your customized toolbar is ready to speed up your workflow.

This simple customization reduces time wasted **searching for features**, helping you work **more intuitively and efficiently**.

Personalizing the Ribbon for Faster Navigation

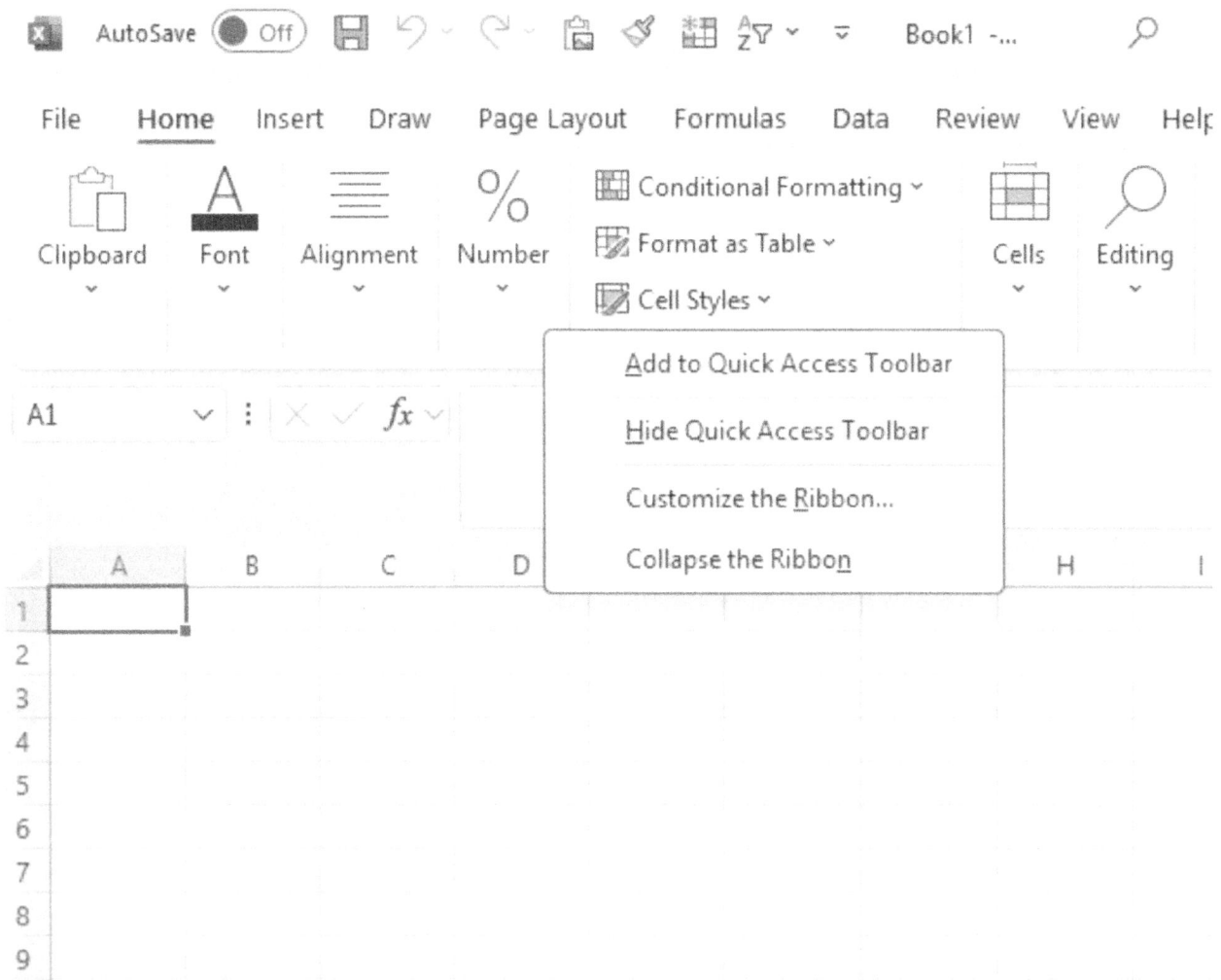

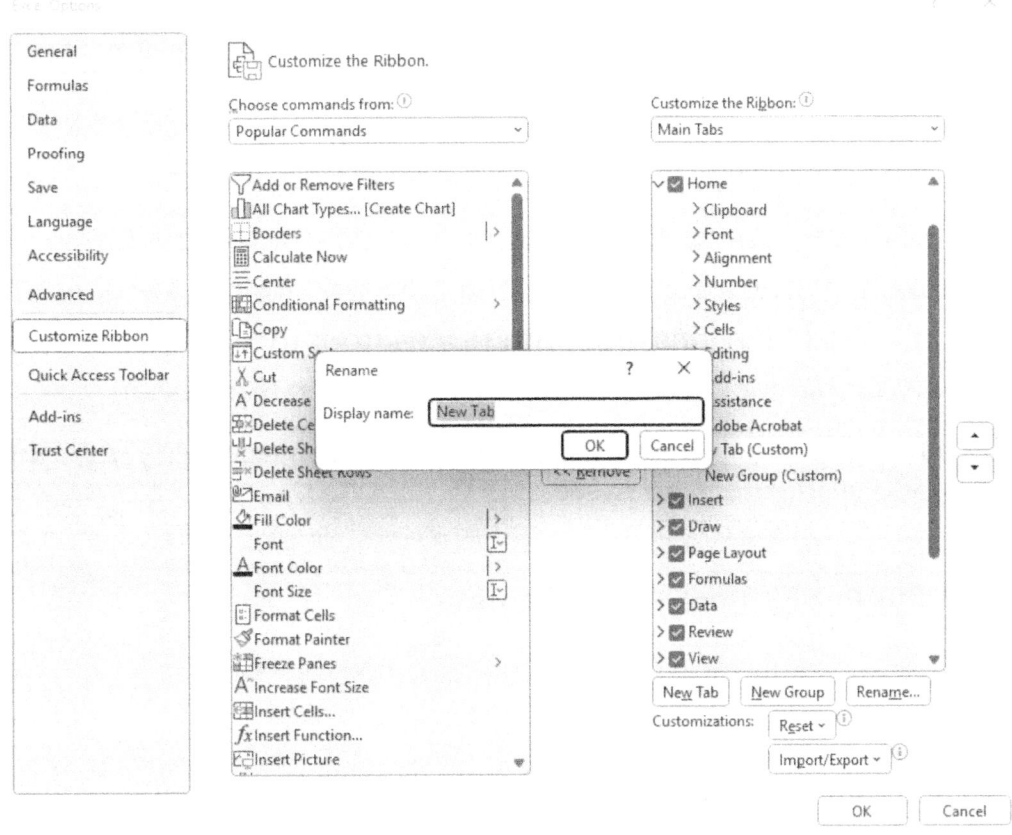

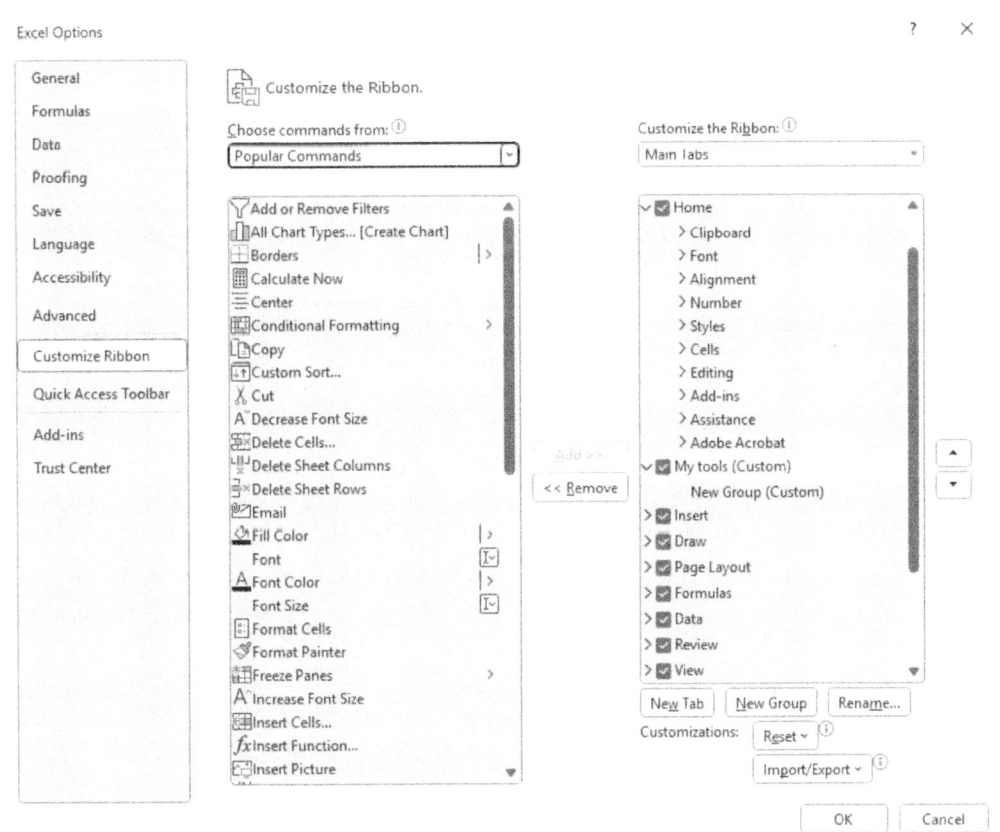

The **Ribbon** is where most of Excel's functionality lives, but **not every command is easy to find**. If you frequently use certain tools that require multiple clicks to access—such as **Text to Columns, Goal Seek, or Remove Duplicates**—you can create **a custom Ribbon tab** that consolidates everything into one easy-to-find location.

To create a custom Ribbon tab:

1. **Right-click anywhere on the Ribbon** and select **Customize the Ribbon**.
2. Click **New Tab** and name it something useful, like **My Tools** or **Productivity Boosters**.
3. Add commonly used functions and commands from the left-hand list.
4. Click **OK**, and your personalized tab will now appear in the Ribbon.

Having all your **most-used tools in one place** eliminates **unnecessary navigation**, making your workflow much **smoother and faster**.

Mastering the Status Bar for Real-Time Insights

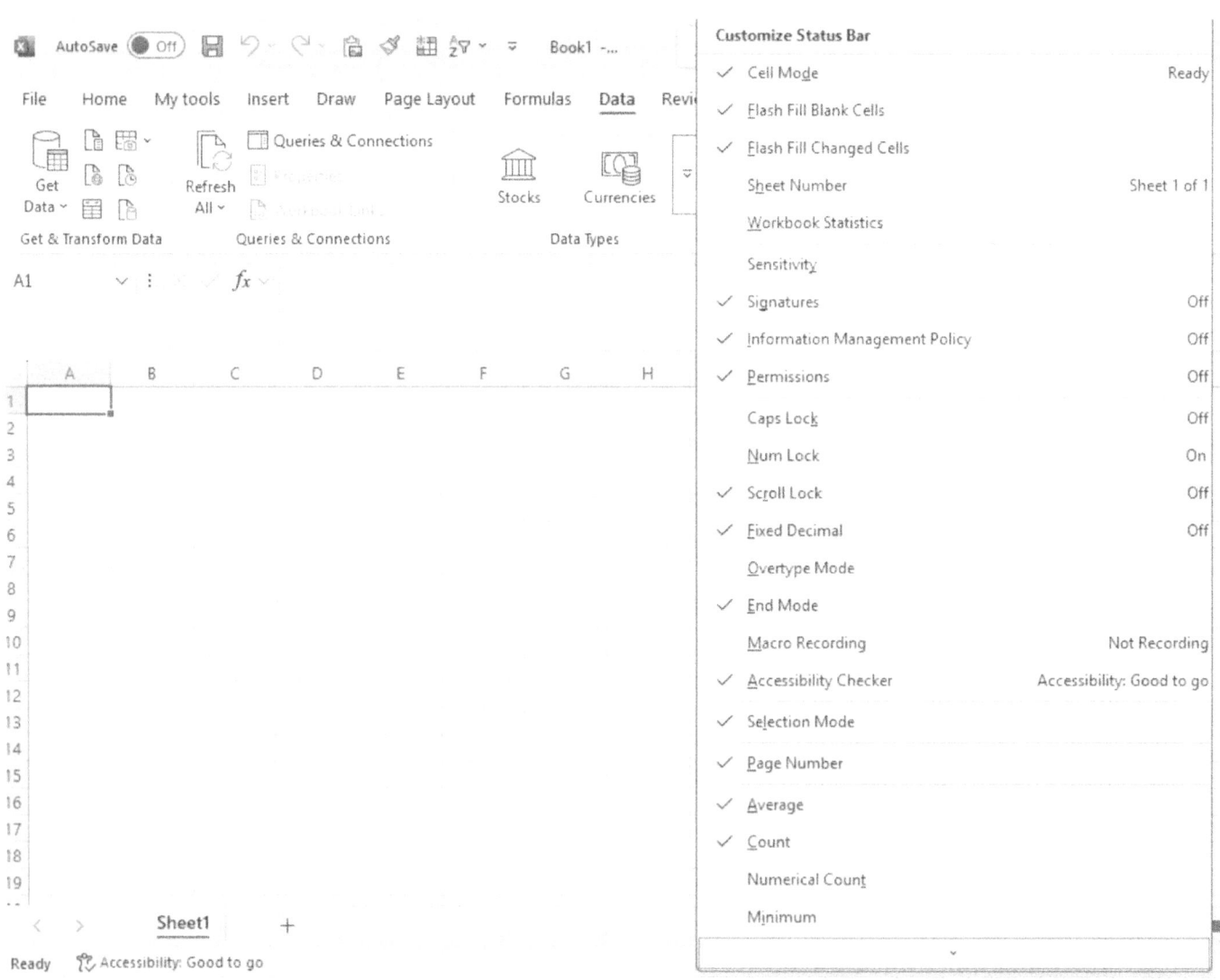

Sensitivity
Signatures Off
Information Management Policy Off
Permissions Off
Caps Lock Off
Num Lock On
Scroll Lock Off
Fixed Decimal Off
Overtype Mode
End Mode
Macro Recording Not Recording
Accessibility Checker Accessibility: Good to go
Selection Mode
Page Number
Average 3
Count 5
Numerical Count 5
Minimum
Maximum
Sum 15
Upload Status
View Shortcuts
Zoom Slider
Zoom 100%

AutoSave Off
Book1
Search
File Home My tools Insert Draw Page Layout Formulas Data Review View Help Acrobat
Get Data
Refresh All
Queries & Connections
Stocks
Currencies
Sort
Filter
Advanced
Text to Columns
What-If Analysis
Forecast Sheet
Outline
Get & Transform Data
Queries & Connections
Data Types
Sort & Filter
Data Tools
Forecast
Sheet1
Ready
Accessibility: Good to go
Average: 3 Count: 5 Sum: 15

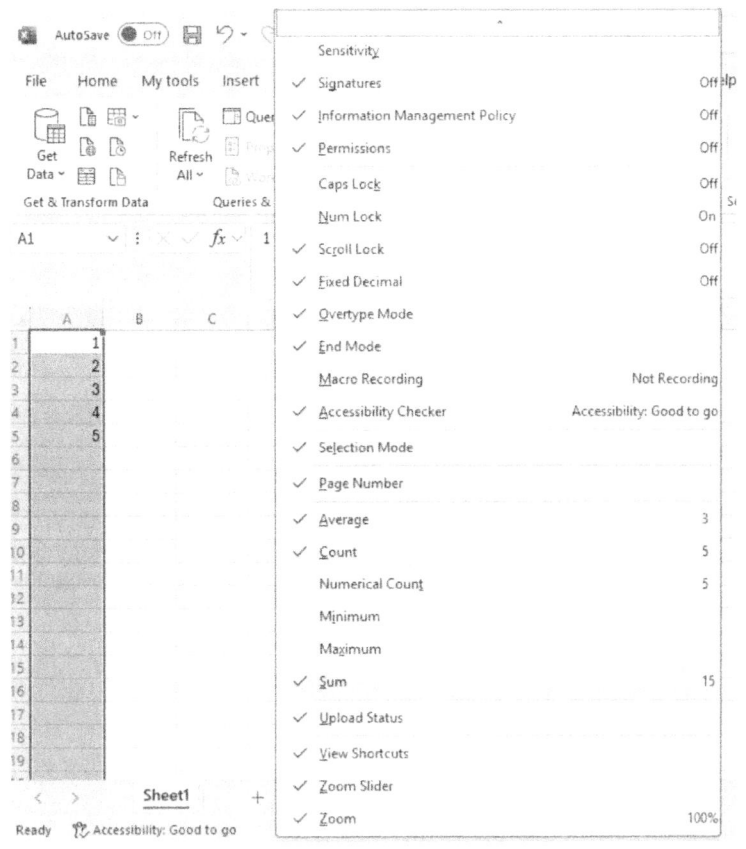

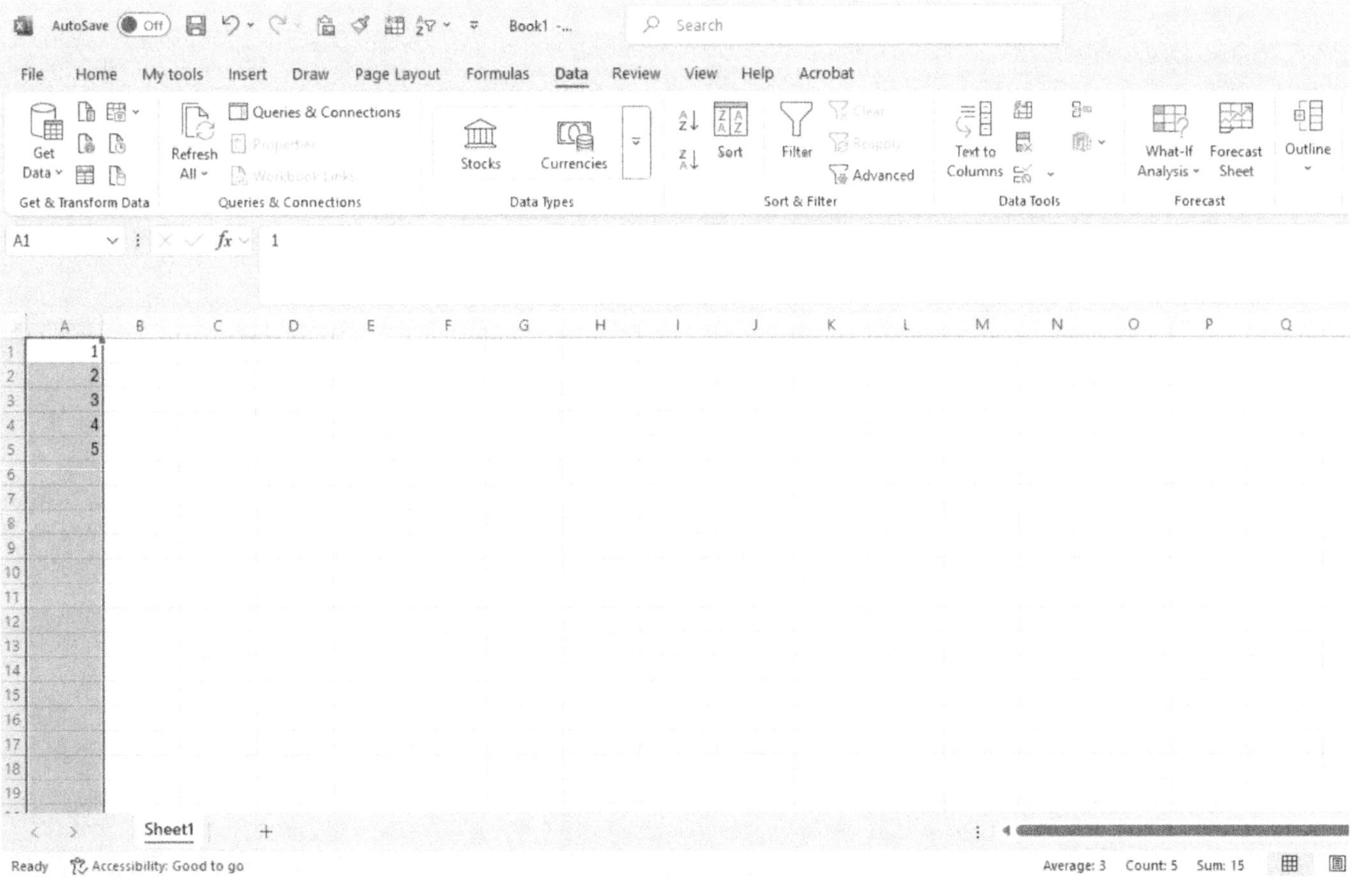

The **Status Bar** at the bottom of the Excel window is more than just a **passive display**—it can provide **real-time insights** without needing formulas. By customizing it, you can instantly view calculations like **sum, average, count, and minimum/maximum values** just by selecting a range of data.

To enable these features:

1. **Right-click on the Status Bar** and select which statistics you want displayed.
2. Try selecting a **column of numbers**—Excel will immediately show **the total, average, and count** without needing a single formula.

This feature is particularly useful when you need **quick calculations without modifying the spreadsheet**, making it a hidden productivity booster.

Optimizing Default Settings for Seamless Workflows

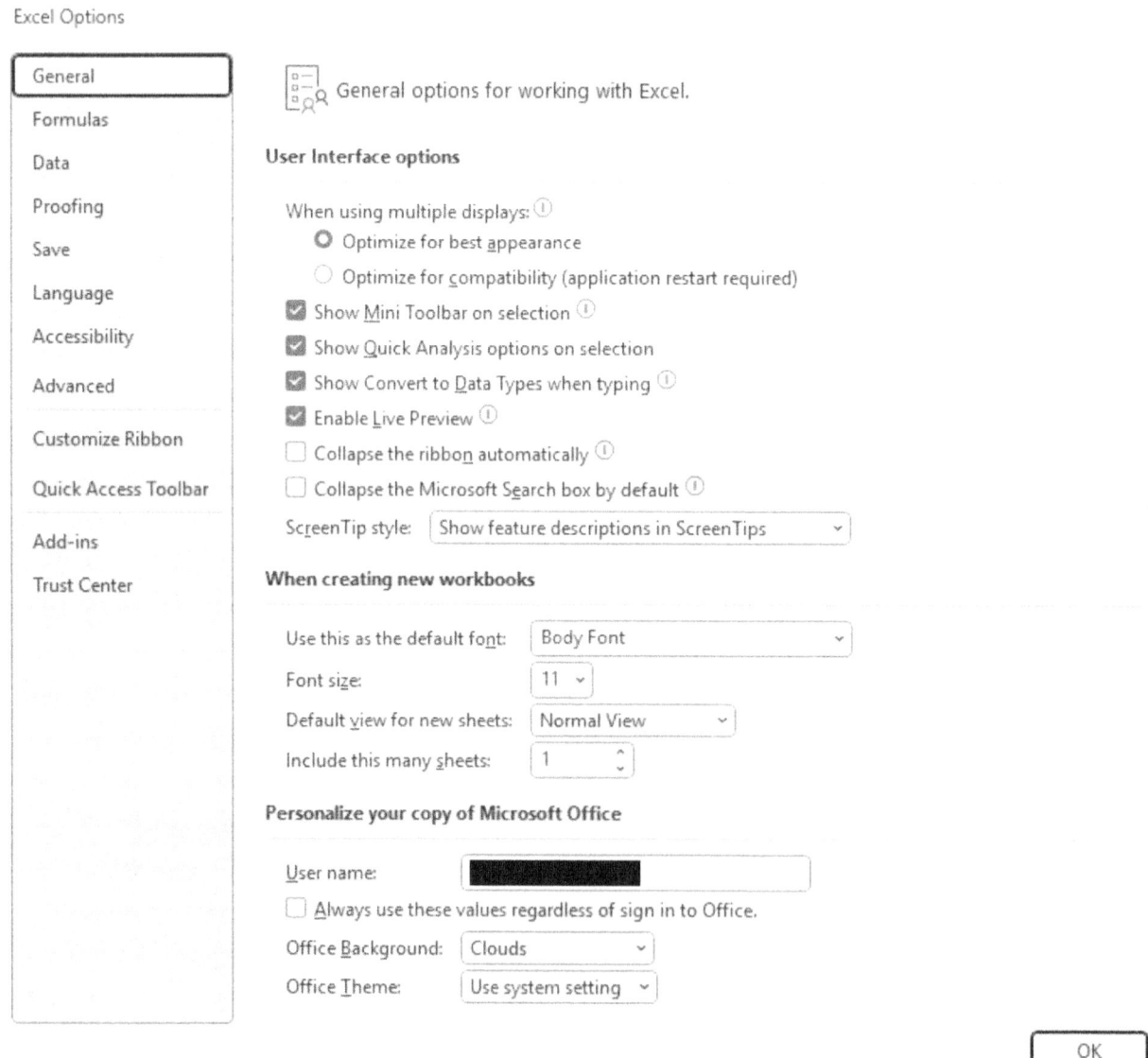

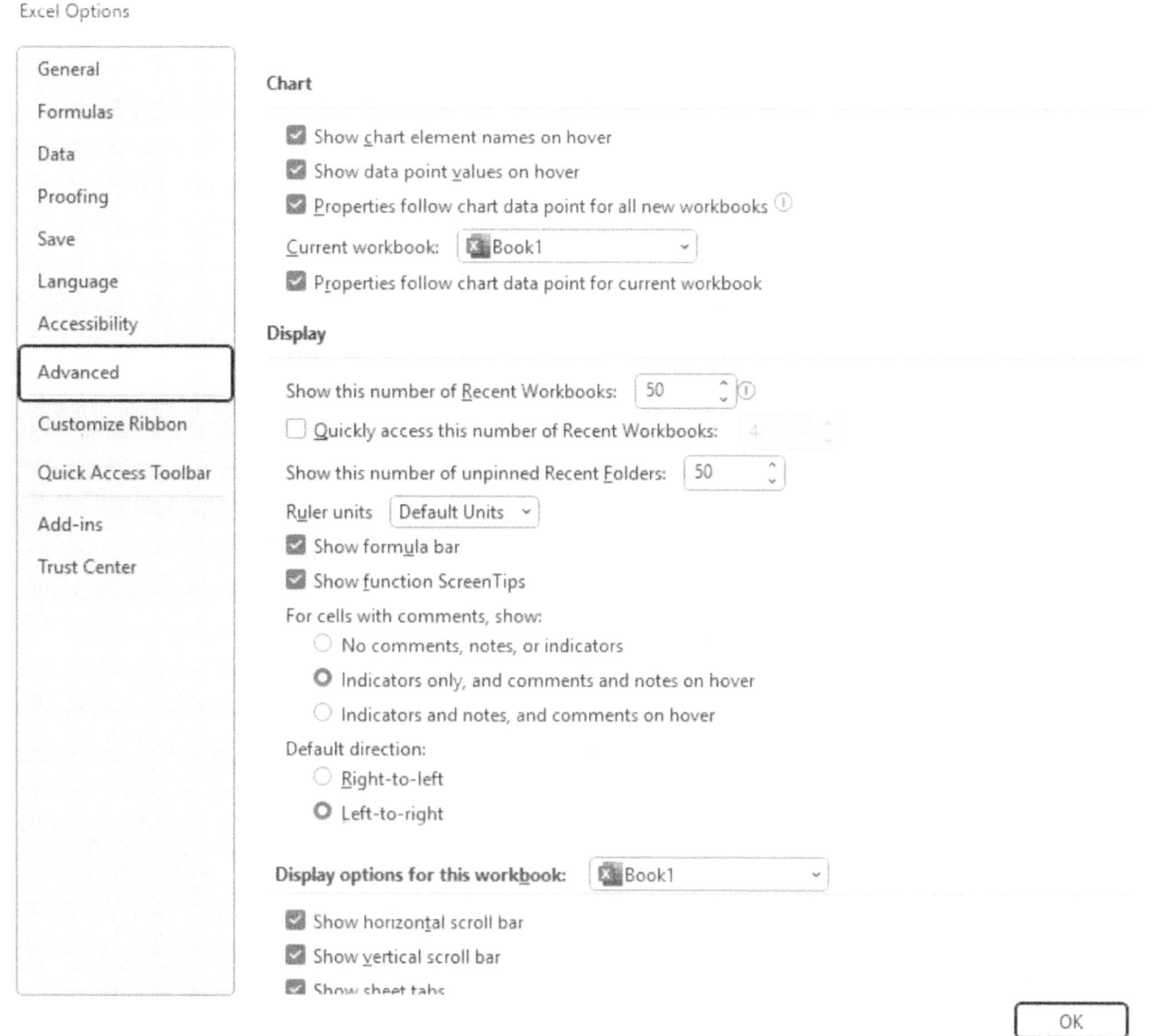

By adjusting Excel's default settings, you can **eliminate unnecessary steps** and create a **more fluid experience**:

- **Set Default Font and Size:** If you always use **Calibri 12pt** or **Arial 10pt**, update Excel's defaults so every new workbook opens with your preferred settings.

- **Change Default Save Location:** If you frequently save files to a shared drive or One-Drive, setting it as the default **prevents constant manual navigation**.

- **Increase the Number of Recent Files Displayed:** In **File › Options › Advanced**, you can set Excel to show **up to 50 recent documents**, ensuring quick access to your most-used files.

Small tweaks like these may seem insignificant at first, but together, they **add up to substantial time savings** over weeks and months, making your Excel experience **faster, smoother, and frustration-free**.

Essential Tools and Features You Need to Master

Mastering Excel isn't just about knowing formulas—it's about understanding the **essential tools and features** that transform the way you work. If you're still clicking through menus, manually formatting tables, or repeatedly entering the same formulas, you're **wasting valuable time**. The features covered here will help you **streamline your workflow, reduce errors, and work with data more efficiently**.

The Power of Tables: Turning Raw Data into Dynamic Reports

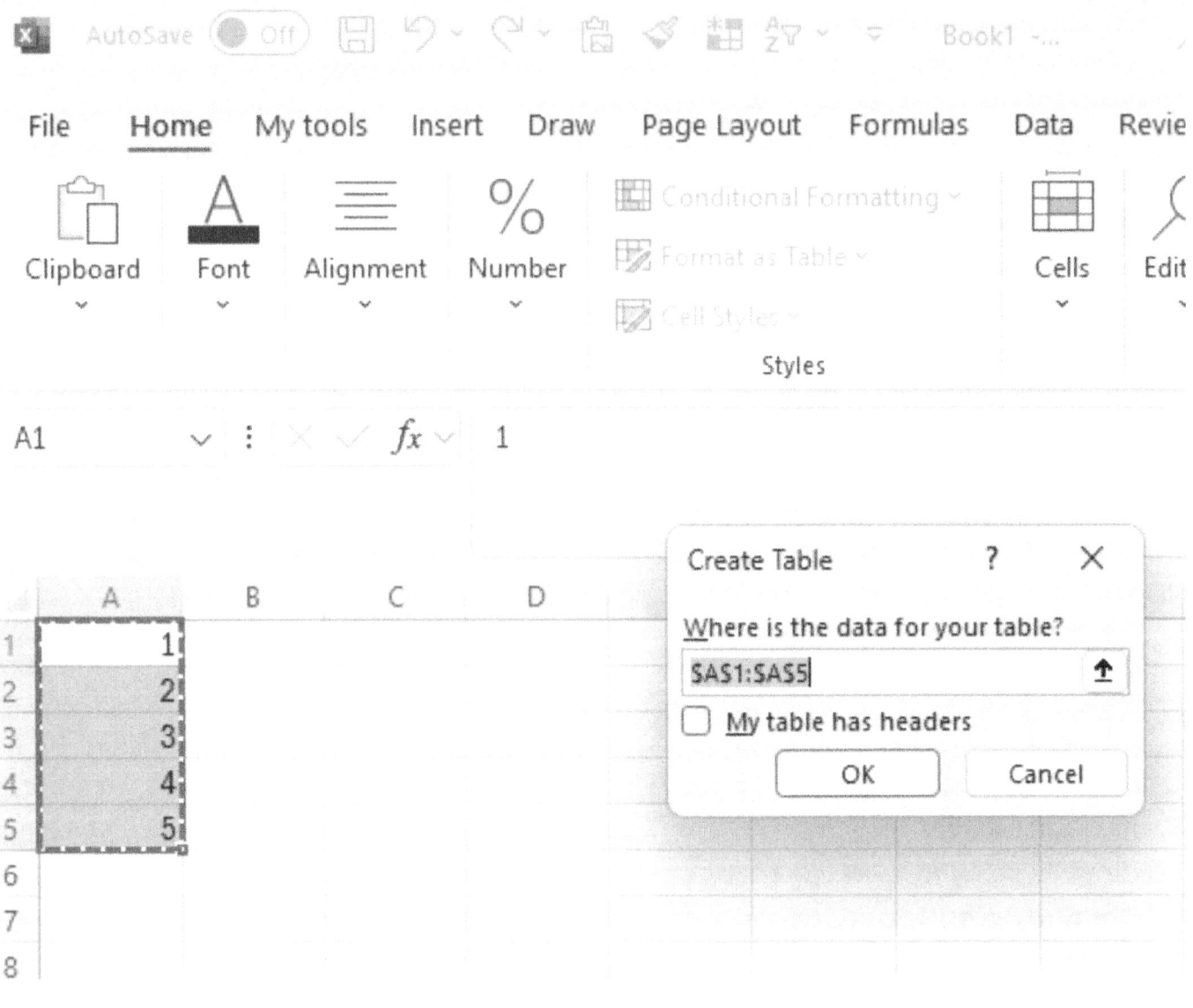

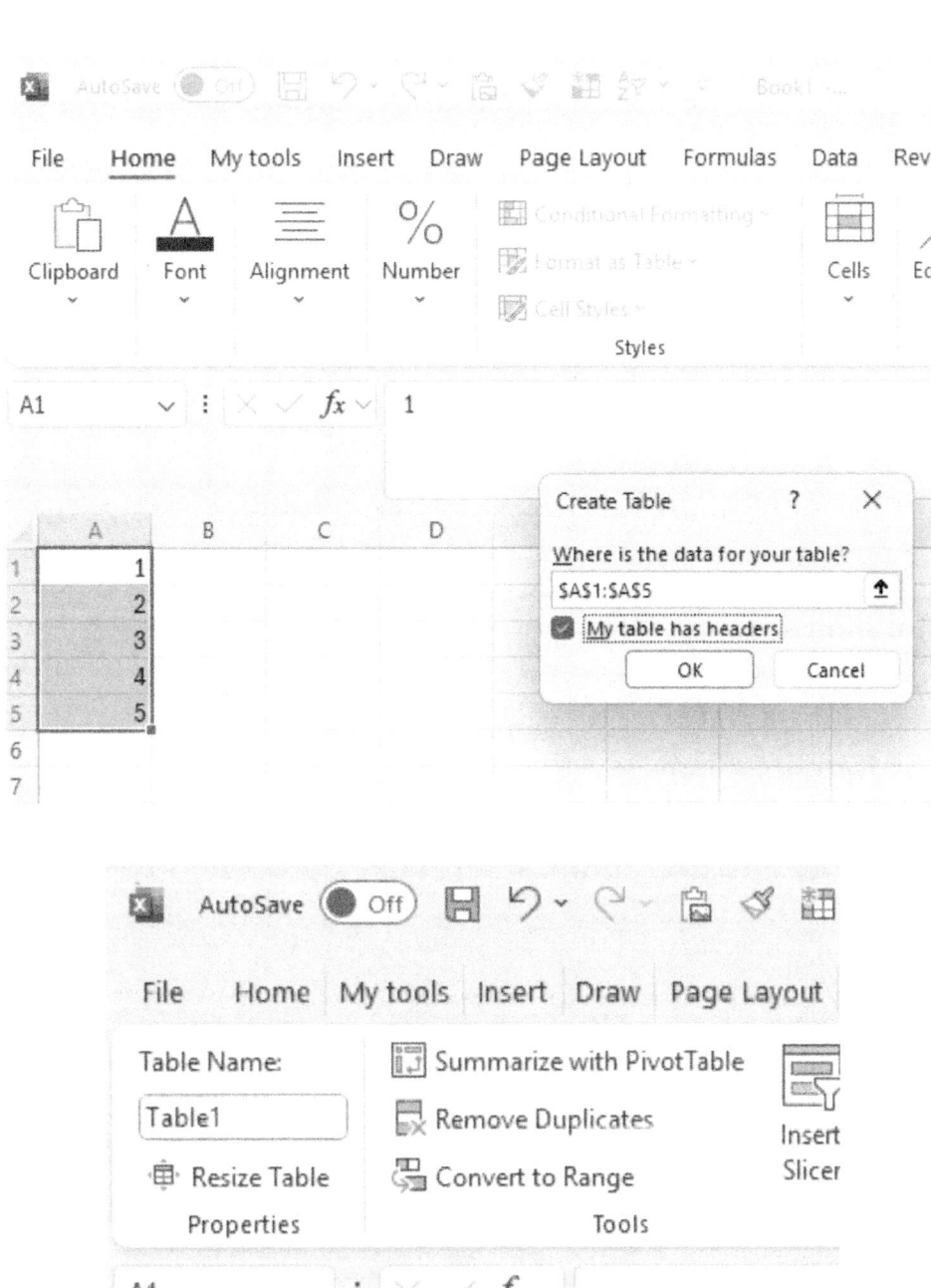

If you're still working with plain spreadsheets, it's time to embrace **Excel Tables**. Unlike a basic dataset, a Table **automatically expands, applies structured formatting, and enables dynamic referencing**.

Why is this a game-changer? Imagine you have a **sales dataset** with hundreds of rows. If you add new data at the bottom, traditional formulas **don't automatically update**—you'd have to adjust ranges manually. But with Tables, everything **updates dynamically**.

To convert a range into a Table:

1. Select your dataset and press **Ctrl + T**.
2. Make sure "My table has headers" is checked.
3. Click **OK**—Excel instantly formats it as a dynamic Table.

Once created, you can:

- **Sort and filter effortlessly** with dropdowns on each column.
- **Use structured references in formulas instead of cell ranges (e.g., `=SUM(Sales[Revenue])` instead of `=SUM(B2:**B100)`)**.
- **Auto-expand formulas**—any new row automatically carries down formulas, reducing manual work.

Tables **turn static data into a dynamic, interactive dataset**—an absolute must for efficiency.

Conditional Formatting: Instantly Spot Key Trends

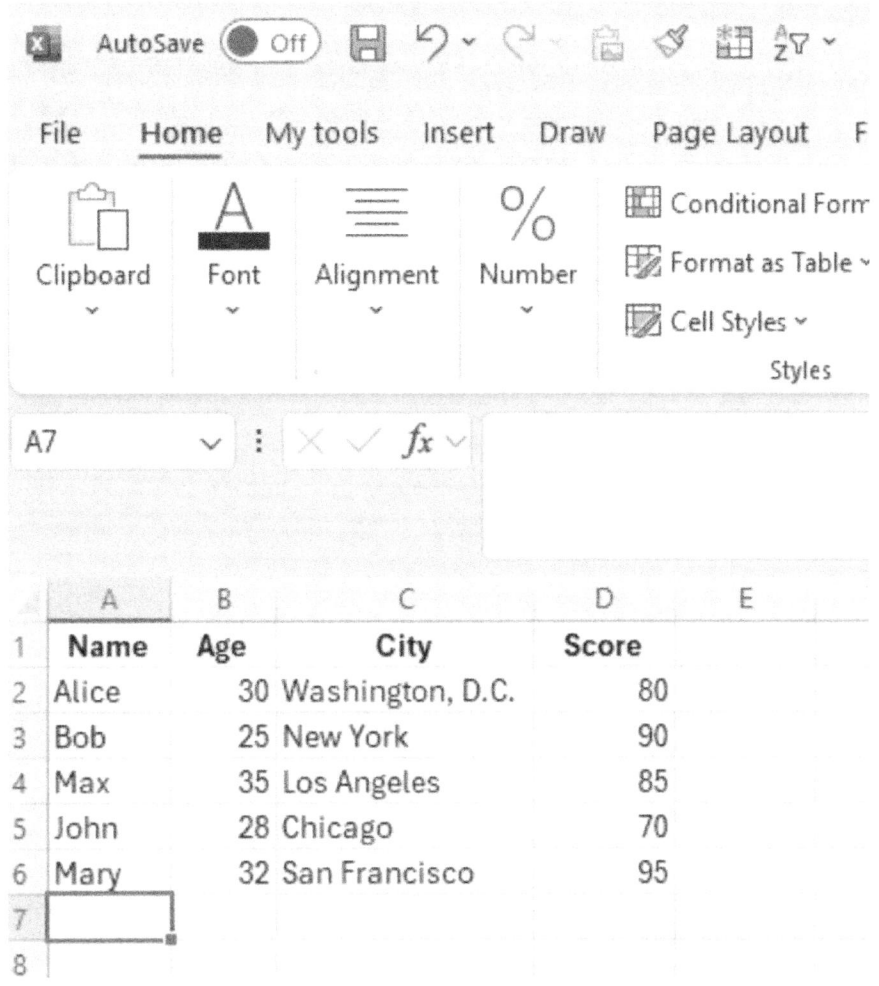

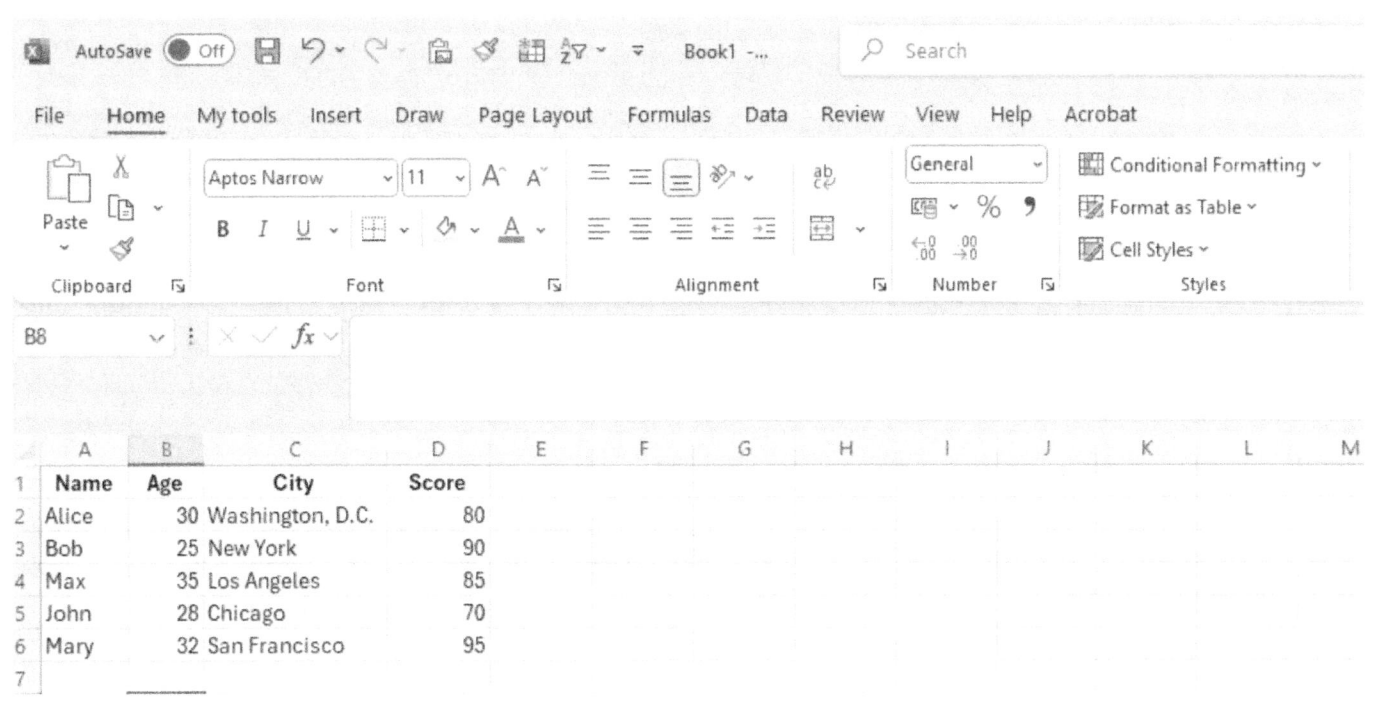

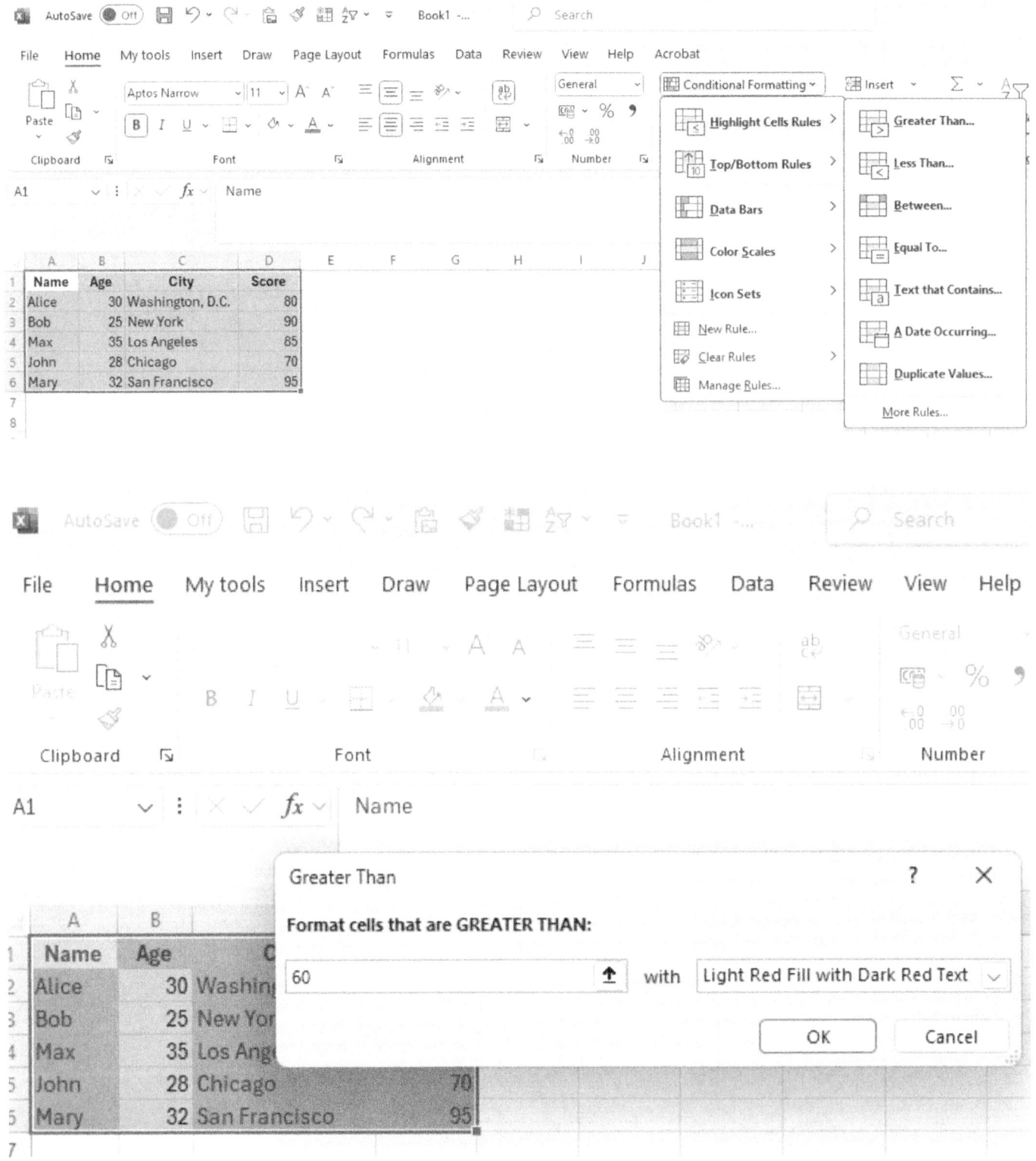

Scanning through rows of numbers to find **outliers, trends, or errors** is both time-consuming and prone to mistakes. **Conditional Formatting** allows you to highlight data based on **specific conditions**, drawing attention to important figures automatically.

Some key applications:

- **Highlight overdue invoices** in red.
- **Shade high-performing sales numbers** in green.
- **Use data bars** to create in-cell bar charts, visually representing data differences.

To apply Conditional Formatting:

1. Select the data range.
2. Click **Home > Conditional Formatting** and choose a rule (e.g., "Highlight Cell Rules" > "Greater Than").
3. Enter the criteria (e.g., highlight cells greater than $10,000 in bold red).

Now, Excel **works for you**, drawing your attention where it's needed **without manually scanning rows of numbers**.

PivotTables: The Ultimate Data Analysis Tool

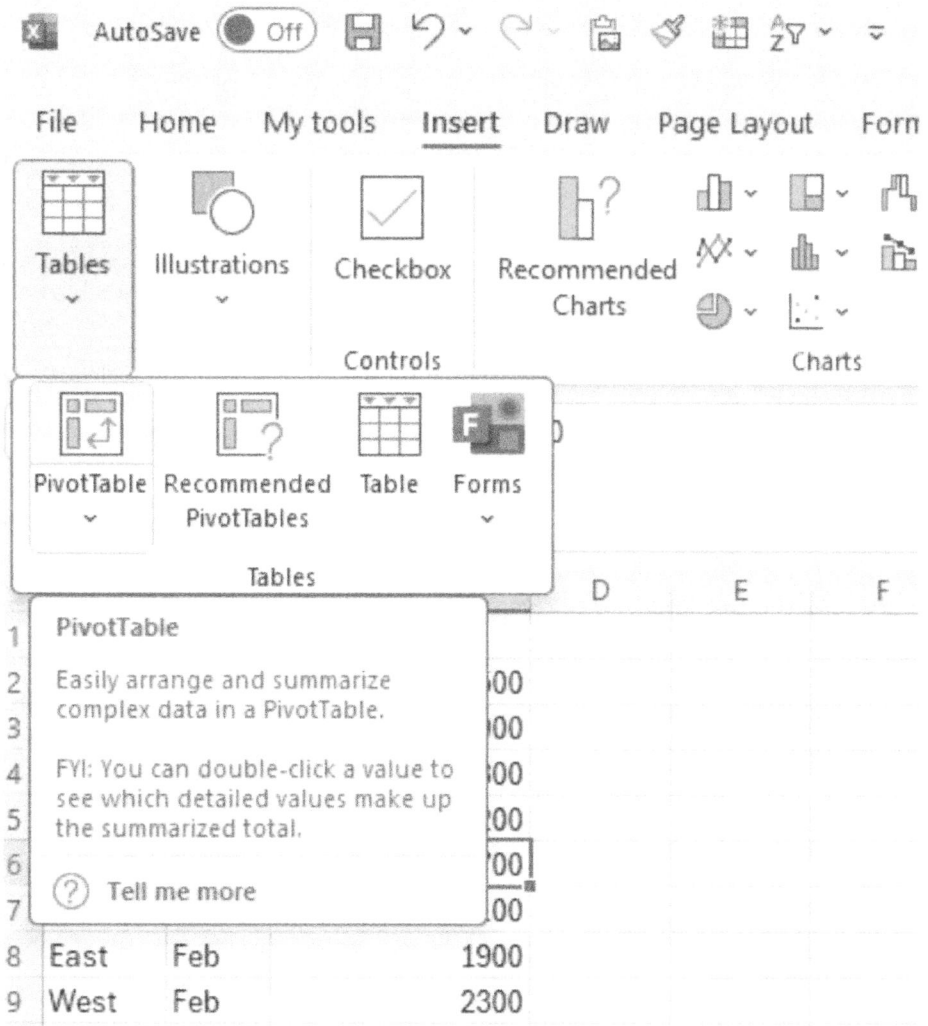

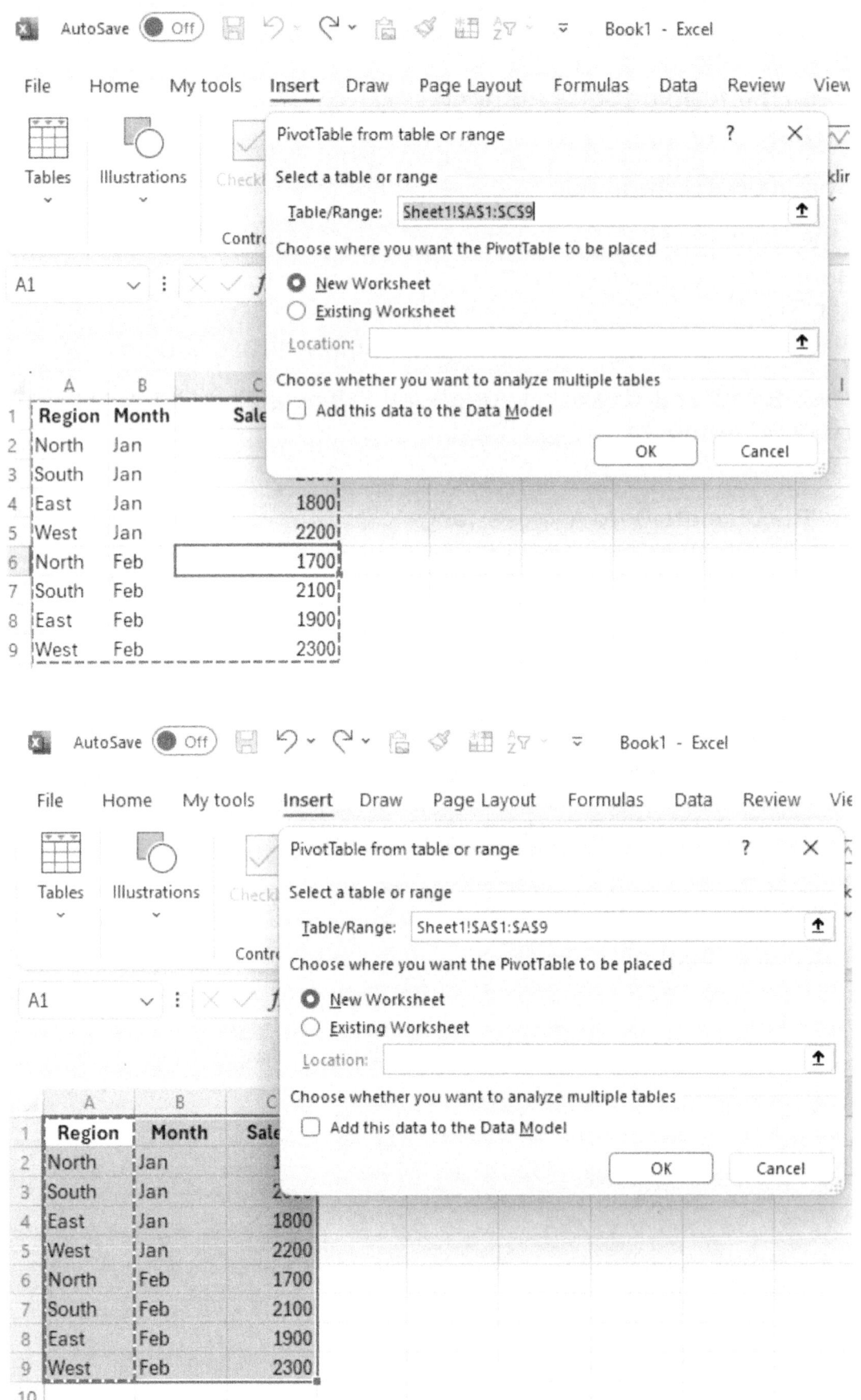

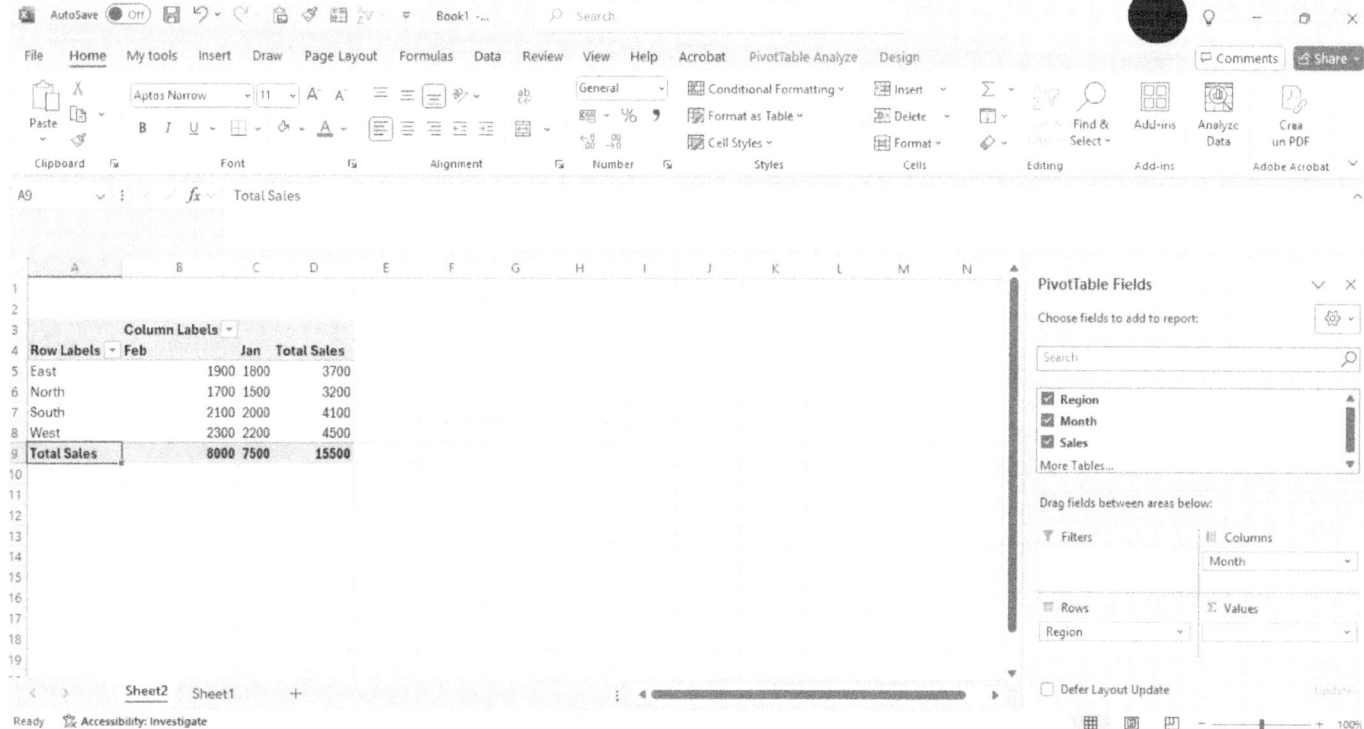

If there's one feature that separates **Excel experts from casual users**, it's **PivotTables**. Instead of writing endless formulas, PivotTables let you **summarize, analyze, and reorganize data with just a few clicks**.

Let's say you're analyzing **monthly sales data** for different regions. Without PivotTables, you'd need multiple **SUMIFs, COUNTIFs, and manual sorting**. With a PivotTable, you can:

- **Group sales by region or product category**.
- **Filter by month or quarter dynamically**.
- **Drag and drop fields** to instantly restructure reports.

To create a PivotTable:

1. Click anywhere inside your dataset.
2. Go to **Insert › PivotTable**.
3. Choose "New Worksheet" and click **OK**.
4. Drag fields from the right-hand panel into the **Rows, Columns, Values, and Filters** sections.

PivotTables **turn messy data into clear, actionable insights**—essential for anyone dealing with reports and analysis.

AutoFill & Flash Fill: The Secret to Speeding Up Data Entry

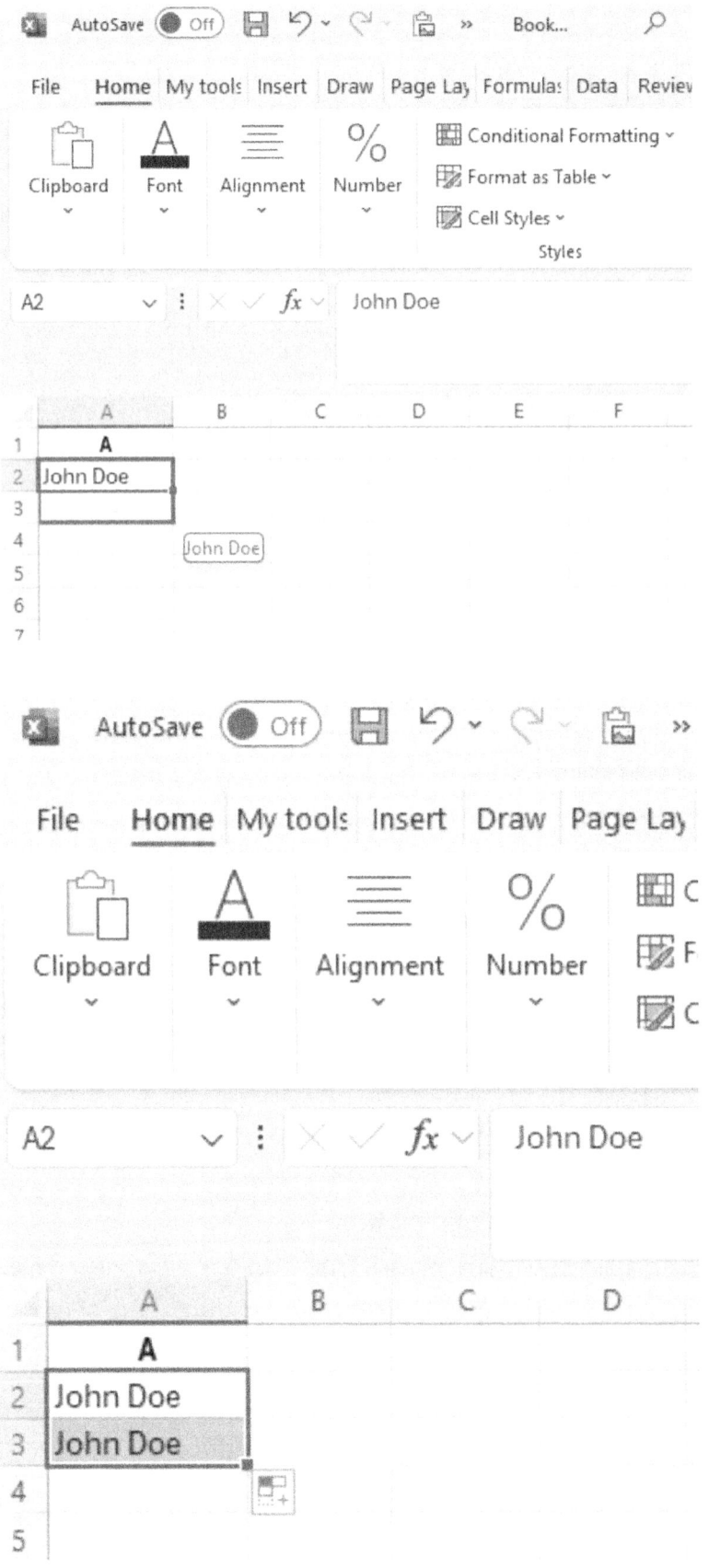

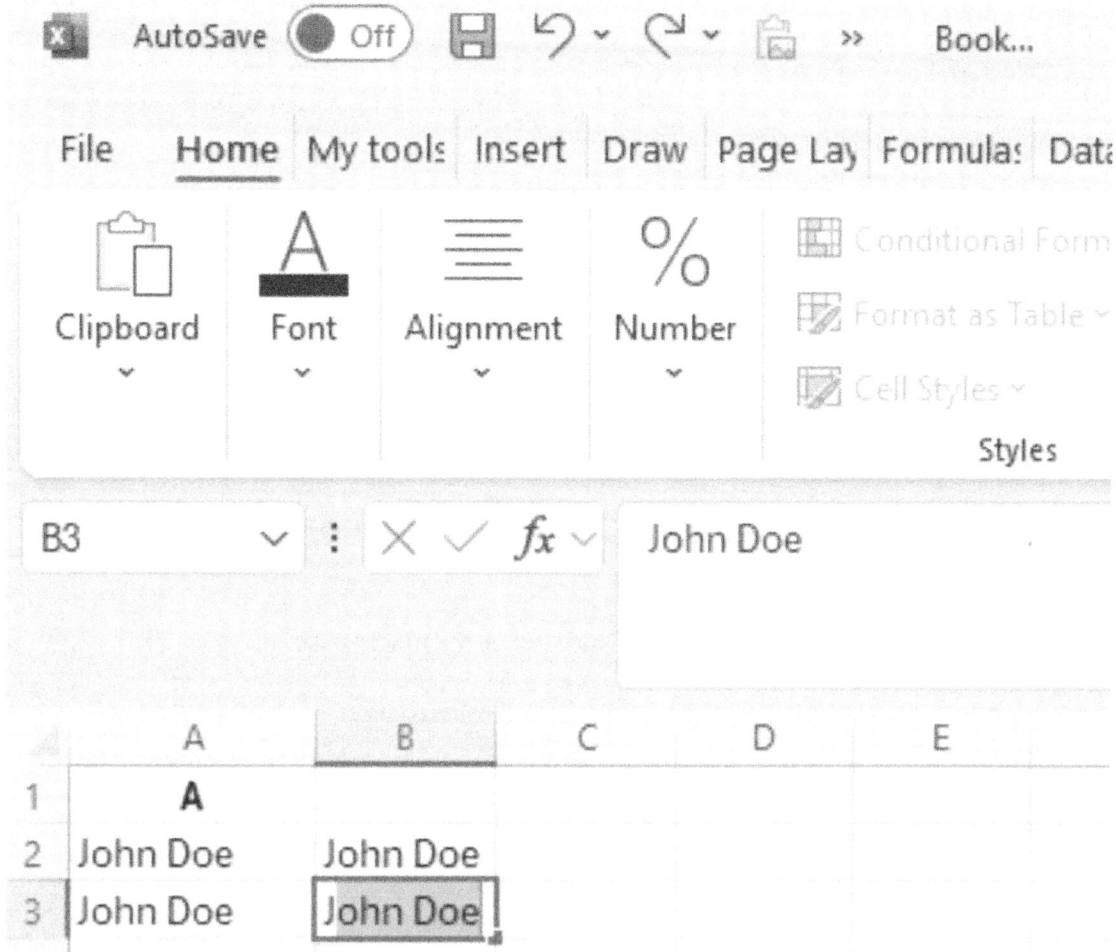

Manually entering data is one of the **biggest productivity killers** in Excel. If you find yourself **retyping similar information**, these two features will save **hours of work**:

- **AutoFill:** Dragging the fill handle (bottom-right corner of a cell) can instantly copy patterns (e.g., dates, numbers, or custom sequences).
- **Flash Fill:** Excel detects patterns in your entries and fills the rest **automatically**.

Example:

If column A contains **"John Doe"**, and you want **only the first names** in column B, start typing "John" in B2. Excel will suggest filling the rest—press **Enter**, and it's done.

These features **remove the need for repetitive typing** and allow you to focus on higher-value tasks.

Why These Features Matter

When combined, these essential tools **turn Excel from a basic spreadsheet tool into a powerful productivity machine**. By mastering Tables, Conditional Formatting, PivotTables, and automation features, you **eliminate tedious work, speed up your tasks, and gain better insights—positioning yourself as an Excel expert in your workplace**.

CHAPTER 2

EXCEL SHORTCUTS AND PRODUCTIVITY HACKS: WORK SMARTER, NOT HARDER

Master the keyboard shortcuts and techniques that
eliminate 60% of your daily manual work in Excel

The Most Powerful Keyboard Shortcuts for Instant Speed

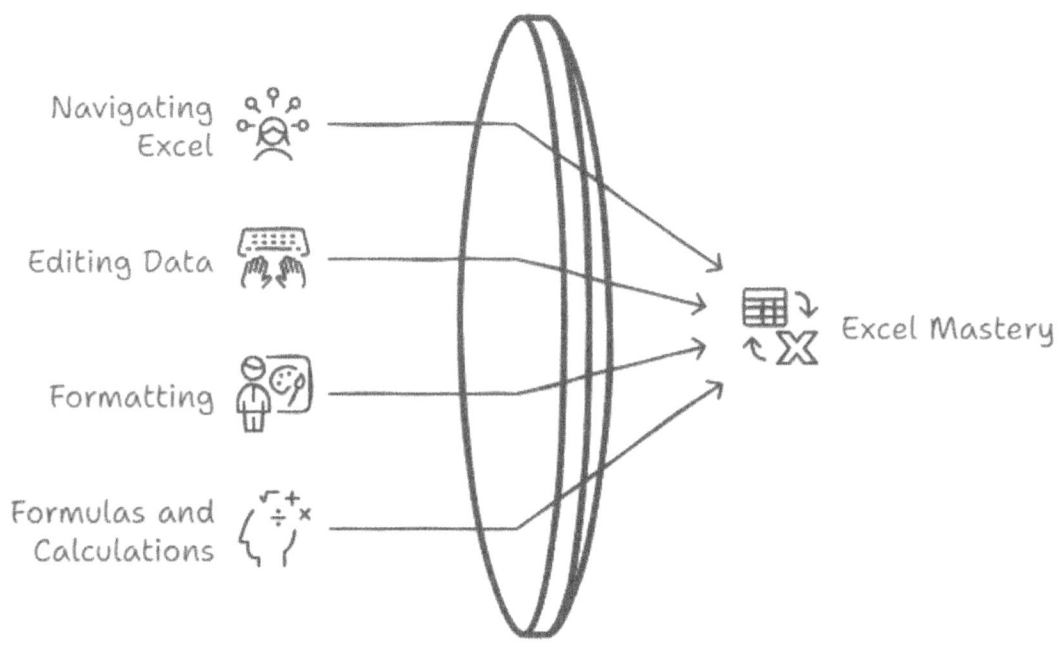

If you're still relying on your mouse to navigate Excel, you're working **twice as hard** as you need to. Every click and menu selection adds **unnecessary seconds** to your workflow—seconds that add up to hours over time. **Keyboard shortcuts are the secret weapon of every Excel expert**. They help you work faster, eliminate repetitive tasks, and make you look effortlessly skilled in front of your colleagues.

But here's the challenge: **there are hundreds of Excel shortcuts**. The key isn't memorizing all of them—it's **learning the ones that deliver the most impact for the tasks you perform daily**. Below, we focus on the shortcuts that will save you the most time **without overwhelming you with unnecessary combinations**.

Navigating Excel Like a Pro

Before diving into formulas and formatting, let's start with **basic navigation**—because if you're still clicking around cell by cell, you're wasting valuable time.

- **Move to the last filled cell in a row or column:** `Ctrl + Arrow Key`
- Perfect for jumping through large datasets without scrolling endlessly.
- **Select an entire column:** `Ctrl + Space`
- **Select an entire row:** `Shift + Space`
- Need to format or analyze a specific column? These shortcuts make it effortless.
- **Jump between worksheets:** `Ctrl + Page Up/Page Down`
- If your workbook has multiple sheets, this shortcut makes flipping between them feel seamless.

Entering and Editing Data Efficiently

Data entry is where Excel users waste **the most time**. These shortcuts will **cut your workload in half**.

- **Copy and paste faster:**
- `Ctrl + C` (Copy) > `Ctrl + V` (Paste) > `Ctrl + X` (Cut)
- **Bonus:** Use `Ctrl + Alt + V` to open Paste Special, where you can paste only values, formats, or formulas.
- **Fill down or fill right:**
- `Ctrl + D` (Fill Down) > copies the cell above.
- `Ctrl + R` (Fill Right) > copies the cell to the left.
- Perfect for quickly duplicating formulas across multiple cells.
- **Insert today's date instantly:** `Ctrl +;`
- If you often log dates in reports, this shortcut will save you from manually typing them out.

Mastering Formatting on the Fly

Proper formatting makes data more readable, but clicking through the menus to apply bold, italics, or number formats **slows you down**. Use these instead:

- **Bold/Italic/Underline:**
- `Ctrl + B` (Bold), `Ctrl + I` (Italic), `Ctrl + U` (Underline)
- Formatting text should be as quick as in Microsoft Word.
- **Auto-adjust column width:** `Alt + H + O + I`
- No more dragging column borders—this shortcut automatically resizes to fit the content.
- **Apply currency format instantly:** `Ctrl + Shift + $`

- Useful for finance professionals who work with dollar values regularly.

Speeding Up Formulas and Calculations

Formulas are at the core of Excel's power, but entering them manually **can be tedious**. These shortcuts help **write and calculate formulas faster**:

- **Start a formula instantly:** `=`
- No need to click the formula bar—just type `=` in a cell and start calculating.
- **Autosum entire columns/rows:** `Alt + =`
- **Instantly calculates the sum of selected numbers without manually typing `=SUM(A1:A100)`.**
- **Recalculate the entire workbook:** `F9`
- If your workbook has complex formulas, hitting `F9` forces Excel to update everything instantly.

Master These, and You'll Work Twice as Fast

Learning these shortcuts isn't just about **saving a few seconds**—it's about developing a workflow that lets you **focus on analysis and insights** instead of wasting time on repetitive actions. Once you incorporate them into your daily work, **Excel will feel smoother, faster, and more intuitive than ever before**.

Customizing Ribbons and Quick Access for Faster Workflows

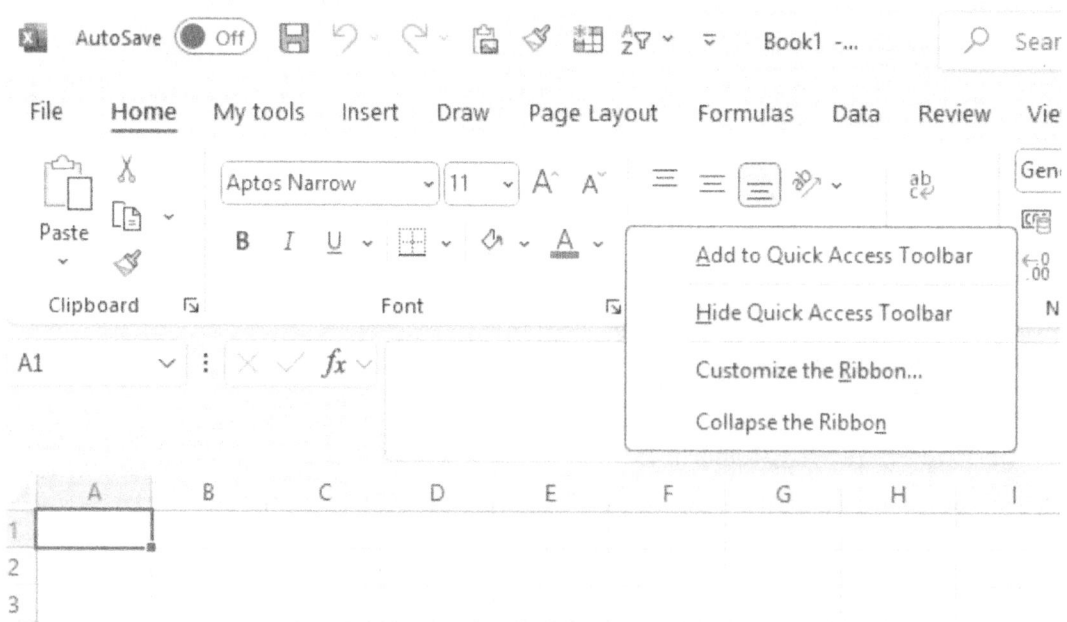

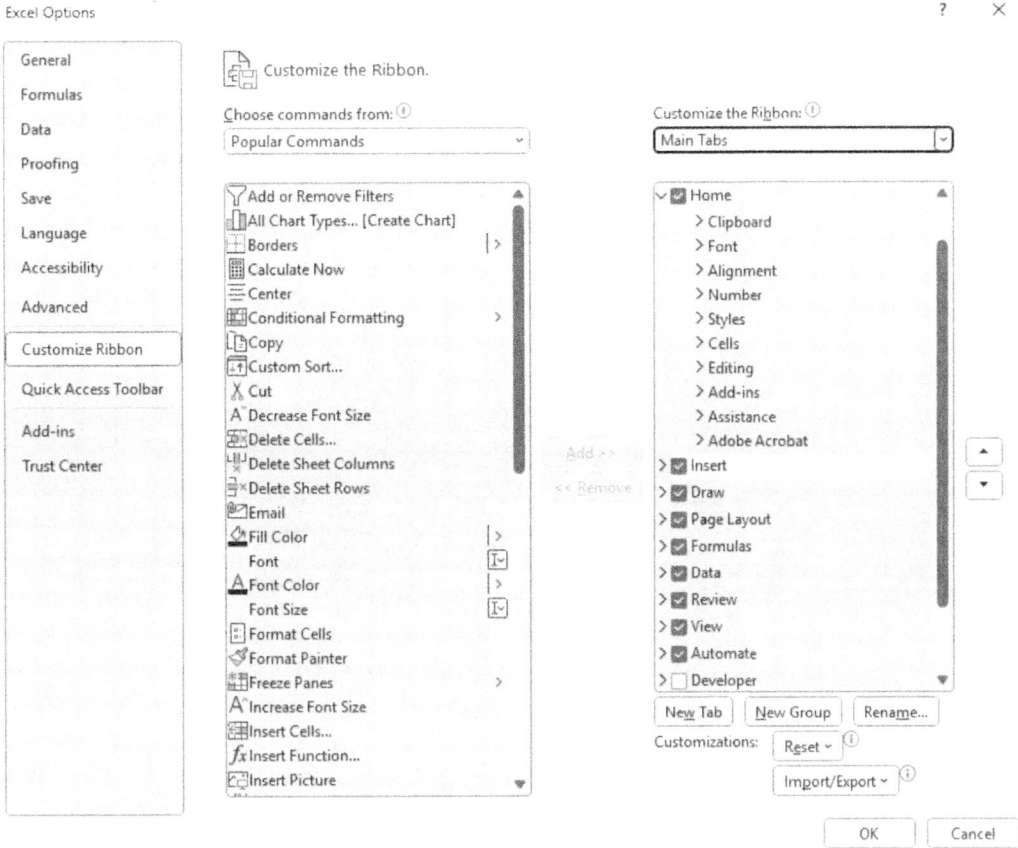

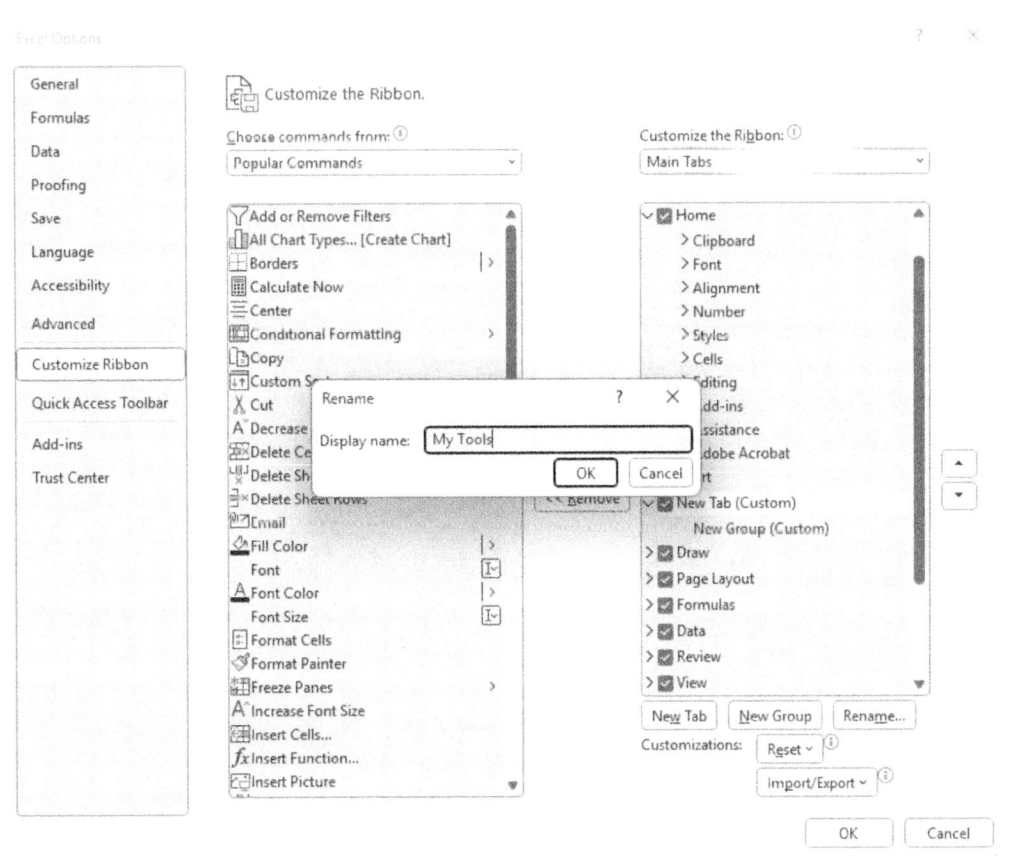

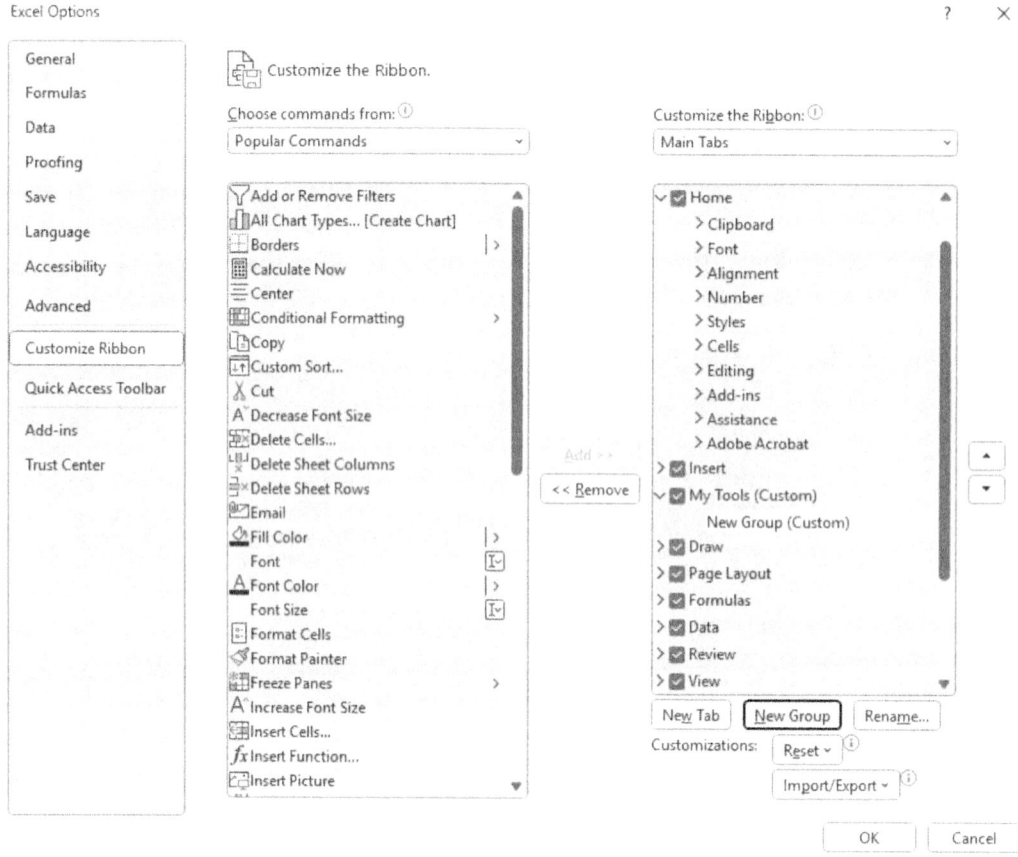

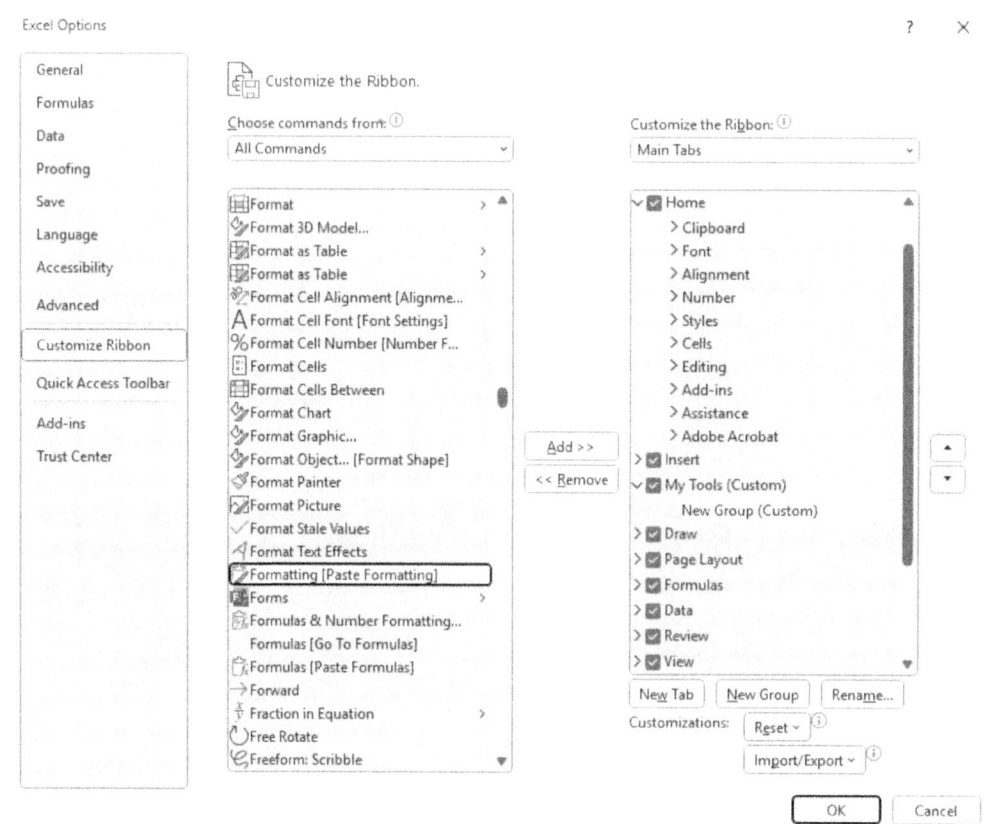

Excel's default interface is designed to serve a **wide range of users**, but it's not optimized for your specific workflow. If you find yourself **clicking through multiple tabs** to find the same functions over and over again, you're **wasting time** that could be better spent analyzing data or automating processes. By customizing the **Ribbon and Quick Access Toolbar (QAT)**, you can **bring your most-used tools to the forefront**, making Excel work for you—not the other way around.

Why Customization Matters

Think of Excel like your **kitchen**—if your most-used utensils are buried in the back of a drawer, cooking becomes frustrating and inefficient. The same applies to Excel: if the tools you need are hidden within multiple Ribbon tabs, **you're adding unnecessary steps to every task**. Customizing your interface allows you to:

- **Eliminate unnecessary clicks** and menu navigation.
- **Create a personalized workspace** tailored to your tasks.
- **Work faster and with less frustration**—no more searching for the same tools.

Creating a Custom Ribbon Tab: Your Personalized Productivity Hub

The **Ribbon** (the toolbar at the top of Excel) organizes functions into tabs like **Home, Insert, Formulas, and Data**. While useful, these default tabs **aren't always structured to fit your workflow**. Instead of constantly switching between them, you can **create a custom tab** that consolidates your most-used commands into a **single, easy-to-access section**.

To create your own **custom Ribbon tab**:

1. **Right-click anywhere on the Ribbon** and select **Customize the Ribbon**.
2. Click **New Tab**, then rename it (e.g., "My Tools" or "Efficiency Hub").
3. Click **New Group** to categorize your functions (e.g., "Formatting,").
4. Add commands from the left panel by selecting them and clicking **Add >>**.
5. Click **OK**, and your personalized Ribbon tab will now appear in Excel.

The Quick Access Toolbar: One-Click Efficiency

The **Quick Access Toolbar (QAT)** is the **small bar at the top-left of Excel**, above the Ribbon. By default, it contains basic commands like **Save, Undo, and Redo**—but you can add **any tool you frequently use**, making repetitive actions instant.

To customize your **QAT**:

1. Click the **dropdown arrow** next to the toolbar.
2. Select **More Commands** to open the customization panel.
3. Choose functions like **Paste Special, Format Painter, Freeze Panes, or Sort & Filter** and click **Add >>**.

4. Click **OK**, and your most-used commands will now be available with a **single click**.

This small change can **eliminate dozens of unnecessary clicks** every day, saving valuable time.

Organizing Your Tools for Maximum Speed

Not all commands are created equal—some you use daily, others only occasionally. A well-organized Ribbon and QAT ensures that **your most critical tools are instantly accessible** while keeping lesser-used ones within reach but out of the way.

Here's how to **prioritize your most important functions**:

• Place **data cleaning tools** (Remove Duplicates, Text to Columns) in one section.
• Group **formatting functions** (Bold, Conditional Formatting, Borders) together.
• Add **automation tools** (Macros, Power Query) if you frequently work with large datasets.

By structuring your interface around **how you actually work**, you can move through Excel **with precision and efficiency**, reducing frustration and boosting productivity.

PART 2

DATA MANAGEMENT AND ORGANIZATION – FROM CHAOS TO CLARITY

CHAPTER 3

STRUCTURING DATA: THE ART OF CREATING CLEAN AND RELIABLE SPREADSHEETS

Build error-free, professional databases that colleagues trust and managers can understand at a glance

Designing Error-Free Databases with Proper Formatting

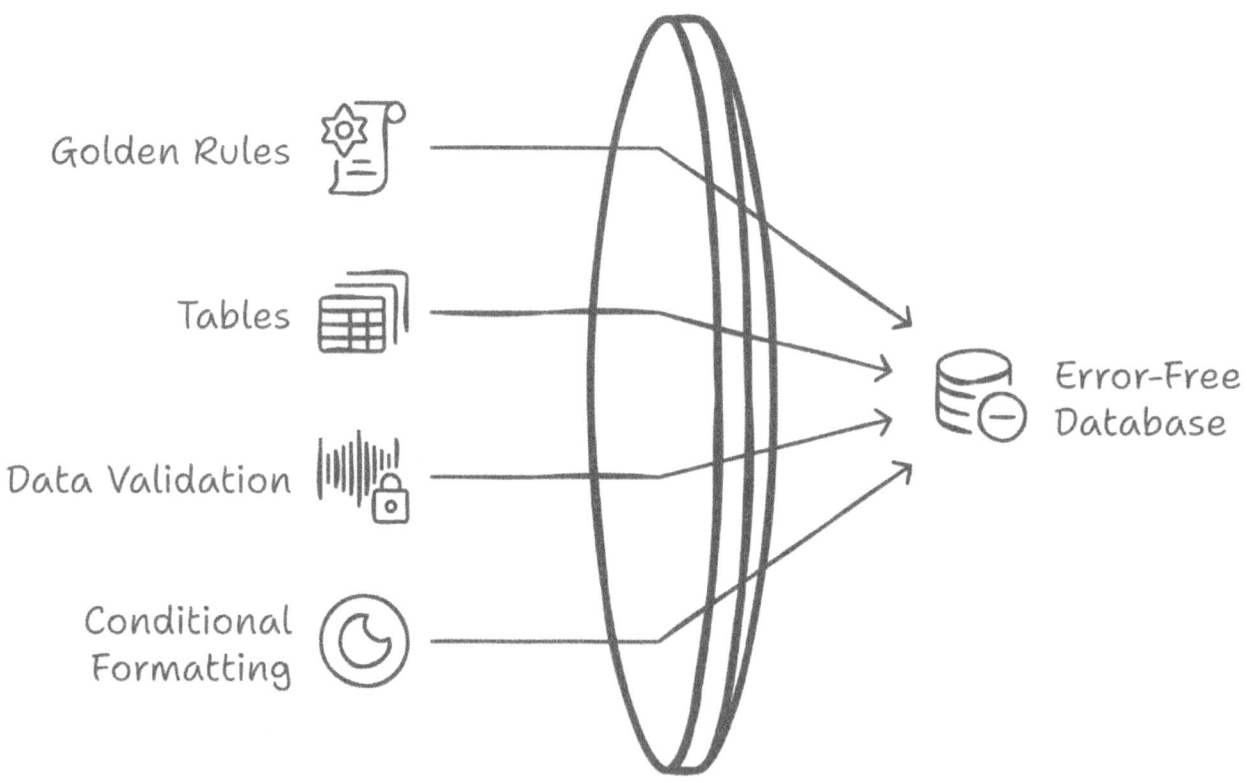

Achieving Database Perfection

A well-structured Excel database is the foundation of **accurate data analysis, streamlined workflows, and error-free reporting**. Without proper formatting, your spreadsheets can quickly become a **minefield of inconsistencies, duplicate entries, and formula errors**. The key to **creating a reliable database** is to implement **clear formatting rules** that ensure consistency, readability, and error prevention from the start.

The Golden Rules of a Well-Structured Database

Before diving into Excel tools, it's essential to understand **what makes a database clean and reliable**. A well-designed Excel database should:

- **Follow a structured layout:** Data should be organized in a **tabular format**, with each column representing a distinct field (e.g., Name, Date, Amount).
- **Avoid merged cells:** Merging cells may seem convenient for formatting, but it disrupts data sorting and calculations.
- **Use column headers effectively:** Headers should be **clear and descriptive**, making it easy to understand what each column represents.
- **Keep formatting consistent:** Dates, numbers, and text should follow a **uniform format** to prevent formula errors.
- **Minimize manual data entry:** Wherever possible, use **dropdown lists and data validation** to enforce accuracy.

Using Tables for Dynamic and Error-Free Data Management

Converting your raw dataset into an **Excel Table** (`Ctrl + T`) is one of the best ways to **reduce errors and automate formatting**. Unlike plain spreadsheets, Tables:

- **Automatically expand** to include new data without manually adjusting formulas.
- **Retain consistent formatting**, making reports look professional.
- **Enable structured referencing**, which prevents broken formulas when adding new rows.

For example, instead of using a formula like `=SUM(A2:A100)`, a Table allows you to use `=SUM(Sales[Revenue])`, ensuring **dynamic range updates** when new data is added.

Data Validation: Preventing Errors Before They Happen

The most effective way to maintain a **clean and reliable database** is to **prevent errors before they occur**. Excel's **Data Validation** tool allows you to set rules for **what users can enter** in specific columns.

How to Apply Data Validation:

AutoSave
Off
Book1
Search
File
Home
Insert
My Tools
Draw
Page Layout
Formulas
Data
Review
View
Help
Acrobat
Get & Transform Data
Queries & Connections
B2
Status
Data Validation
Settings
Input Message
Error Alert
Validation criteria
Allow:
List
Ignore blank
In-cell dropdown
Data:
between
Source:
=$B$2:$B$3
Apply these changes to all other cells with the same settings
Clear All
OK
Cancel
Name
Status
John Doe
Approved
Jane Smith
Pending
Bob Brown
Approved
Alice White
Pending

AutoSave
Off
File
Home
Insert
My Tools
Draw
Page Layout
Get Data
Refresh All
Queries & Connections
Properties
Workbook Links
Get & Transform Data
Queries & Connections
B2
Approved
Name
Status
John Doe
Approved
Approved
Pending
Jane Smith
Bob Brown
Approved
Alice White
Pending

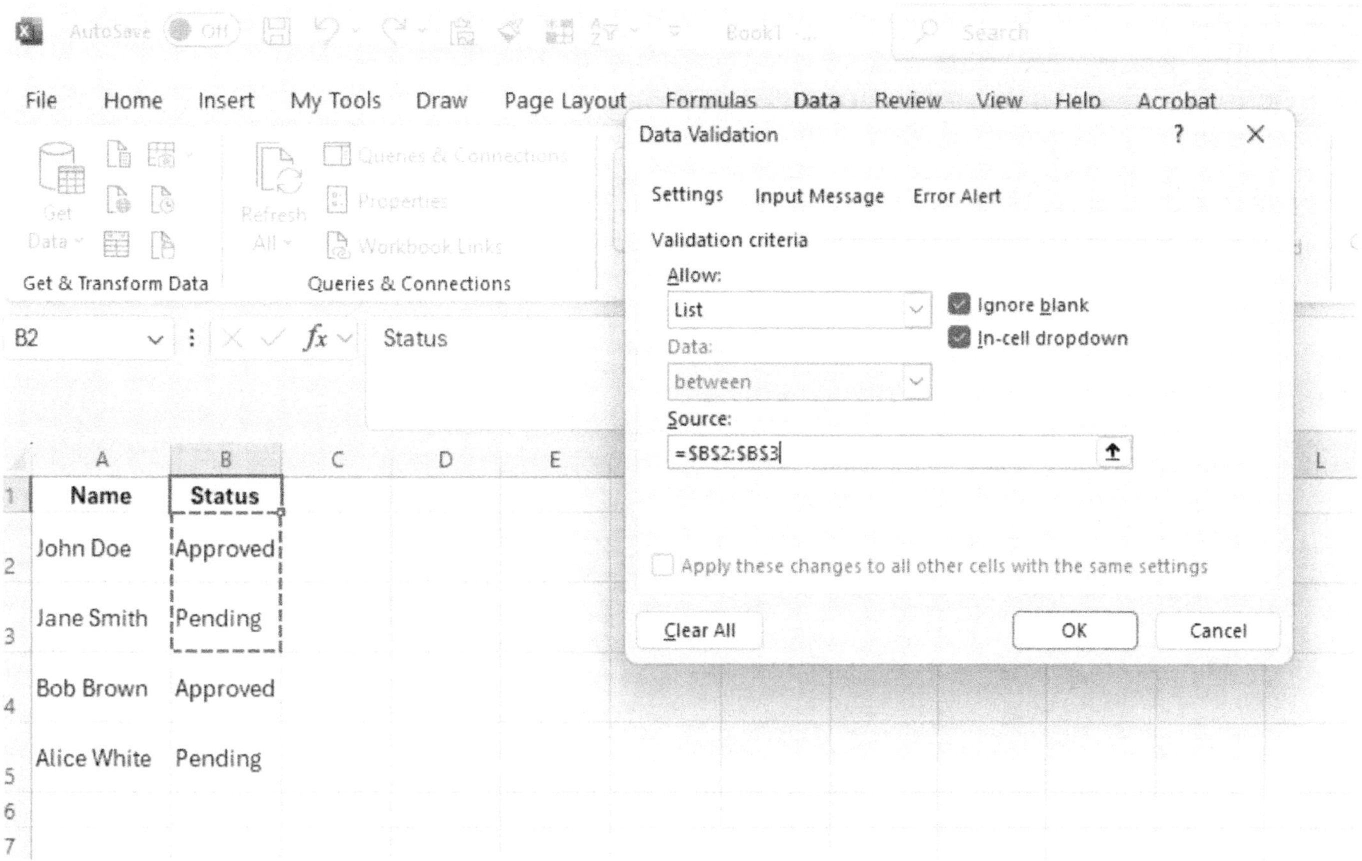

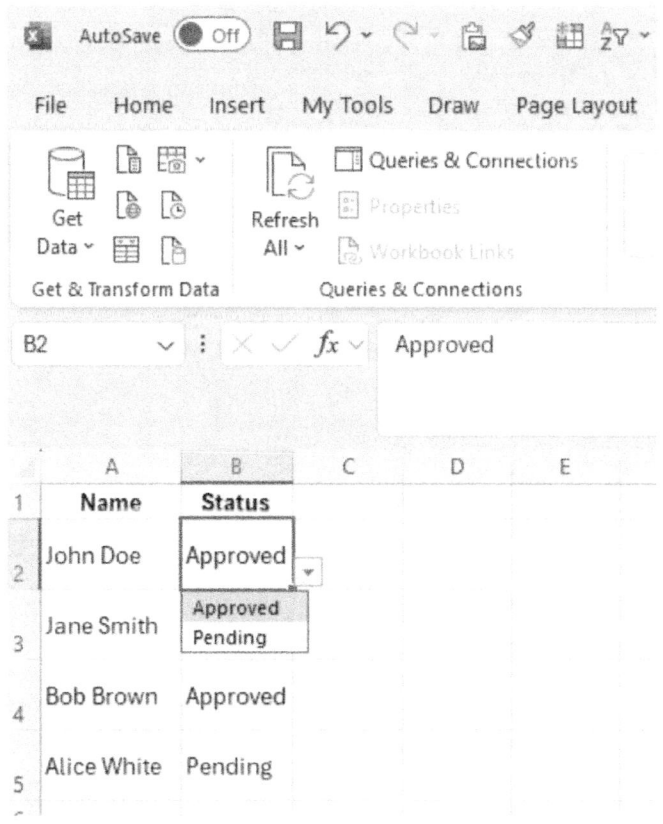

1. Select the column where you want to restrict input (e.g., "Status" should only allow "Approved" or "Pending").
2. Go to **Data > Data Validation** and choose the appropriate rule (e.g., a **list of predefined values**).
3. Enter allowed values or criteria, then click **OK**.

This simple feature prevents **typos, inconsistent entries, and invalid data** from corrupting your database.

Conditional Formatting: Instantly Spot Errors

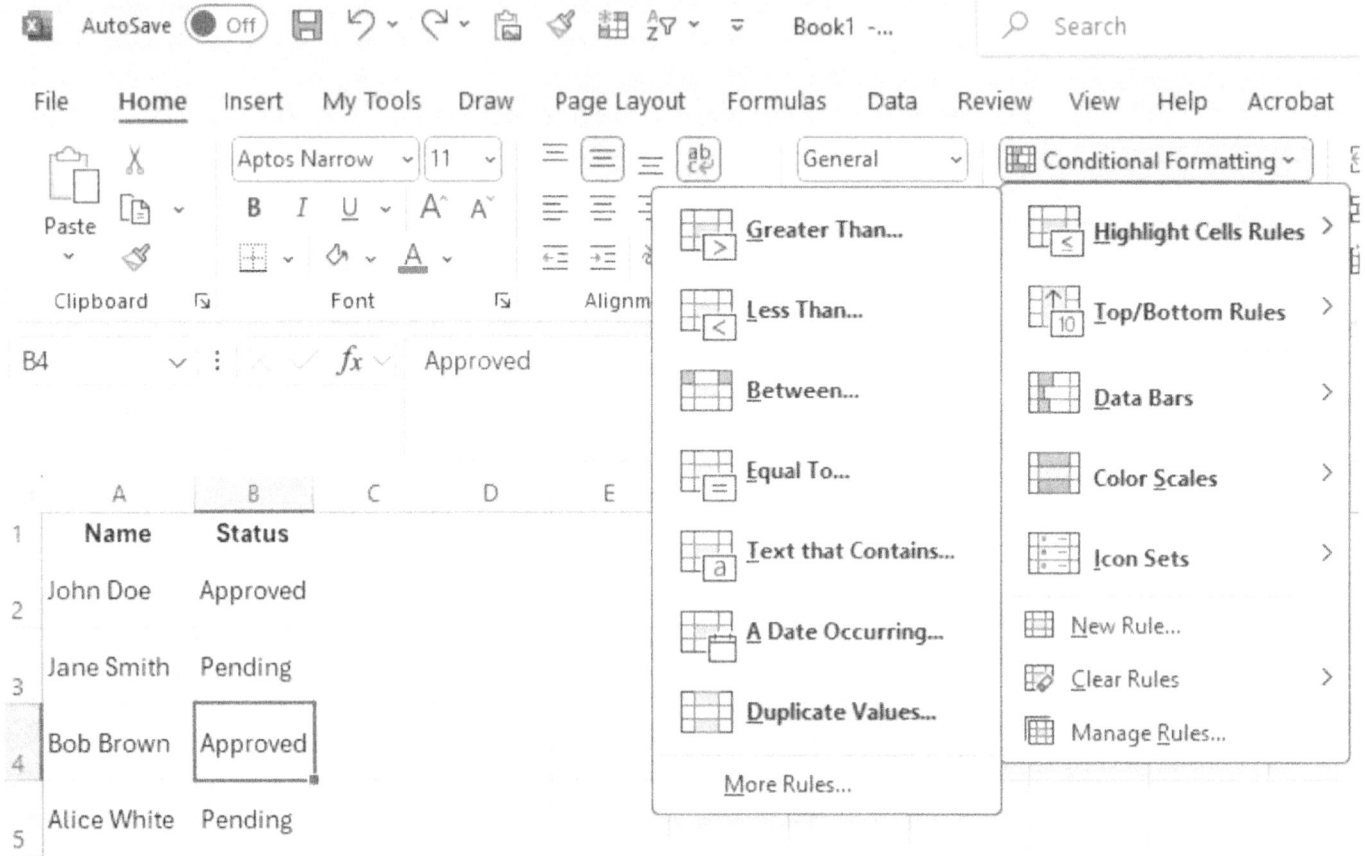

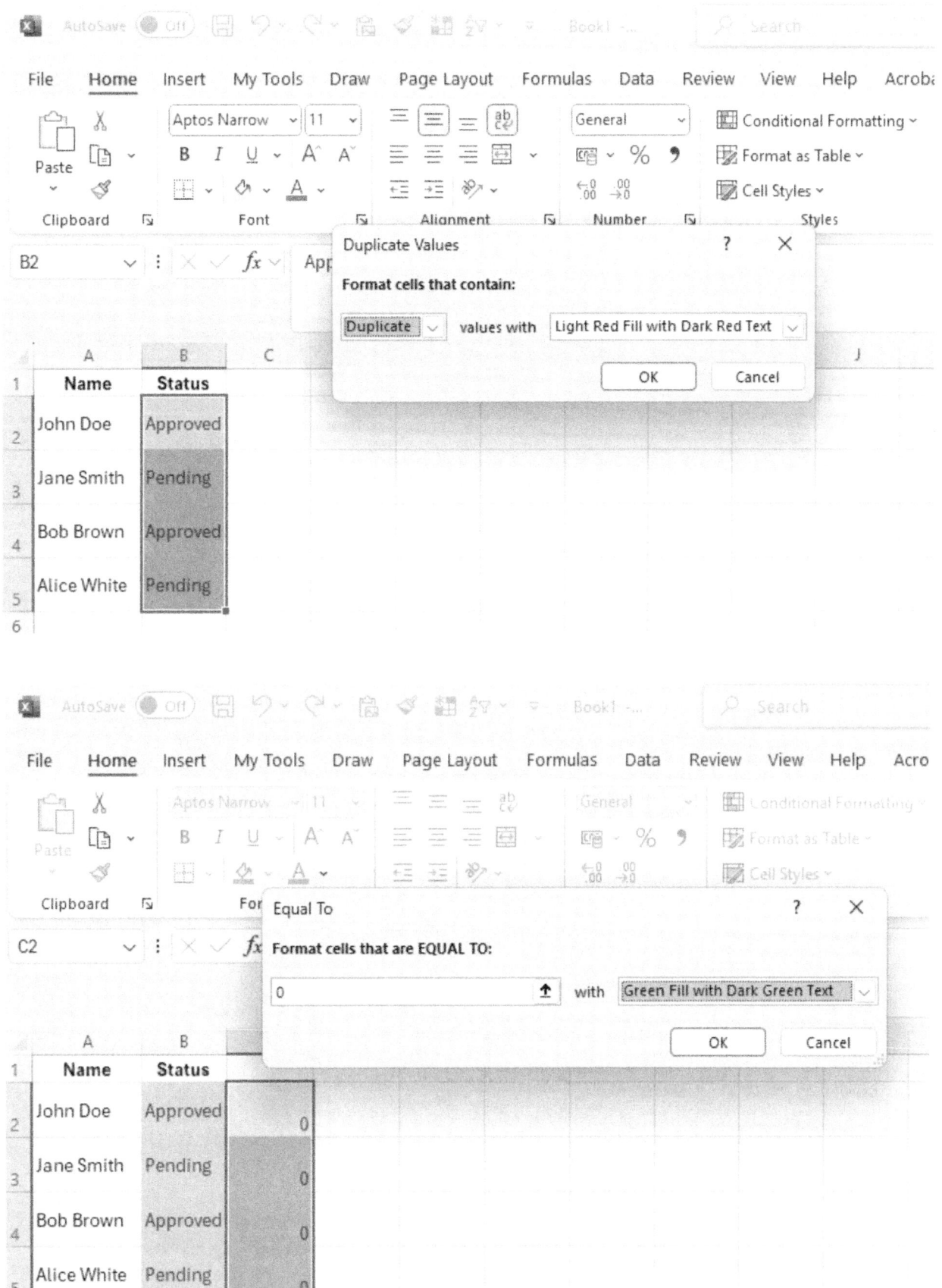

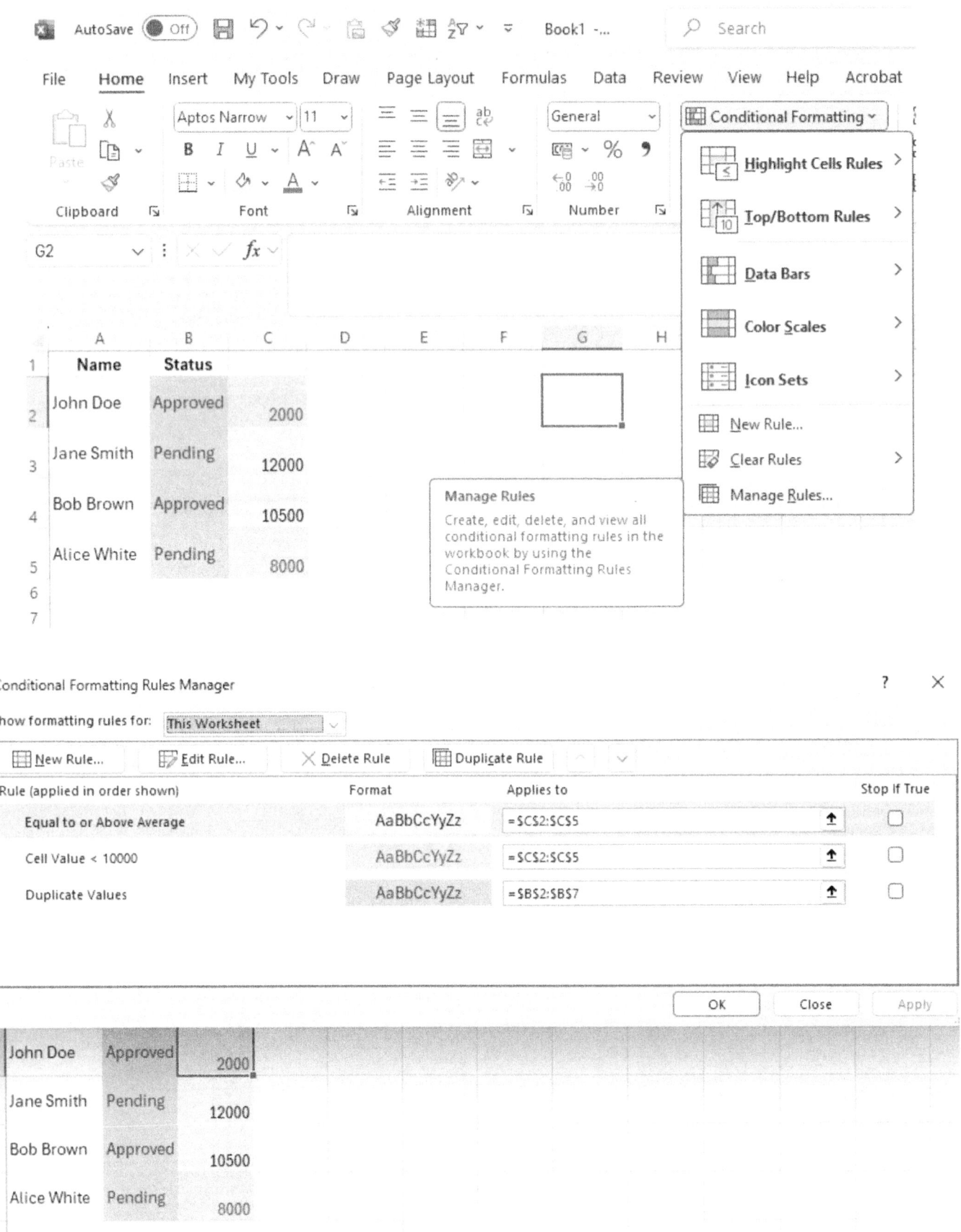

Even with well-structured data, mistakes happen. **Conditional Formatting** acts as an **early warning system**, highlighting errors before they affect calculations.

Some useful formatting rules include:

* **Duplicate detection:** Highlight duplicate entries in key columns (`Home > Conditional Formatting > Highlight Duplicate Values`).
* **Missing values:** Apply a color rule to flag empty cells in mandatory fields.
* **Out-of-range numbers:** Automatically shade cells that exceed predefined limits (e.g., expenses over $10,000).

These simple formatting tools **bring attention to inconsistencies**, allowing you to correct errors before they cause larger issues.

By implementing these **structured formatting practices**, you ensure that your database remains **clean, error-free, and scalable**, saving **time, frustration, and costly mistakes** in the long run.

Importing, Cleaning, and Organizing Large Data Sets

Handling large datasets in Excel can feel overwhelming, especially when dealing with **inconsistent formats, missing values, and redundant entries**. Without a structured approach, data can quickly become a mess, making analysis unreliable and time-consuming. **Mastering data import, cleaning, and organization is essential to transforming raw numbers into accurate, usable insights**.

Importing Data: Bringing in External Information Efficiently

Most professionals don't manually enter data into Excel; they import it from **CSV files, databases, online sources, or other applications like Google Sheets or SAP**. However, importing data without proper formatting often leads to errors—misaligned columns, missing fields, or unwanted characters.

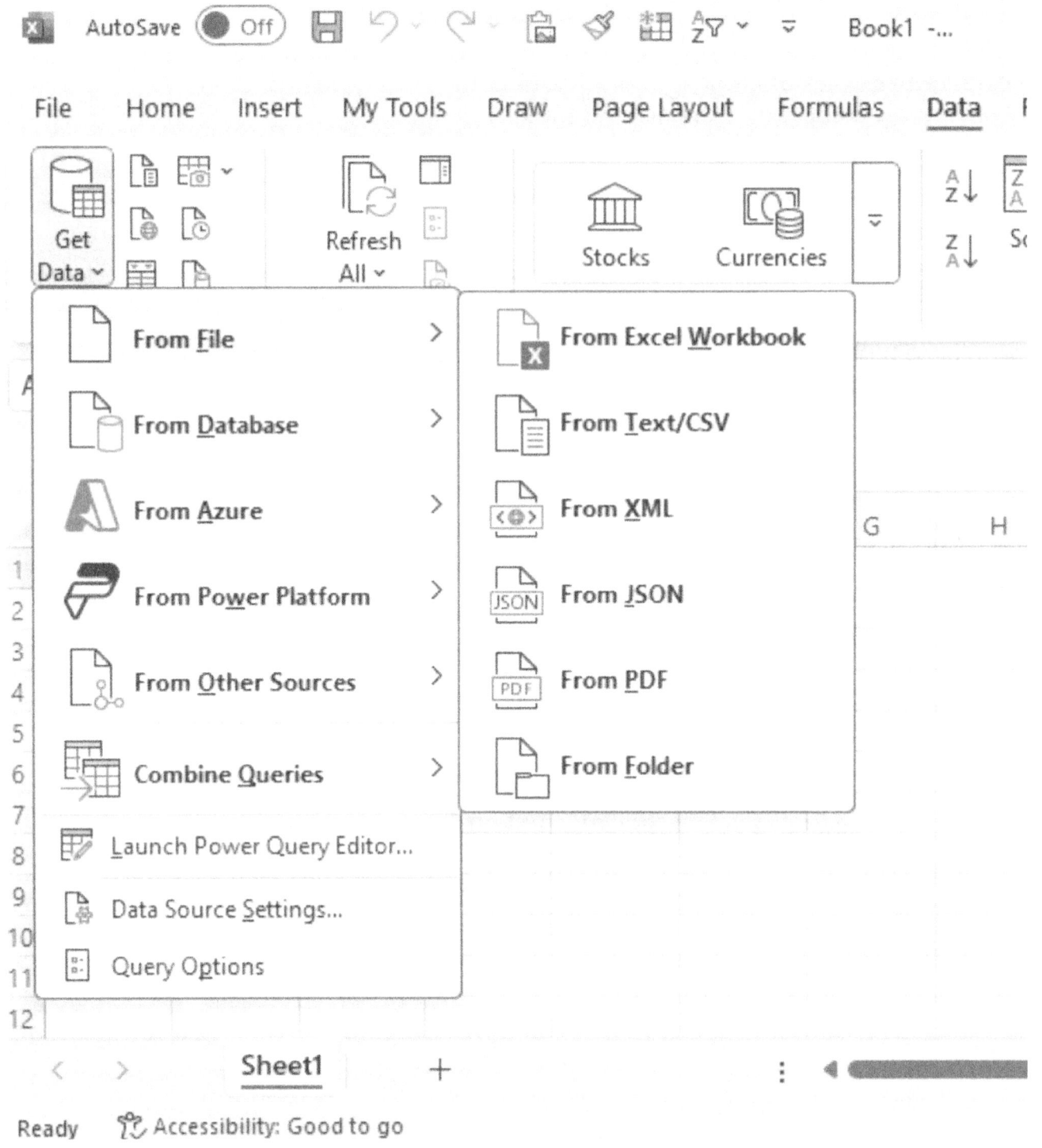

1. Use "Get & Transform" (Power Query) for Large Datasets

- Instead of manually opening a CSV file, use Data > Get Data to connect Excel directly to the source.

- This ensures that data refreshes automatically whenever updates are made, eliminating manual re-importing.

2. Check for Encoding Issues

- Some CSV files don't import special characters correctly. Ensure the file uses UTF-8 encoding to prevent errors.

3. Avoid Hard-Coded Imports

- Instead of copying and pasting data from external sources, link to the file so updates can be retrieved dynamically.

Cleaning Data: Eliminating Errors and Inconsistencies

Once data is imported, it's rarely perfect. Issues like **duplicate entries, inconsistent formatting, and missing values** can lead to **inaccurate analysis and misleading conclusions**. Cleaning data efficiently ensures that every entry is **valid, standardized, and ready for analysis**.

Using Power Query for Automated Data Cleaning

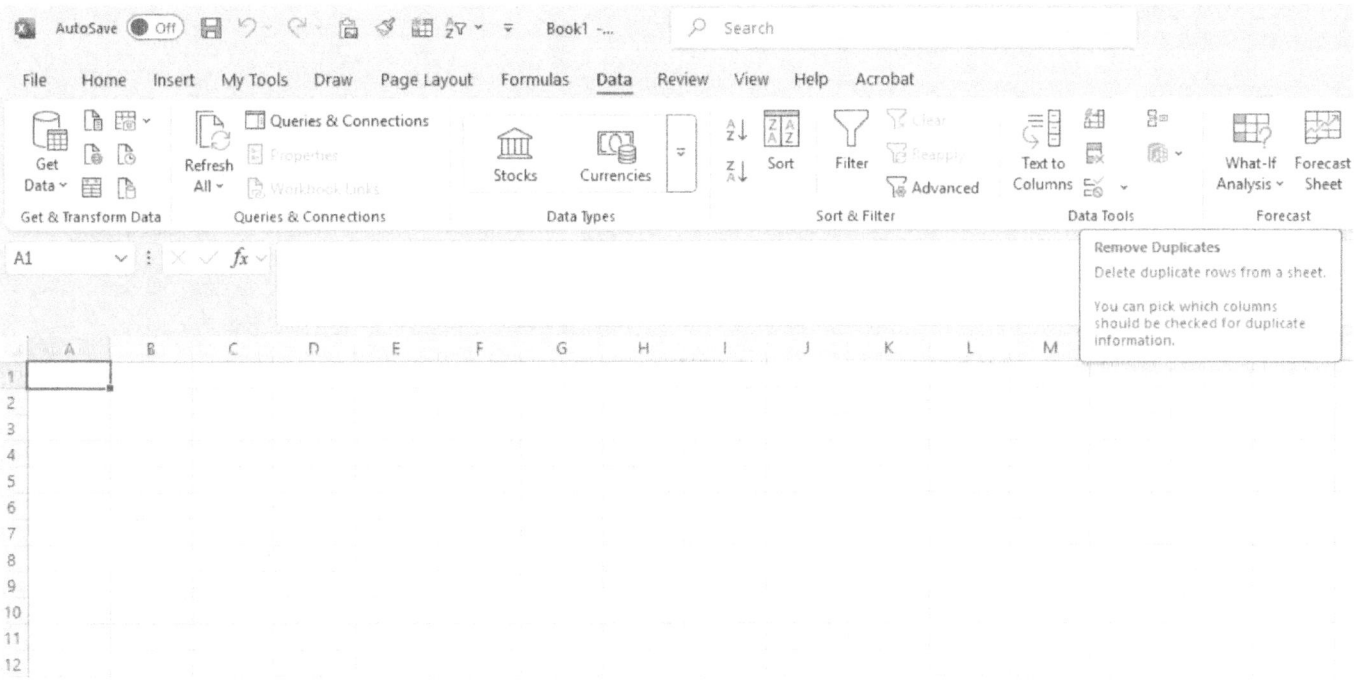

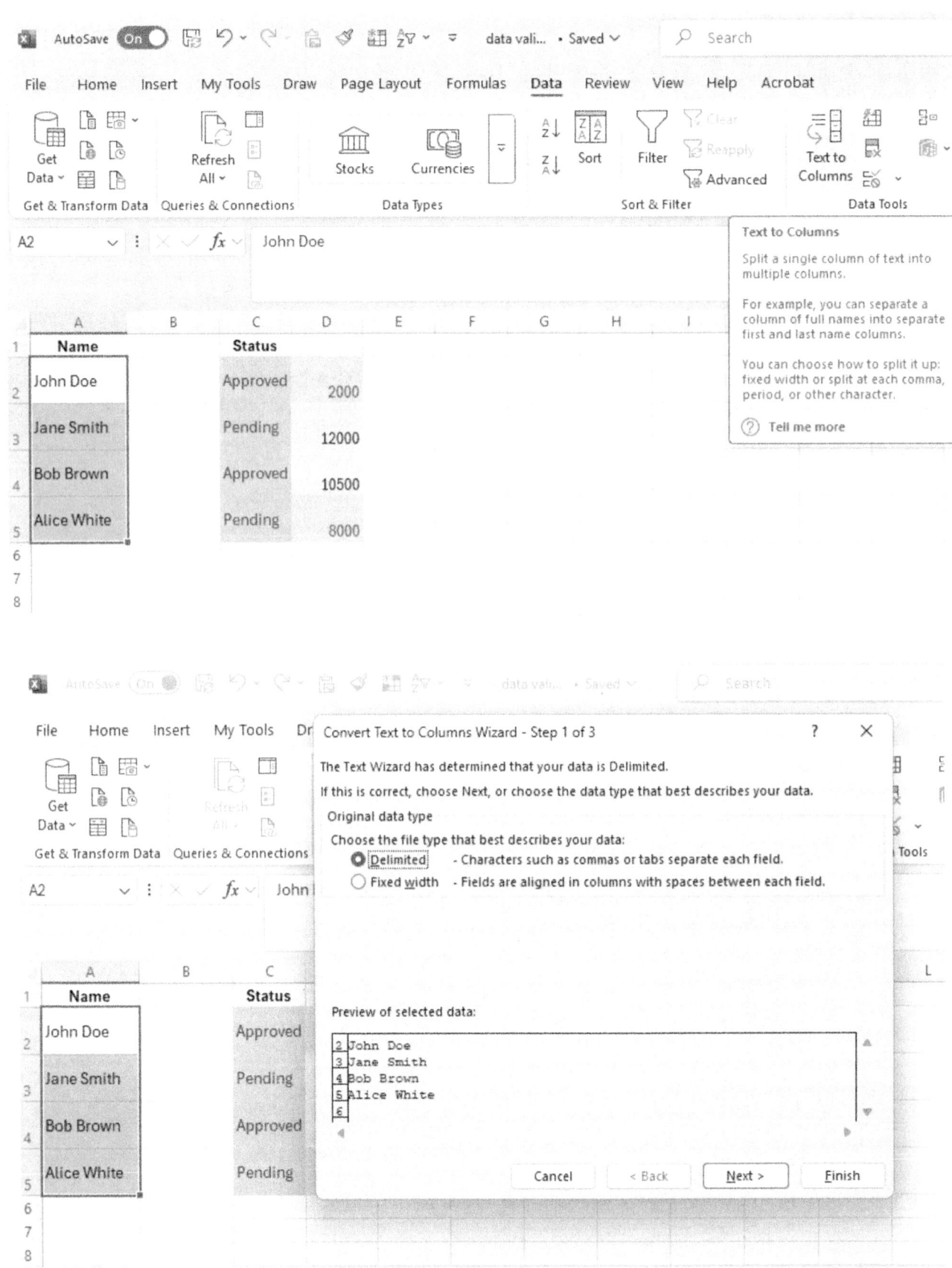

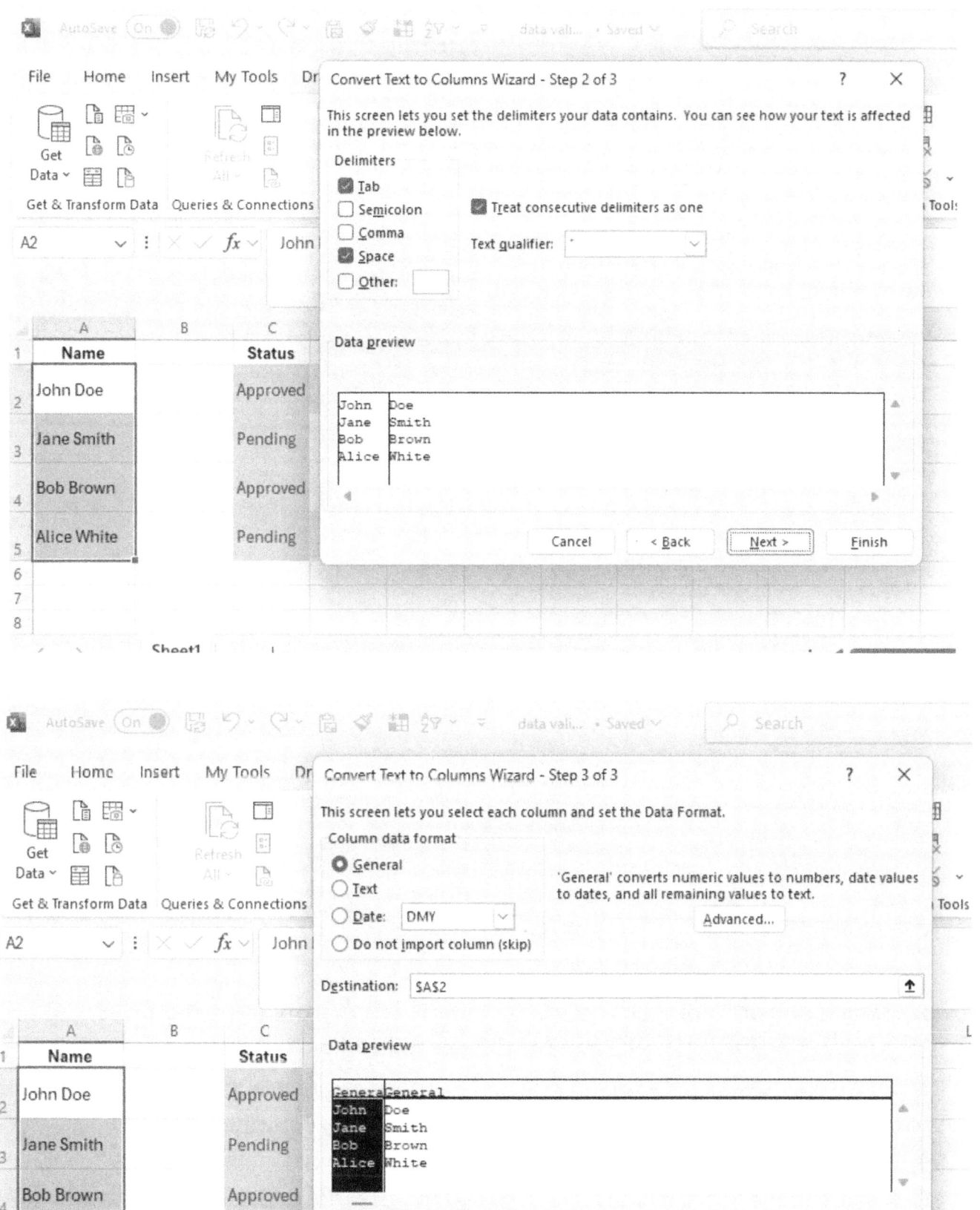

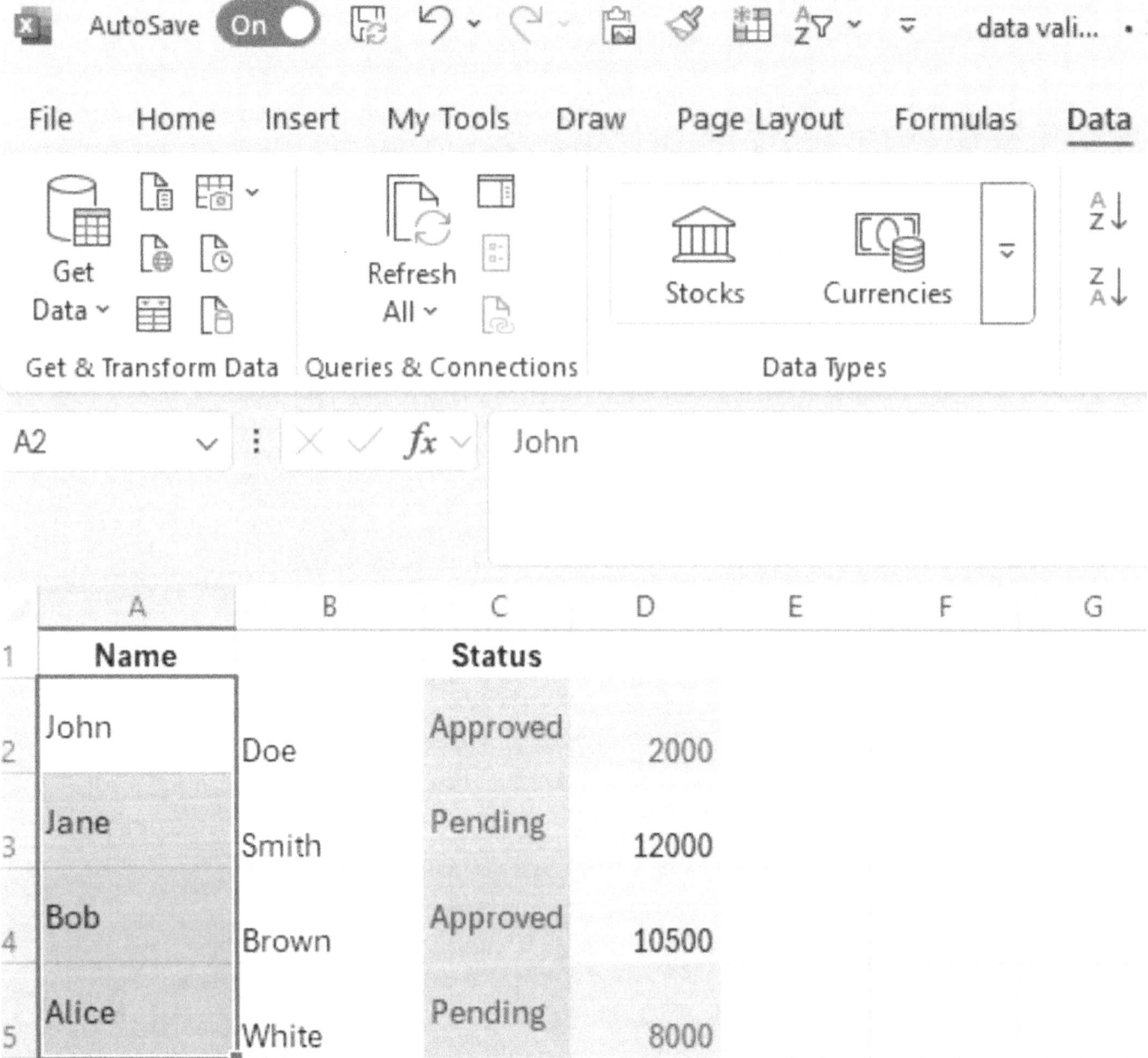

Power Query is one of Excel's most **powerful tools for data transformation**, allowing users to **clean, reshape, and structure datasets automatically**. With Power Query, you can:

- **Remove duplicate values** with one click (`Home > Remove Duplicates`).
- **Split combined data** (e.g., separating "First Last" into "First" and "Last").
- **Replace missing or incorrect values** (e.g., replacing blank cells with "N/A" or zero).
- **Standardize case formatting** (convert all text to uppercase, lowercase, or proper case).

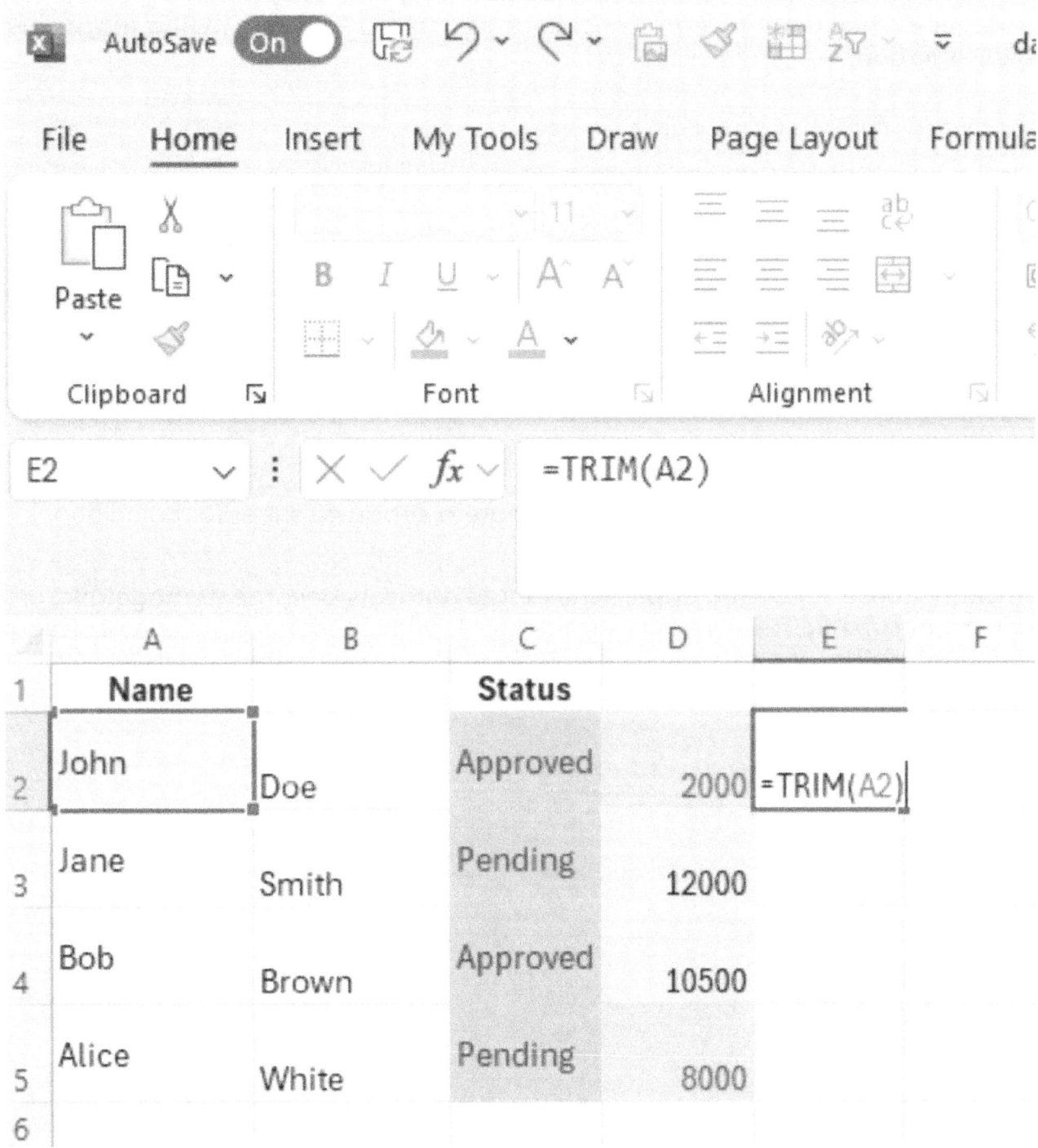

For datasets that don't require Power Query, Excel provides built-in tools to clean up data:

- **Use TRIM to remove unwanted spaces:** `=TRIM(A2)` eliminates extra spaces that can cause lookup errors.
- **Find and replace errors quickly** (`Ctrl + H`) to remove incorrect characters.
- **Use Flash Fill (`Ctrl + E`)** to quickly recognize and apply formatting patterns.

Organizing Data: Structuring for Analysis

A properly organized dataset **minimizes manual work, speeds up reporting, and enhances accuracy**. Once data is clean, it should be structured for **efficient filtering, analysis, and automation**.

Best Practices for Structuring Large Datasets

1. **Use Tables (`Ctrl + T`) for Dynamic Ranges**

- Automatically expands when new data is added.
- Simplifies structured references for formulas (`=SUM(Sales[Revenue])`).

2. **Apply Filters for Quick Analysis**

- Enable AutoFilter (`Ctrl + Shift + L`) to sort and analyze specific data subsets.
- Use advanced filters to extract unique records or multiple conditions.

3. **Keep Data Separate from Calculations**

- Raw data should remain untouched; create a separate sheet for calculations and reports.

By following these structured approaches, large datasets become **manageable, clean, and instantly usable**, helping you extract insights with confidence instead of struggling with chaotic data.

CHAPTER 4

FORMATTING THAT MATTERS: MAKING DATA VISUALLY IMPACTFUL

Transform complicated numbers into visually impressive reports that highlight your analytical skills and attention to detail

Conditional Formatting for Instant Insights

Raw data alone is rarely useful—**patterns, trends, and key insights often get lost in a sea of numbers**. That's where **Conditional Formatting** comes in. This feature allows you to **visually highlight important data points automatically**, making it easier to spot trends, outliers, and critical information at a glance. **Instead of manually scanning rows and columns, let Excel do the work for you.**

Why Conditional Formatting is a Game-Changer

Imagine you're preparing a **sales performance report** and need to quickly identify **underperforming regions** or highlight **top-performing sales reps**. You could:

- **Manually search through the data**—time-consuming and prone to error.
- **Sort and filter repeatedly**—useful but requires constant adjustment.
- **Use Conditional Formatting**—where Excel **automatically colors cells based on your criteria**, making important figures stand out instantly.

Conditional Formatting transforms **static spreadsheets into interactive dashboards, helping you make faster, data-driven decisions.**

Common Uses of Conditional Formatting

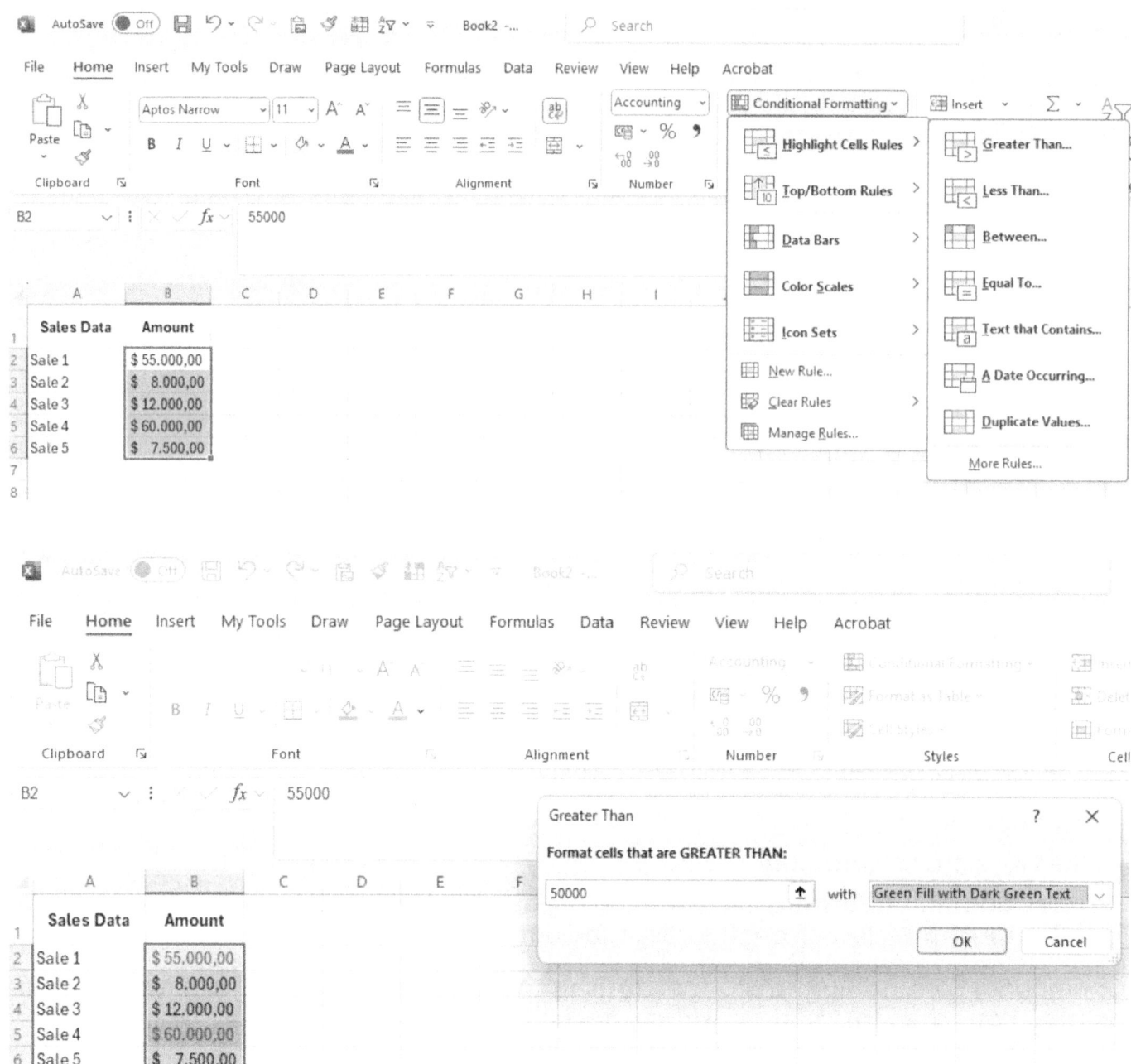

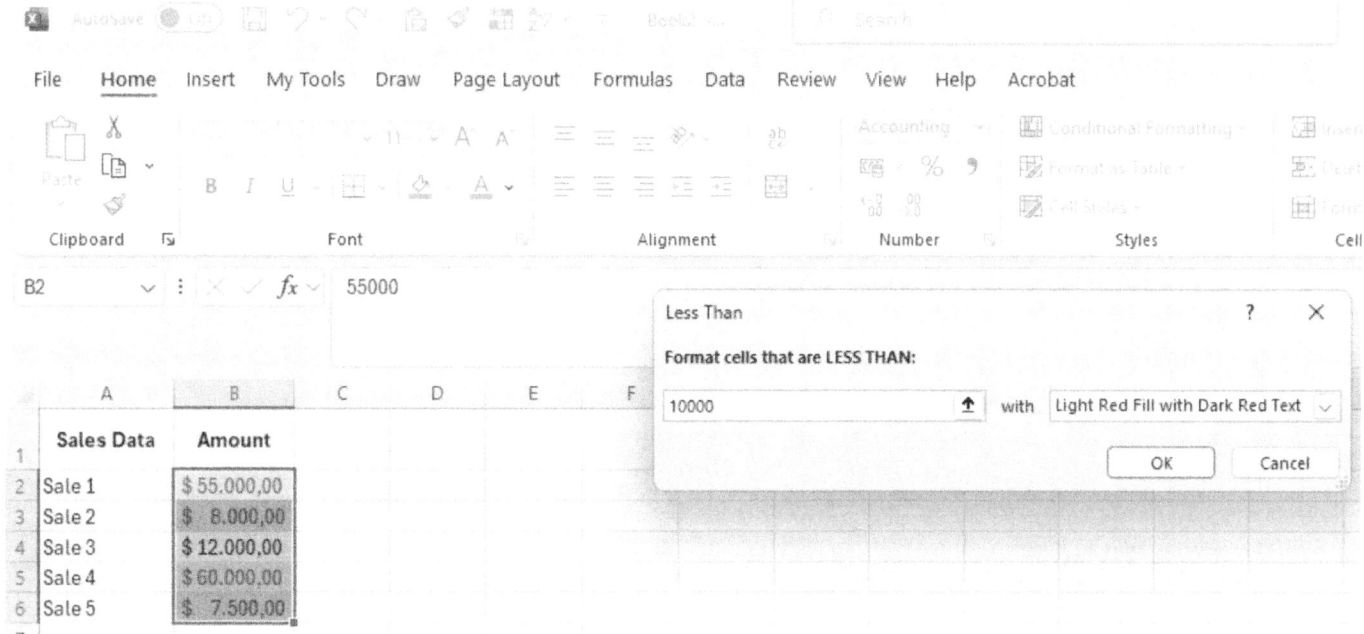

Highlighting Values Above or Below a Certain Threshold

Let's say you want to highlight all sales **above $50,000 in green** and all sales **below $10,000 in red**:

1. Select the **sales column**.
2. Go to **Home › Conditional Formatting › Highlight Cell Rules › Greater Than...**
3. Enter **50000** and choose **Green Fill with Dark Green Text**.
4. Repeat for values **less than 10000**, using **Red Fill with Dark Red Text**.

Now, high performers stand out in green, and areas of concern are **immediately visible in red**—no manual checking required.

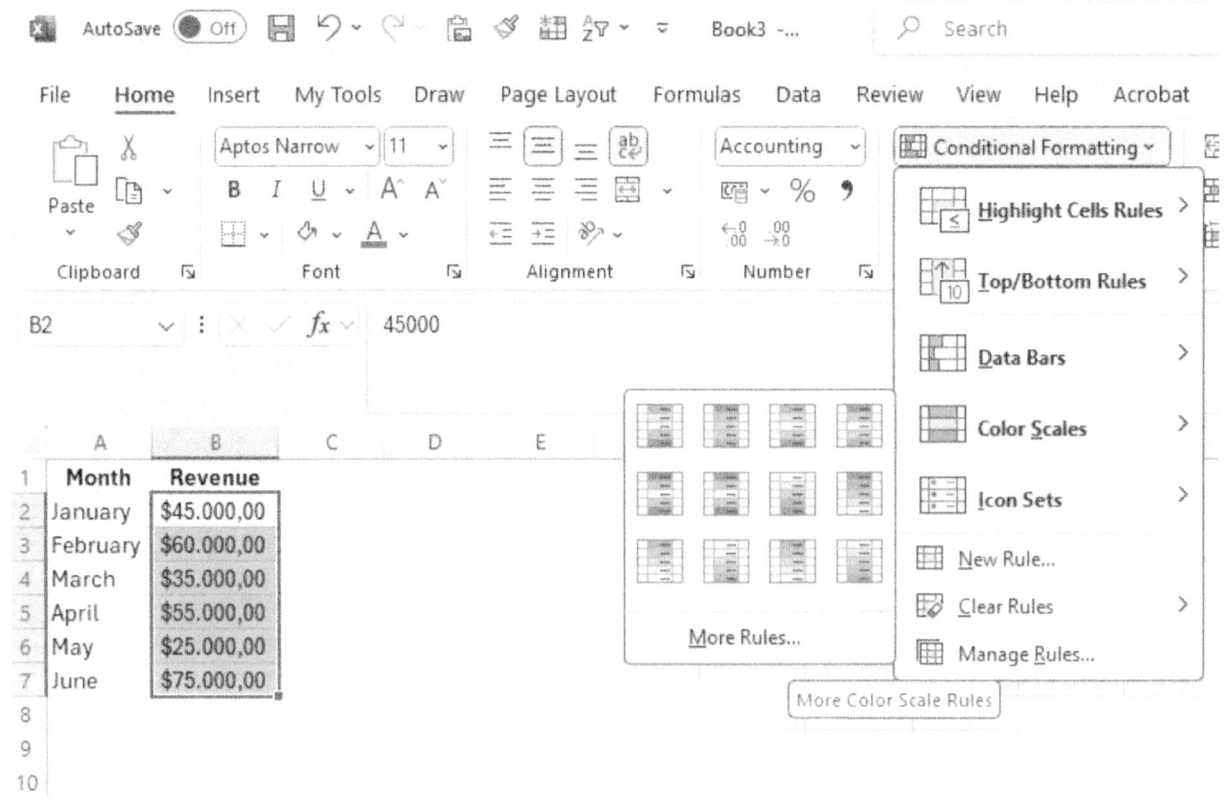

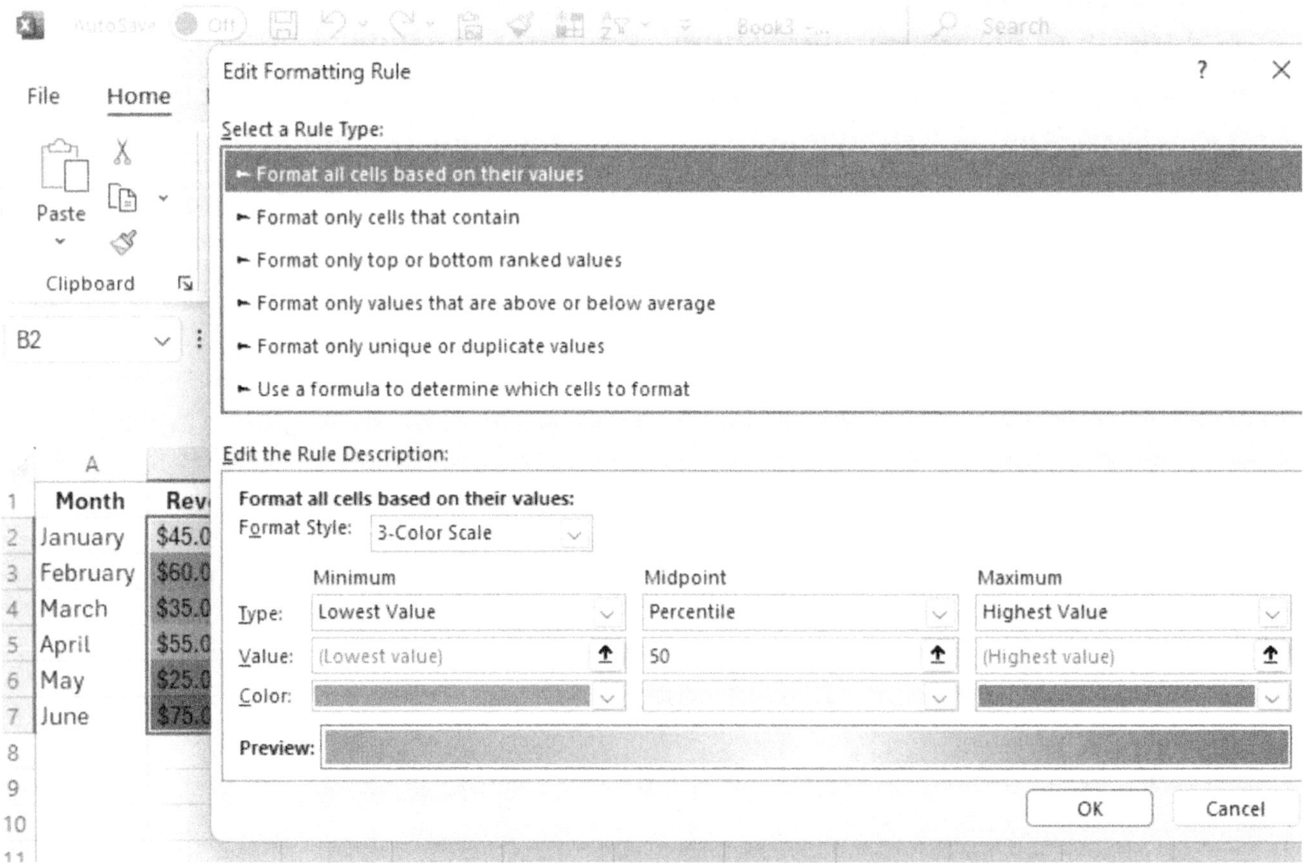

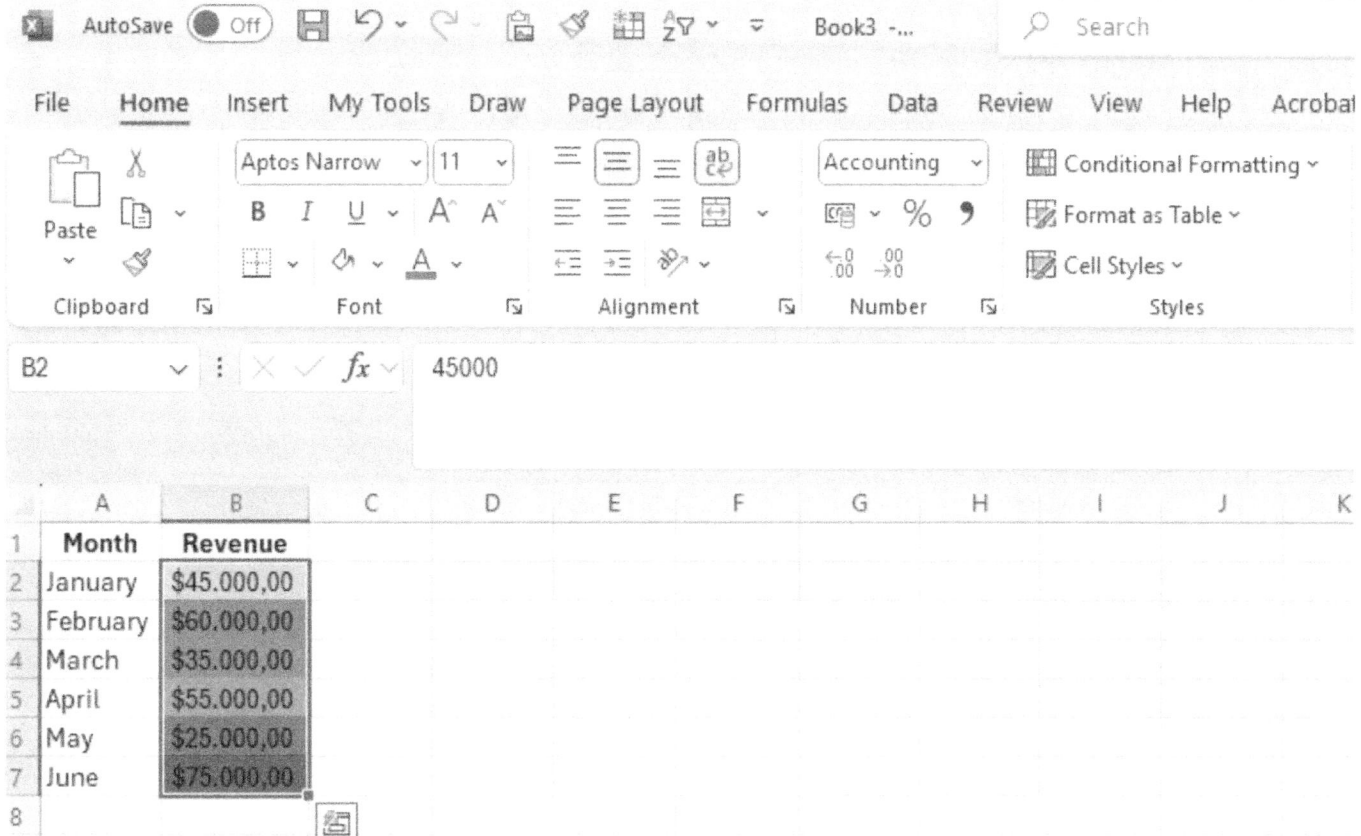

Instead of using rigid threshold-based formatting, **color scales** provide a **gradient effect**, making **relative comparisons** easier.

Example: If you're analyzing **monthly revenue trends**, a **green-to-red color scale** can visually show which months performed best (green) and worst (red), helping you **spot seasonal trends without calculations**.

To apply:

1. Select the **revenue column**.
2. Click **Conditional Formatting › Color Scales** and choose a color scheme (e.g., **Green-Yellow-Red** for high-to-low values).

Now, you instantly **see patterns** without sorting or filtering.

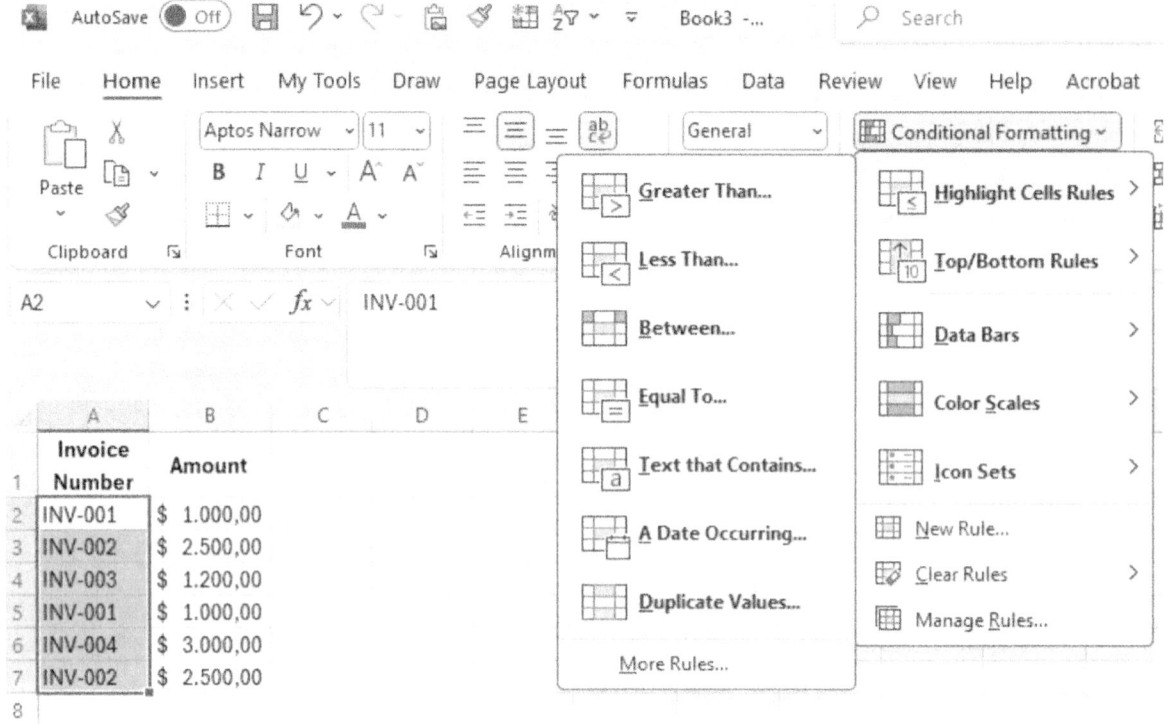

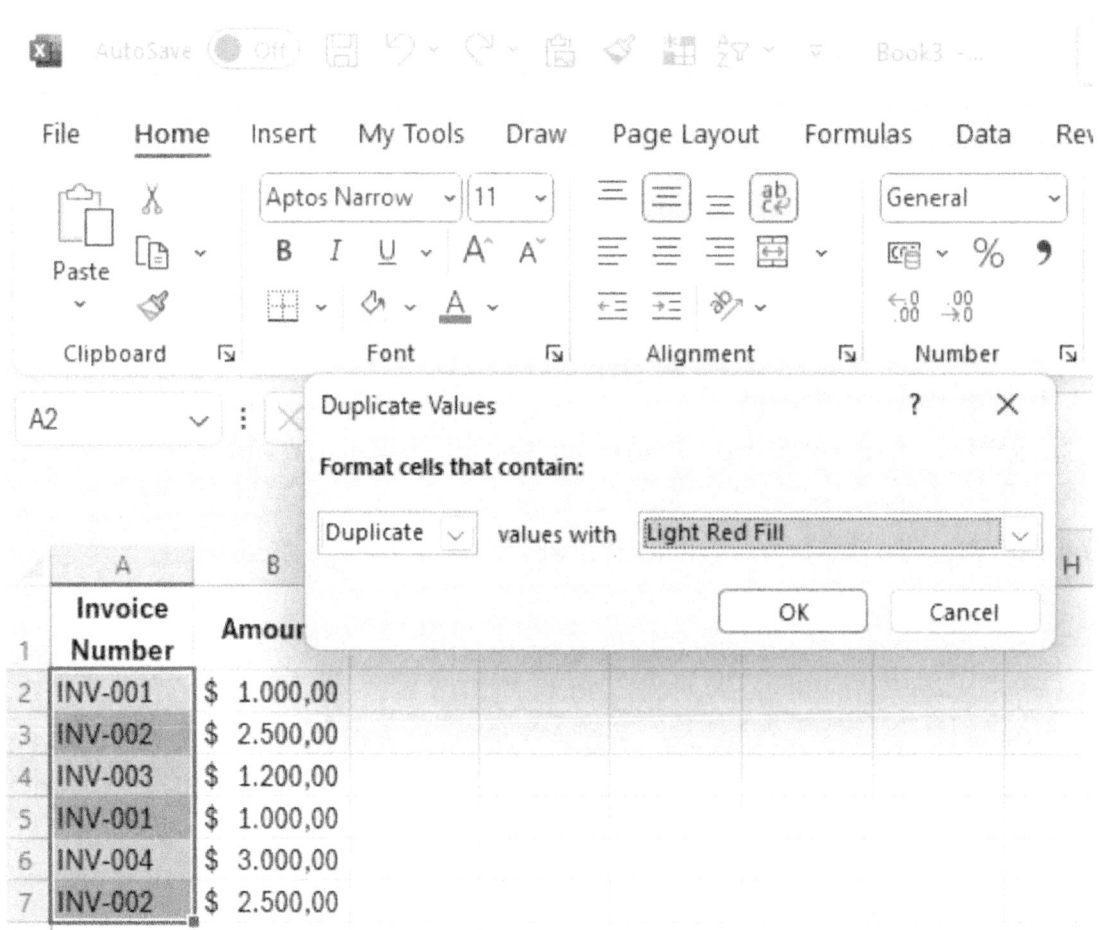

Duplicate entries can wreak havoc on reports, leading to **miscalculations and misleading insights**. Instead of manually searching for duplicates, let Excel do it:

1. Select the **column with potential duplicates** (e.g., **Invoice Numbers**).
2. Click **Conditional Formatting > Highlight Cell Rules > Duplicate Values**.
3. Choose a highlight color (e.g., **light red fill**).

Now, duplicate values **instantly pop out**, ensuring cleaner data and preventing costly mistakes.

Making Data-Driven Decisions Faster

By applying **Conditional Formatting strategically**, you can:

- **Spot trends instantly** instead of relying on filters.
- **Identify problems before they escalate** (e.g., overdue payments, low-performing sales regions).
- **Reduce manual effort**, freeing up time for analysis rather than data-checking.

With just a few clicks, your spreadsheets become **visually intuitive tools** that highlight key insights, helping you work **smarter, not harder**.

Crafting Professional-Quality Reports and Tables

In the business world, how you present data **matters just as much as the data itself**. A well-structured report or table not only communicates insights **effectively** but also **builds credibility**. Whether you're preparing an executive summary, a financial report, or a performance dashboard, professional formatting ensures **clarity, impact, and readability**.

Designing Reports That Make an Impact

A professional Excel report isn't just a collection of numbers—it's a **story told through data**. To craft a high-quality report, consider:

1. Clarity Comes First: Keep It Clean and Focused

A common mistake in reporting is **overloading the reader with too much information**. A professional report should:

- **Have a clear structure**—title, summary, key findings, and supporting details.
- **Use white space effectively**—avoid clutter by **spacing out sections and aligning elements properly**.
- **Eliminate unnecessary gridlines**—Excel's default grid can make reports look messy. Hide them (`View > Gridlines`) for a cleaner presentation.

2. Choose the Right Font and Colors

- **Fonts:** Stick to professional, easy-to-read fonts like **Calibri, Arial, or Lora**. Avoid script or decorative fonts that can make data hard to read.
- **Colors:** Use **Excel Green (CMYK 85, 10, 100, 10)** for highlights and accents while keeping backgrounds neutral.
- **Contrast:** Dark text on a light background improves readability. Avoid neon colors or excessive bolding.

3. Use Summary Sections and Dynamic Headings

A well-crafted report should **highlight key insights upfront**. Consider using:

- **Bold headers and subheaders** (`Ctrl + B`) for easy navigation.
- **Merged title rows** (`Merge & Center`) to make headings stand out.
- **Summary sections with key takeaways**—avoid forcing the reader to dig through the entire dataset.

Building Professional Tables: The Gold Standard for Readability

Tables are the **backbone of every professional report**. Instead of pasting raw data into a worksheet, **format tables properly** to ensure consistency and usability.

1. Convert Data into an Excel Table (`Ctrl + T`)

Excel's Table feature ensures:

- **Automatic formatting**—each row is clearly distinguished.
- **Filter-ready headers**—drop-down filters are enabled by default.
- **Dynamic expansion**—tables update automatically as new data is added.

2. Apply Consistent Number Formatting

Inconsistent number formats make reports **look amateurish**. Always:

- Use **comma separators** for thousands (e.g., `1.000.000` instead of `1000000`).
- Align numbers **right** and text **left** for readability.
- Format currency fields using **Accounting format** instead of General or Text.

3. Use Conditional Formatting for Visual Cues

Instead of scanning through rows, **let Excel highlight important trends**. Apply:

- **Data Bars** to visualize values at a glance (`Home > Conditional Formatting > Data Bars`).
- **Color Scales** to show performance trends (`Green = Good, Red = Poor`).
- **Icons for KPIs** (e.g., up arrows for growth, down arrows for declines).

CHAPTER 5

DATA VALIDATION: ENSURING ACCURACY AND PREVENTING ERRORS

Create foolproof systems that eliminate embarrassing
data errors in meetings and presentations

Setting Up Intelligent Data Validation Rules

Data entry errors are one of the most common causes of inaccurate reports, flawed analyses, and wasted time in Excel. Whether it's a **mislabeled category, a mistyped number, or an invalid date**, these small mistakes can snowball into **major business issues**. This is where **Data Validation** comes in—an essential tool that allows you to **control, restrict, and guide data entry** to ensure consistency and accuracy.

By setting up **intelligent Data Validation rules**, you can minimize human error, improve the reliability of your datasets, and make sure that **every input meets your business requirements**.

Why Data Validation Matters

Imagine you're managing a **budget spreadsheet** where expenses need to be categorized as "Marketing," "Operations," or "R&D." Without Data Validation, a user might type "Market" instead of "Marketing" or misspell "Operations" as "Opperations." When it's time to filter or analyze expenses, **these small inconsistencies can create chaos**—reports become unreliable, errors must be manually corrected, and key insights may be lost.

Data Validation prevents this by **restricting inputs** to predefined formats, lists, or logical rules, ensuring that every entry is **clean, accurate, and useful.**

Essential Data Validation Rules to Use

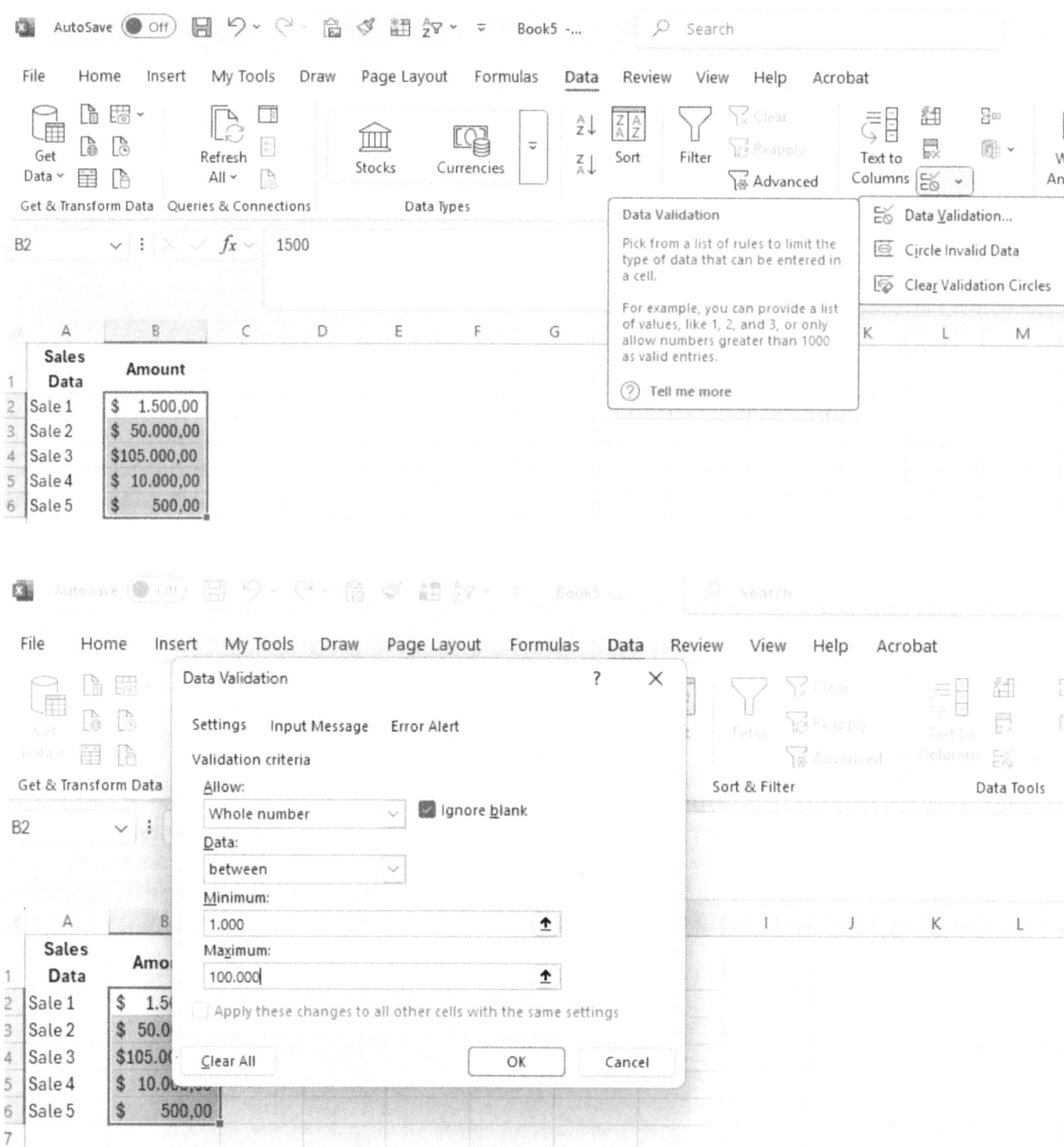

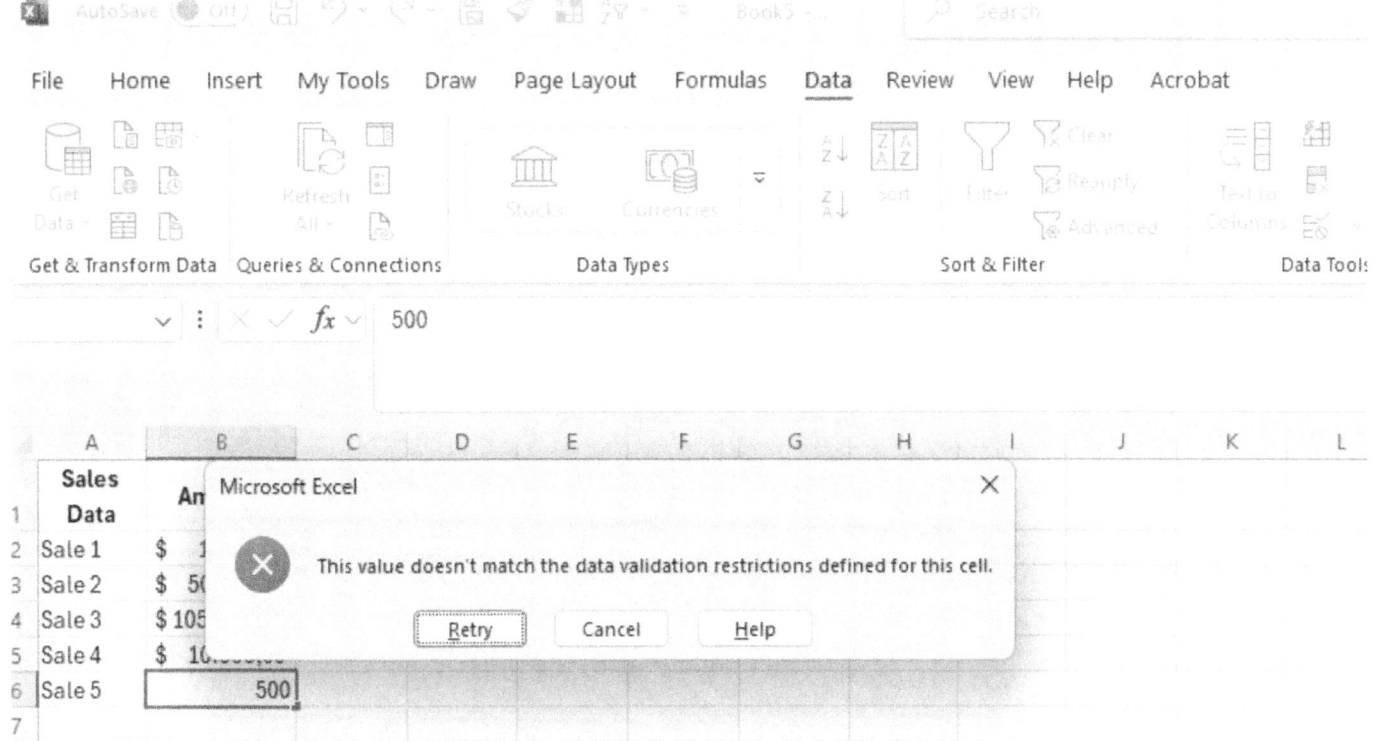

1. Restricting Entries to Specific Ranges (Numbers, Dates, or Text Lengths)

Setting **minimum and maximum limits** prevents errors like entering **negative sales figures or unrealistic dates**.

To enforce a rule where **sales figures must be between $1,000 and $100,000**:

- Select the column where sales data is entered.
- Go to **Data > Data Validation** and choose **Whole Number**.
- Set the minimum to `1000` and maximum to `100000`.
- Click **OK**—now, Excel will reject any invalid values.

This ensures **no impossible or incorrect figures** sneak into your dataset.

2. Creating Logical Input Rules (Custom Formulas)

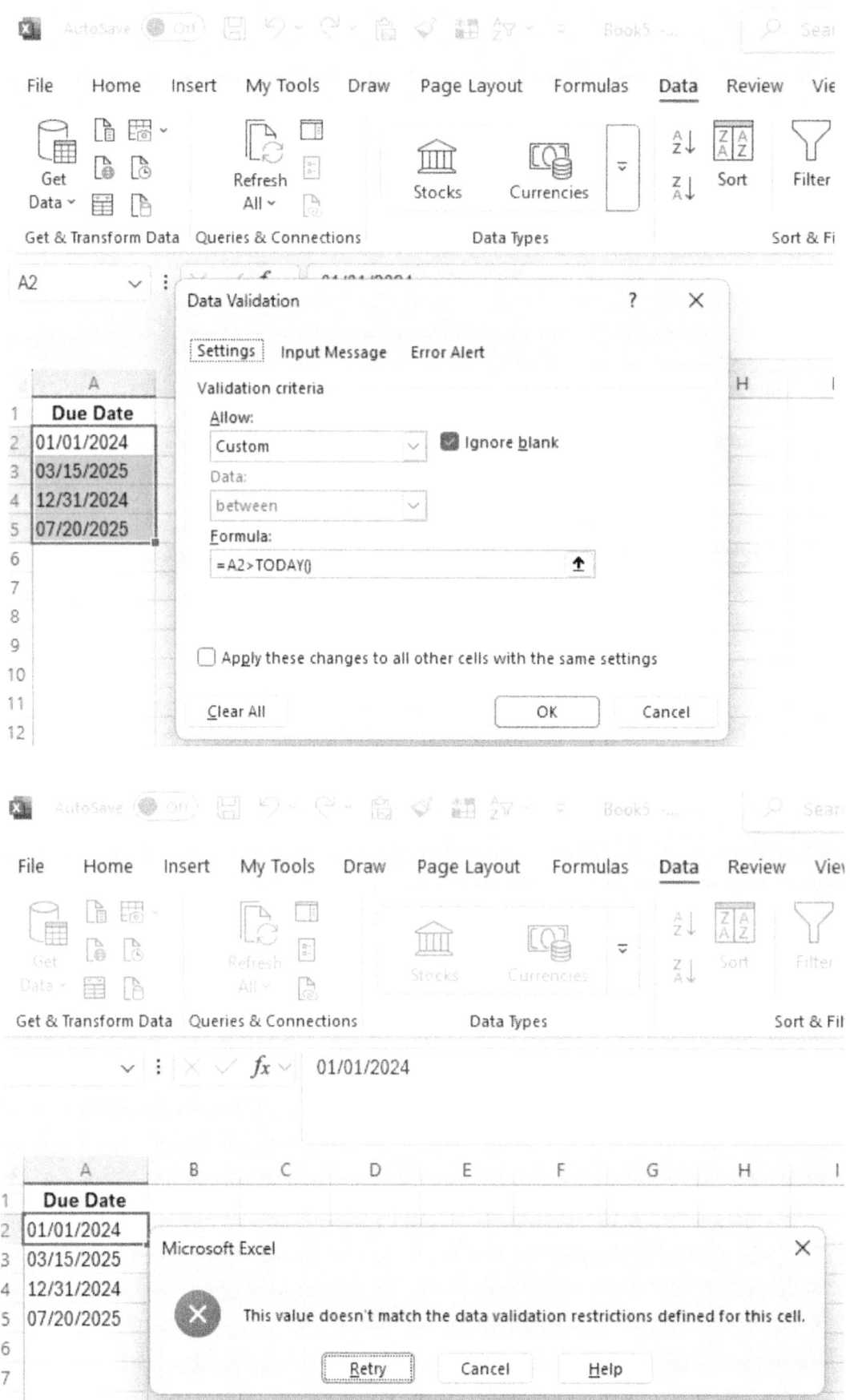

For **more complex validations**, you can use **Excel formulas** to define rules.

Example: If you need a column where **dates must be in the future**, use:

- Select the date column, go to **Data Validation**, and choose **Custom Formula**.
- Enter `=A2>TODAY()`—this rule ensures that only **future dates** can be entered.

Users who try entering past dates will receive an **error message**, guiding them to correct their input.

3. Preventing Duplicate Entries

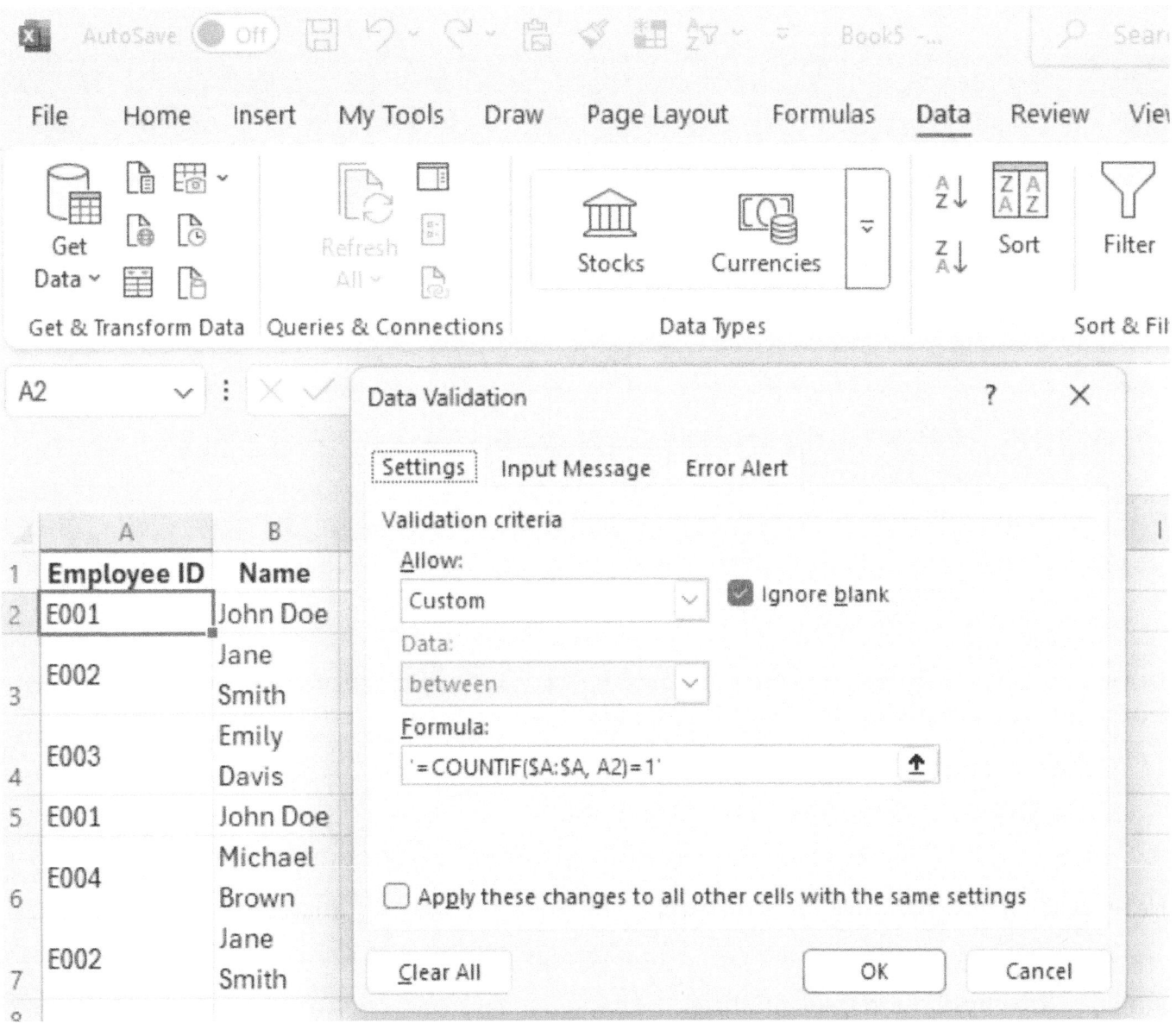

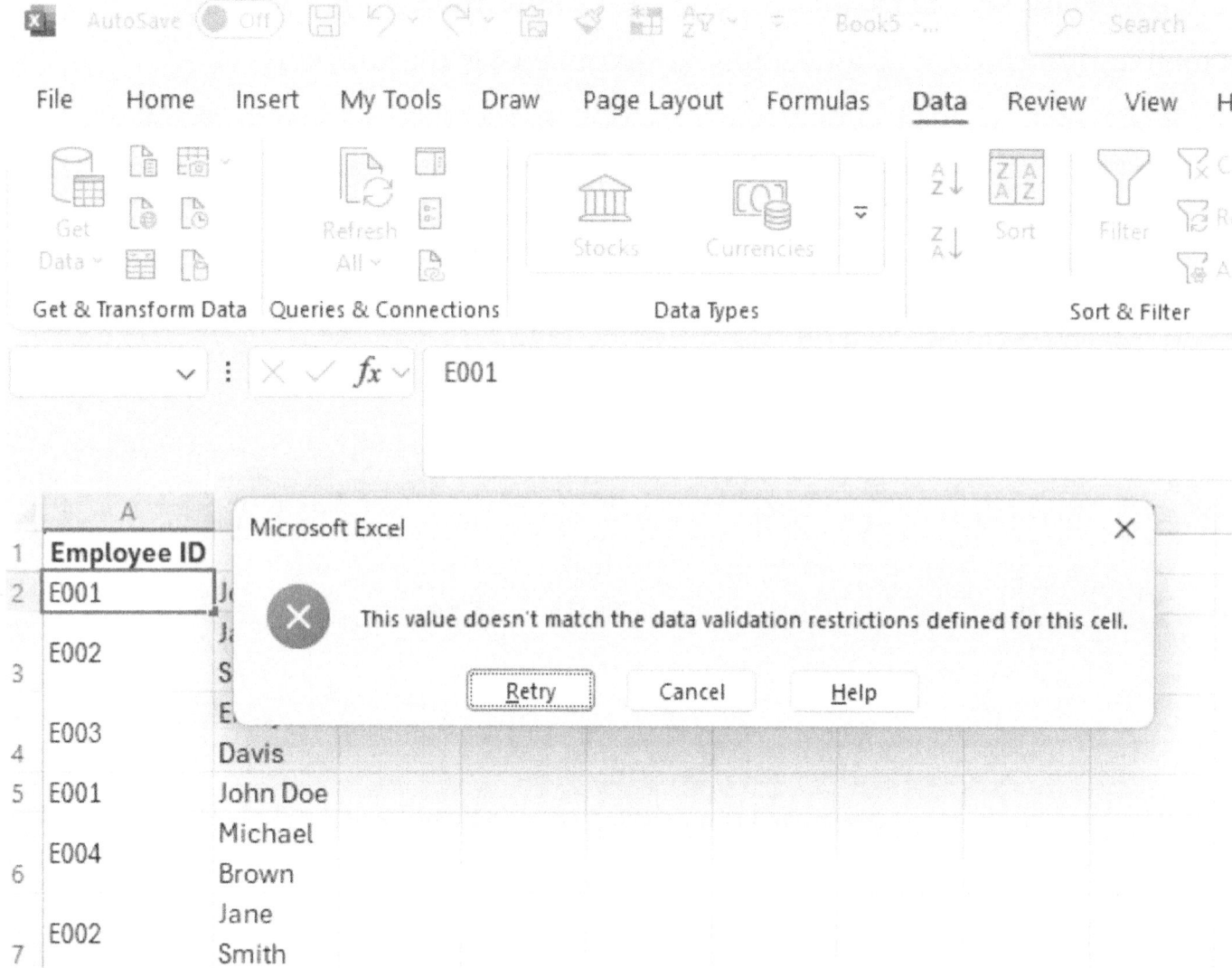

Duplicate entries can cause **serious problems in lists like employee IDs, invoice numbers, or product codes**. To block duplicates:

1. Select the column (e.g., Employee ID).
2. Go to **Data Validation > Custom Formula**.
3. Enter `=COUNTIF($A:$A, A2)=1` to ensure each value appears **only once**.

Now, Excel will **reject duplicate entries**, ensuring unique data integrity.

Making Data Validation User-Friendly

Even the best validation rules are useless if users don't understand **why their entry was rejected**. To make Data Validation intuitive:

*   **Set Up Input Messages** (`Data Validation > Input Message`)—this displays a pop-up hint with instructions before users enter data.

- **Customize Error Alerts (`Data Validation > Error Alert`)—instead of Excel's default vague message, create a clear and friendly warning like:**
- *"Invalid entry. Please enter a date in the future."*

By implementing **intelligent Data Validation rules**, you ensure **error-free data entry**, saving yourself (and your team) from endless corrections and confusion down the line.

Using Drop-Down Lists and Custom Alerts to Guide Users

Data entry errors are one of the biggest productivity killers in Excel. A simple typo, an inconsistent category name, or an invalid entry can throw off calculations, break reports, and create confusion across teams. **Drop-down lists and custom alerts provide a simple yet powerful way to enforce accuracy while guiding users toward correct inputs.** By setting up these tools, you can create structured spreadsheets where errors are minimized, and workflows remain efficient.

Why Drop-Down Lists Are Essential

Imagine you're managing a **project tracking sheet** where team members need to select the project status—options like "In Progress," "Completed," and "On Hold." Without a drop-down list, one person might type "in progress" (lowercase), another might use "IP," and someone else might write "Work in Progress." Now, when you try to filter or analyze the data, **inconsistent inputs create chaos**.

Drop-down lists **eliminate these issues** by restricting inputs to a **predefined set of choices**, ensuring that all data is entered correctly and uniformly.

Creating a Drop-Down List in Excel

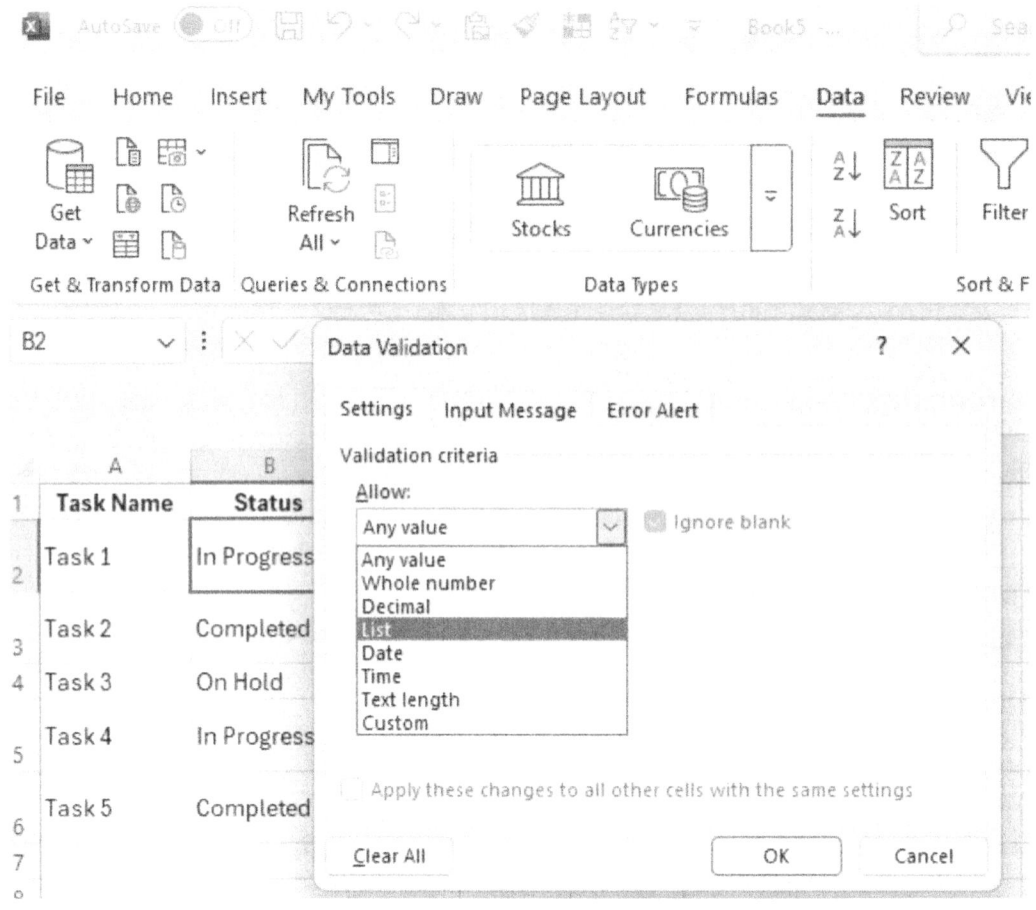

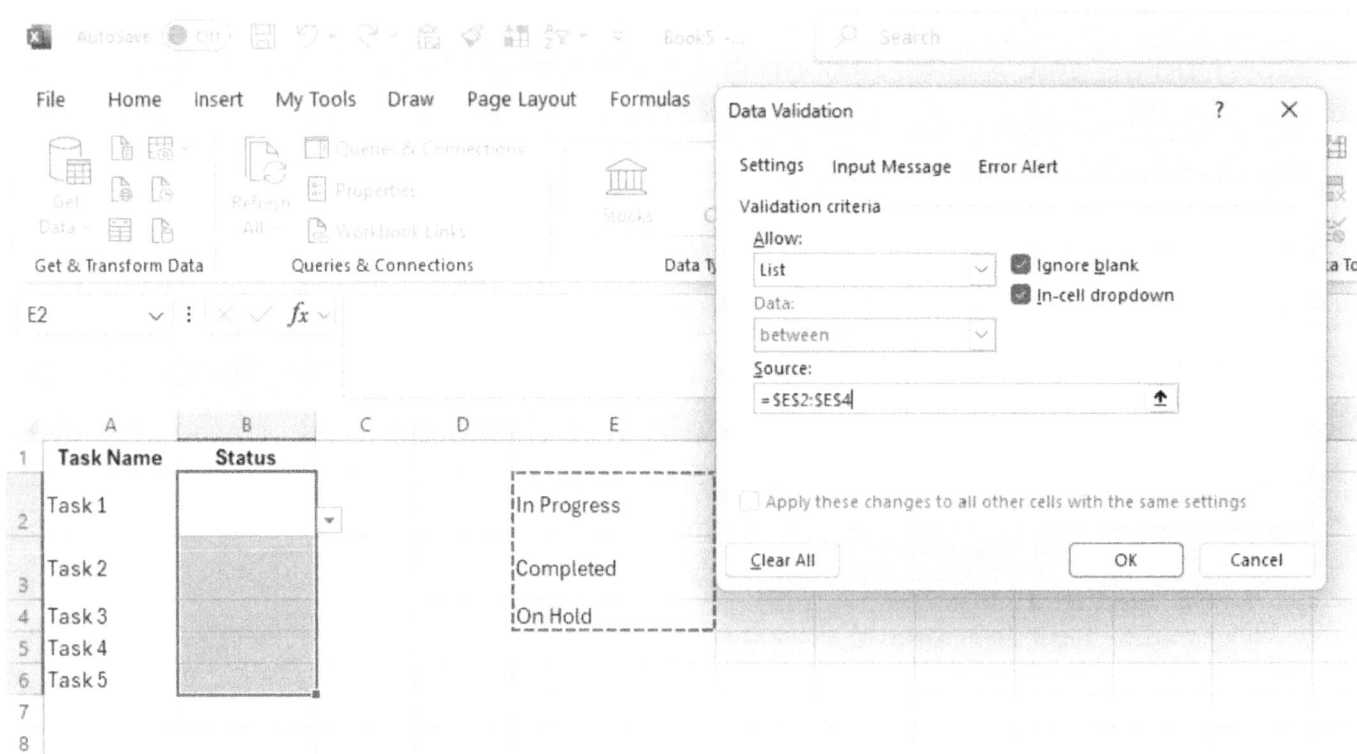

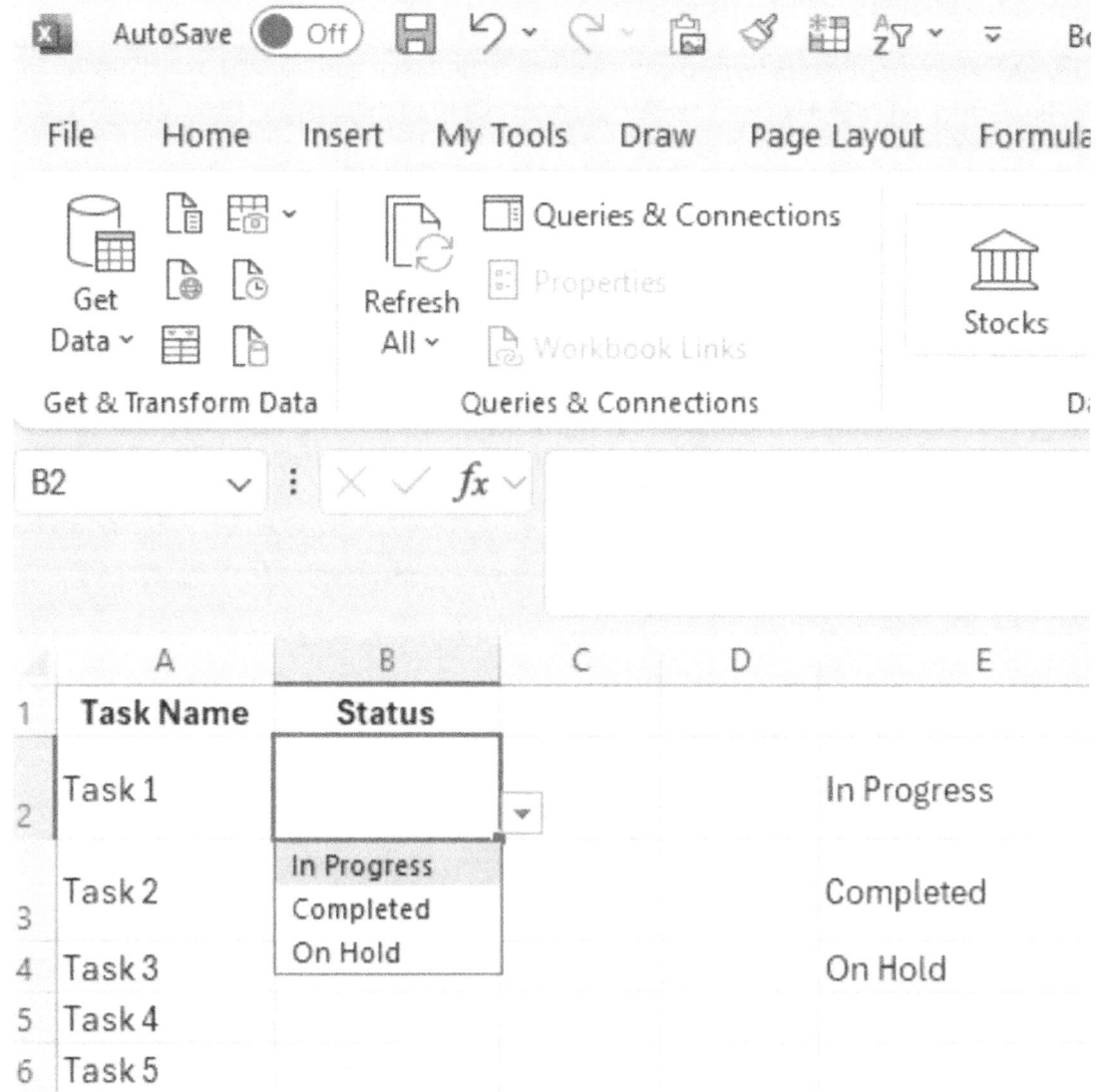

1. **Select the range where the drop-down list will be used.**

- Click on the cell or group of cells where you want users to choose from a predefined list.

2. **Open the Name Manager to create a dynamic range.**

- Go to **Formulas** > **Name Manager** and click **New**.
- In the **New Name** dialog box, enter a name for your list (e.g., `Status`).
- In the **Refers to** field, select the range containing your list items. Click OK to save.

3. **Apply Data Validation to create the drop-down list.**

- Go to **Data** > **Data Validation**.
- Under the **Settings** tab, set **Allow** to **List**.
- In the **Source** field, type `=Status` (or the name you assigned to your list in Step 2).
- Ensure the **In-cell dropdown** checkbox is checked.

4. Confirm and test the drop-down list.

- Click **OK**, and your drop-down list is now ready! Users will only be able to select from the predefined options rather than entering data manually, reducing errors and ensuring consistency.

By following these steps, you create a **dynamic and scalable drop-down list** that automatically updates when new items are added to the source list.

Making Drop-Down Lists More Dynamic

A **static drop-down list** is useful, but what if the available choices **change over time**? Instead of constantly updating the list manually, you can create a **dynamic drop-down list** that updates automatically as new options are added.

Steps to Create a Dynamic Drop-Down List

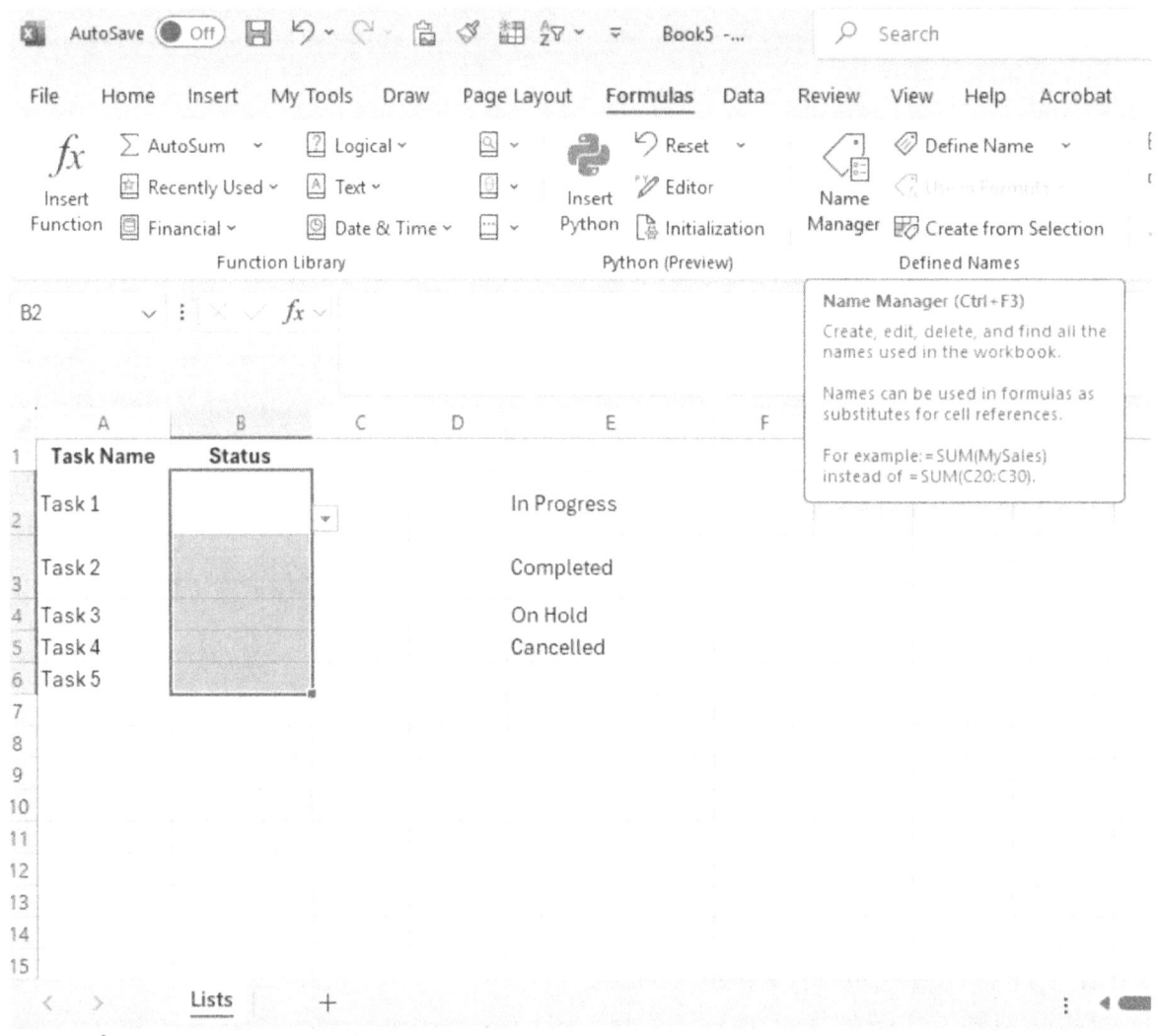

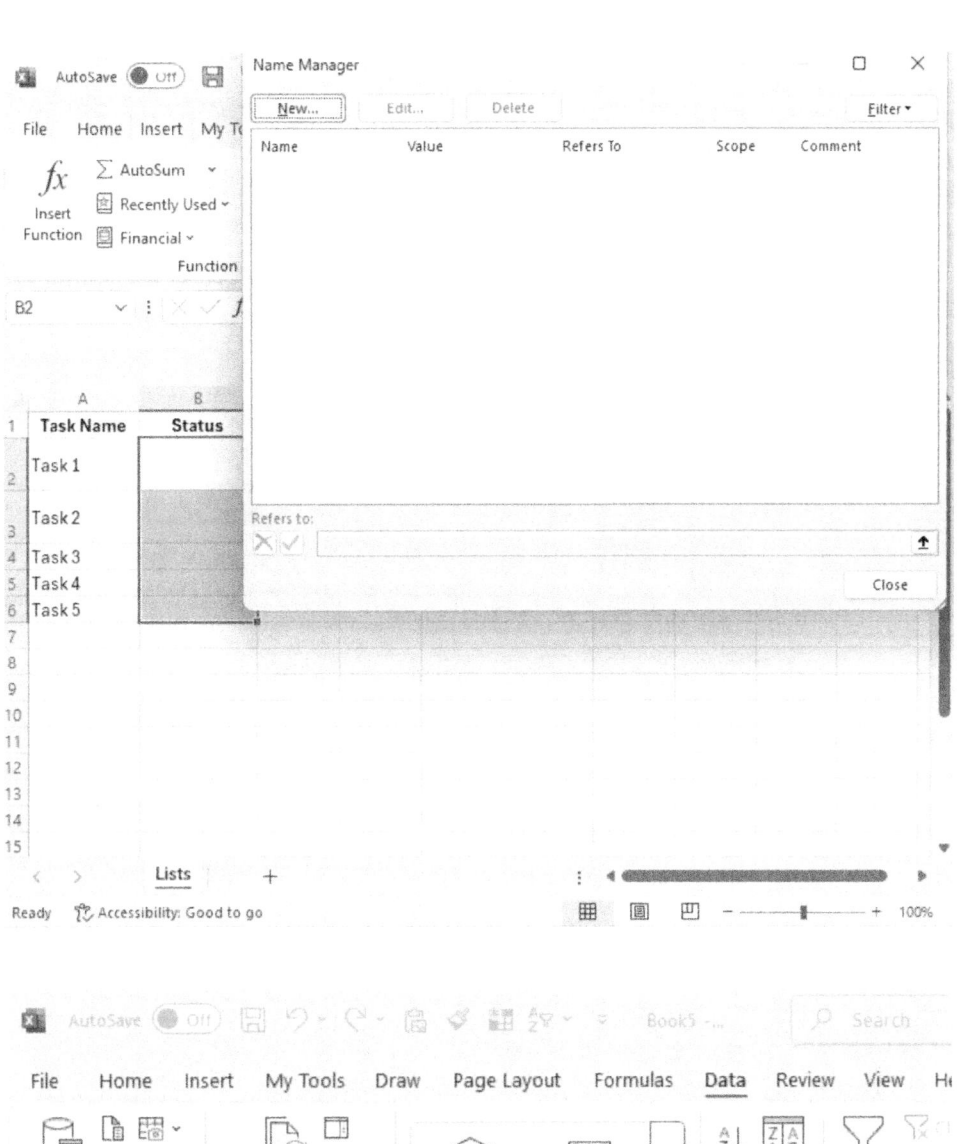

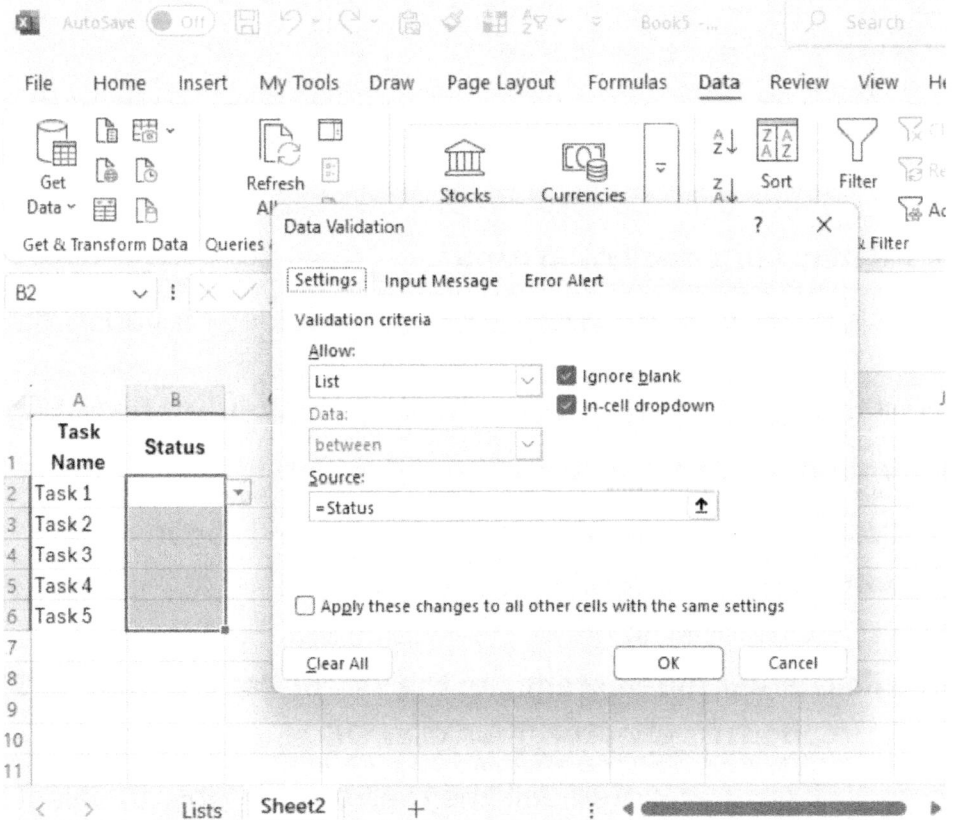

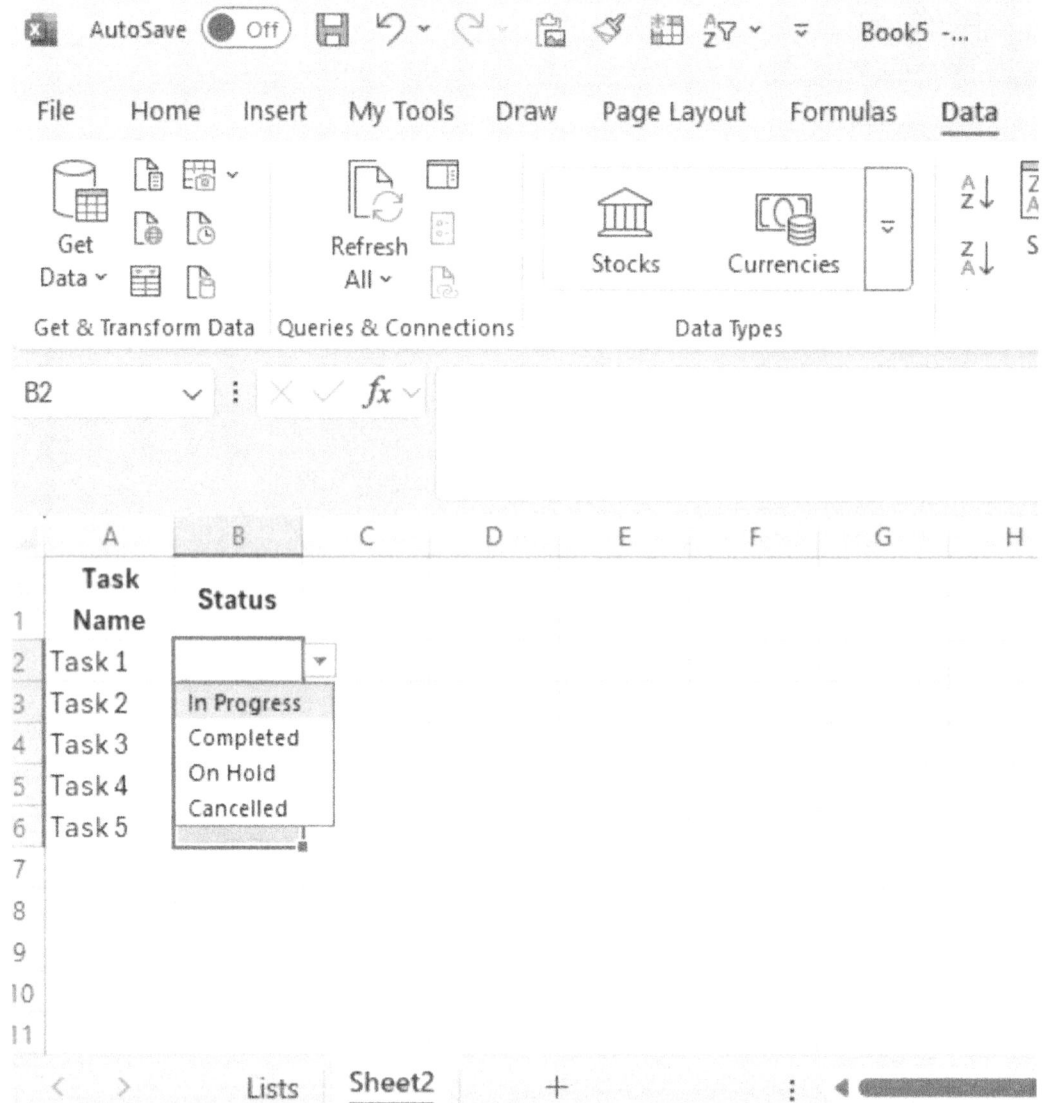

1. **Enter your list items in a dedicated range.**

- In a separate sheet (e.g., named **Lists**), enter the options for your drop-down list in a vertical column.
- For example, if tracking project statuses, list them in **Column A** starting from **A1**.

2. **Apply Data Validation to create the drop-down list.**

- Select the cells where you want the drop-down list to appear.
- Navigate to **Data** > **Data Validation**.
- In the **Settings** tab, choose **List** under the "Allow" drop-down menu.
- **In the Source field, enter the reference to the list range: =Lists!$A$1:$A$4**
- Ensure **In-cell dropdown** is checked, then click **OK**.

Now, when users click on a validated cell, they will only be able to select from the pre-defined list options, ensuring consistent and error-free data entry.

Enhancing User Guidance with Custom Alerts

Even with a drop-down list, users might still make mistakes—entering invalid data or missing required fields. **Custom alerts help guide users in real-time, preventing errors before they happen.**

Setting Up Custom Error Messages

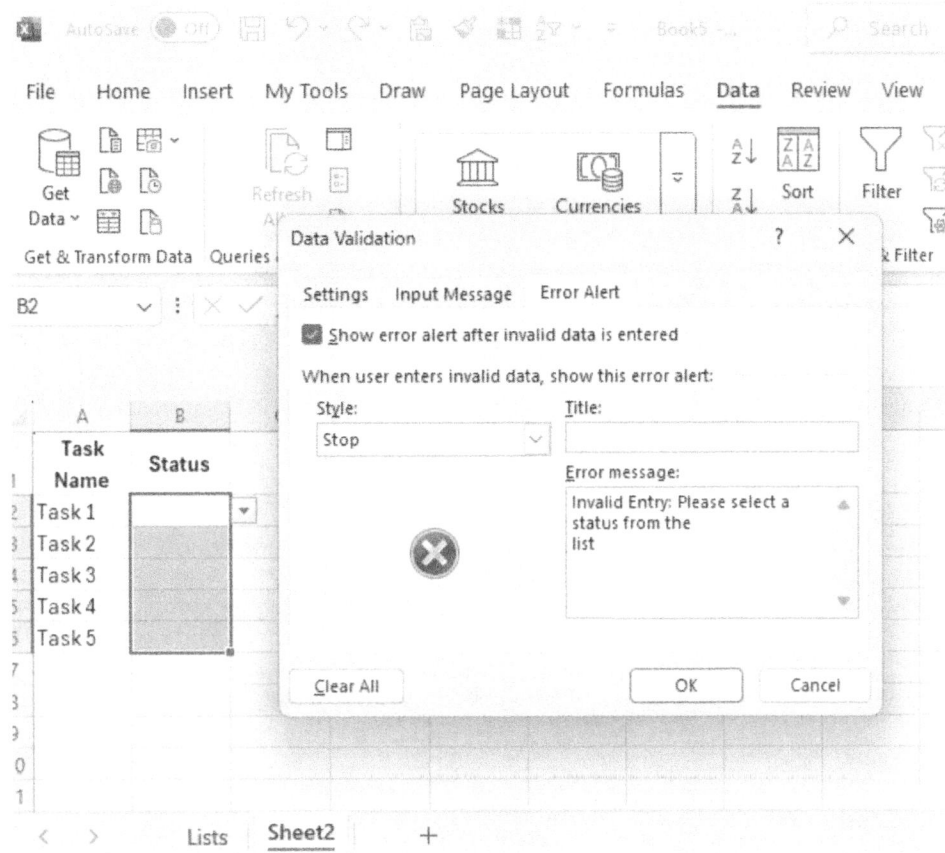

1. Open **Data Validation** (`Data > Data Validation`).
2. Go to the **Error Alert** tab.
3. Choose an alert type:

- **Stop:** Prevents invalid entries completely.
- **Warning:** Allows invalid entries but prompts a cautionary message.
- **Information:** Suggests correct input but doesn't enforce it.

4. Enter a **custom title and message** (e.g., *"Invalid Entry: Please select a status from the list."*).
5. Click **OK**.

Now, if someone tries to enter an incorrect value, they'll get a **clear, informative message**, reducing confusion and mistakes.

PART 3

FORMULAS AND AUTOMATION –
UNLOCKING THE POWER OF EXCEL

CHAPTER 6

MASTERING LOOKUP AND REFERENCE FUNCTIONS

Turn hours of manual searching into instant automated lookups,
finding exactly what you need without asking for help

VLOOKUP, HLOOKUP, and XLOOKUP Demystified

If you've ever found yourself manually searching through a spreadsheet to match data across columns or rows, you already know the frustration of **not having an efficient lookup system** in place. **VLOOKUP, HLOOKUP, and XLOOKUP** are three of Excel's most powerful functions, designed to instantly retrieve the information you need. Whether you're looking up a product price, finding an employee ID, or matching sales figures, these functions eliminate manual work and prevent costly errors.

Understanding VLOOKUP: The Classic Lookup Function

VLOOKUP (Vertical Lookup) is one of Excel's most widely used functions, allowing you to **search for a value in the first column of a table and return a corresponding value from another column**.

When to Use VLOOKUP

- Searching for an **employee's department** based on their ID.
- Retrieving the **price of a product** using a product code.
- Matching **customer details** from a database.

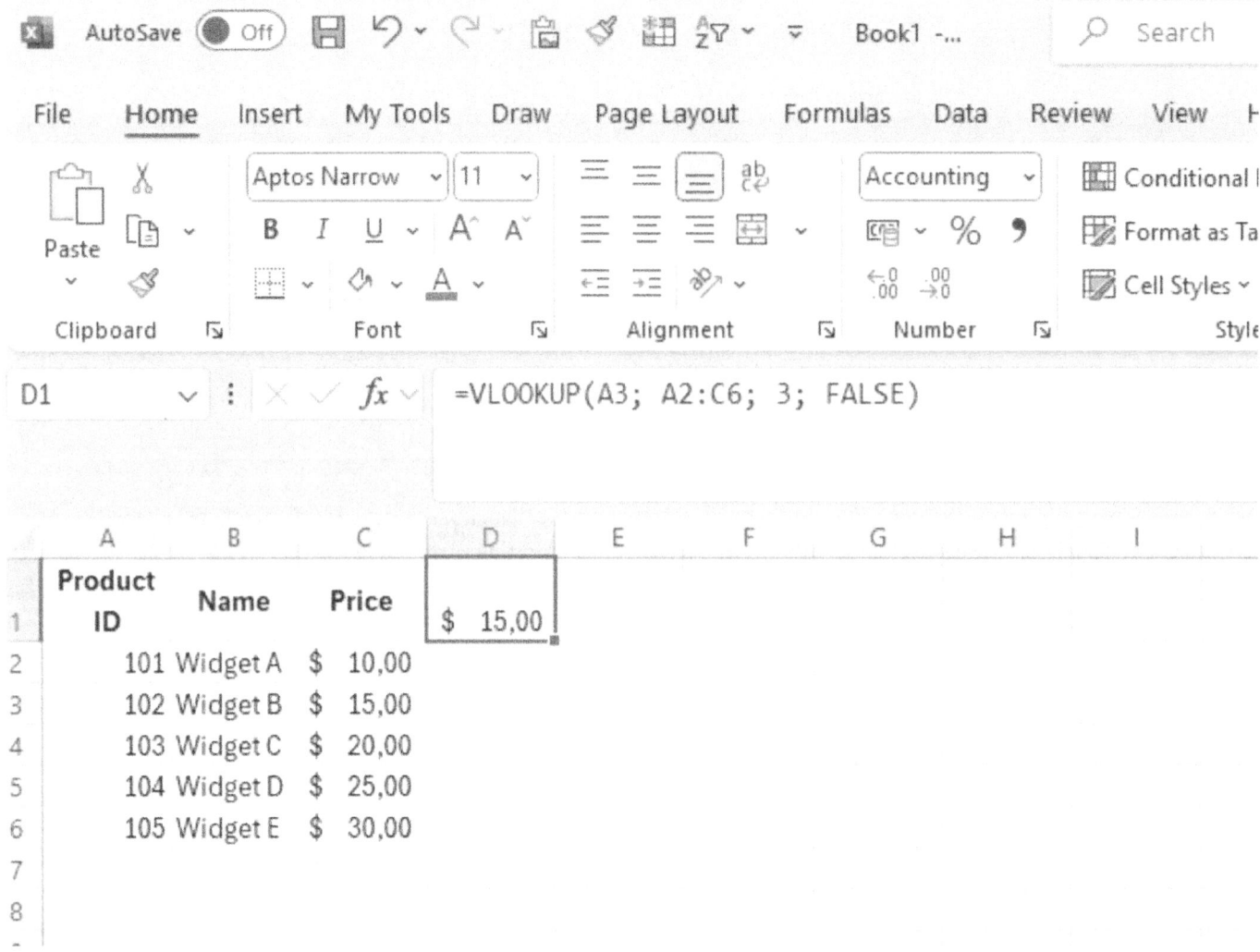

The function follows this syntax:

=VLOOKUP(lookup_value, table_array, col_index_num, [range_lookup])

- **lookup_value:** The value you are searching for.
- **table_array:** The range of data to search within.
- **col_index_num:** The column number where the result is located.
- **range_lookup (optional):** Enter `TRUE` for an approximate match or `FALSE` for an exact match.

Example: Suppose you have a product list in columns A to C, where A contains product IDs, B contains names, and C contains prices. To find the price of Product ID **102**, use:

=VLOOKUP(A3; A2:C6; 3; FALSE)

This searches for 102 in column A and returns the price from column C.

VLOOKUP Limitations:

- It **only searches from left to right**, meaning the lookup column must always be the **first column** in your range.
- If the dataset changes, column numbers may shift, **breaking the formula**.
- It's limited to **vertical searches only**—which brings us to **HLOOKUP**.

HLOOKUP: The Horizontal Counterpart

While **VLOOKUP searches columns**, **HLOOKUP (Horizontal Lookup)** works similarly but searches **rows instead of columns**.

When to Use HLOOKUP

- Looking up **monthly sales data** where months are in the first row.
- Retrieving **grading scales** based on a test score.

HLOOKUP Syntax

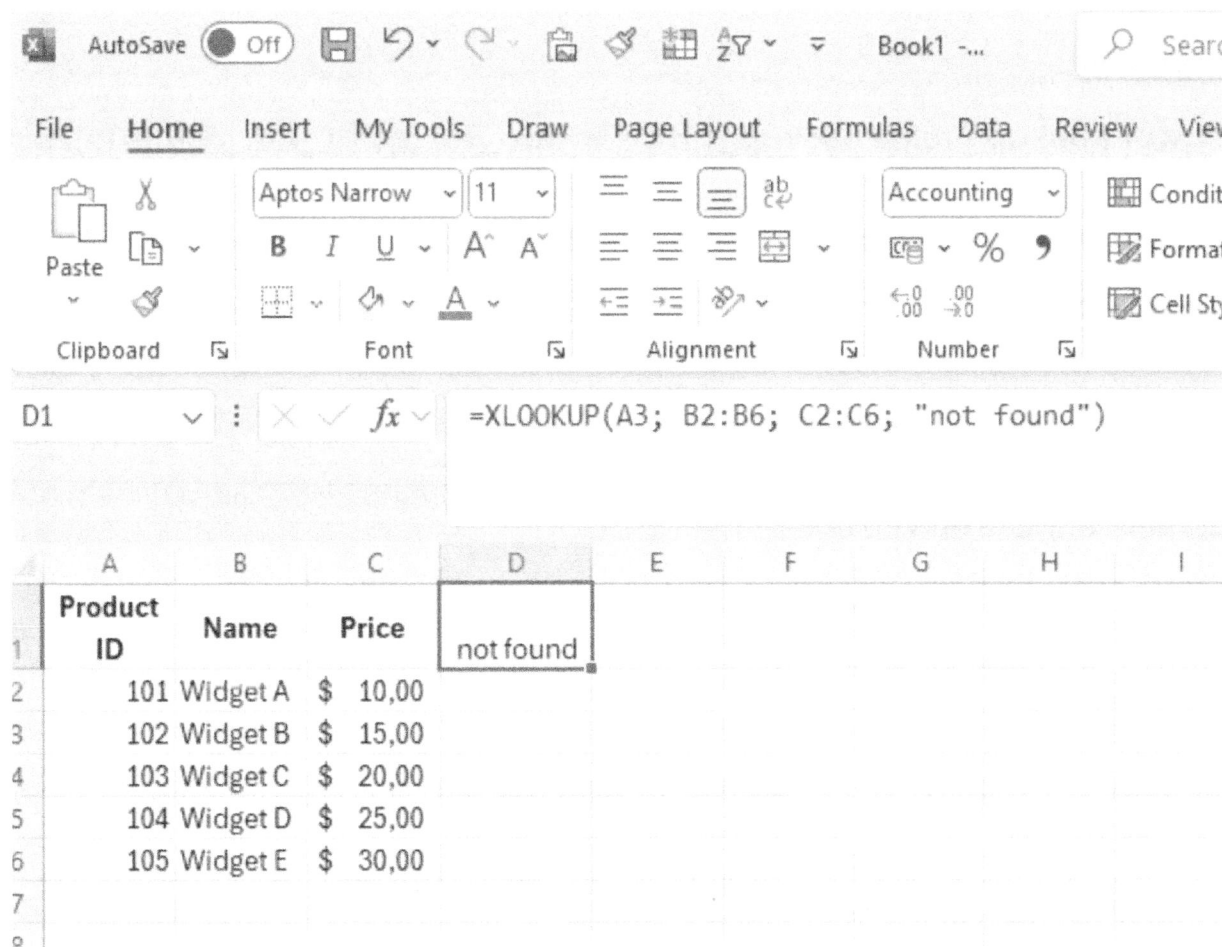

=HLOOKUP(lookup_value, table_array; row_index_num; [range_lookup])

row_index_num: The row number from which to return a value.

For example, if a dataset has months **(Jan, Feb, Mar, etc.)** in row 1 and sales figures in row 2,

=HLOOKUP("Mar"; A1:G2; 2; FALSE)

would return March's sales value.

XLOOKUP: The Ultimate Lookup Solution

VLOOKUP and HLOOKUP have been **Excel staples for years**, but they have **limitations**. Enter **XLOOKUP**, a newer, more **flexible** function introduced in Excel 2019 and Office 365. It solves many of the issues found in the older lookup functions.

Why XLOOKUP is Superior

- **Searches in any direction**—left, right, above, or below.
- **No need for column index numbers**—returns values dynamically.
- **Handles missing values** with built-in error handling.

XLOOKUP Syntax

=XLOOKUP(lookup_value, lookup_array; return_array; [if_not_found]; [match_mode]; [search_mode])

lookup_array & return_array: Allows non-adjacent columns, unlike VLOOKUP.

- **[if_not_found]:** Provides a custom message if the value isn't found.

Example: Searching for a product name in column B and returning its price from column C:

=XLOOKUP("Laptop"; B2:B10; C2:C10; "Not Found")

Unlike VLOOKUP, this formula doesn't require the lookup column to be first, making **XLOOKUP far more reliable and flexible**.

By understanding when and how to use these lookup functions, you'll save **time, reduce errors, and unlock Excel's full potential**, making your data searches **instant and accurate**.

Using INDEX and MATCH for Next-Level Searches

If you've ever struggled with **VLOOKUP's limitations**—like its inability to search to the left, its requirement for a fixed column index, or its lack of flexibility—then it's time to upgrade to **INDEX and MATCH**. These two functions, when combined, create a **powerful, dynamic lookup system** that can handle complex data searches with ease.

Unlike VLOOKUP, which requires the lookup column to be the first in your dataset, **INDEX and MATCH work together to find values anywhere**—in any column or row, no matter their position. This makes them an **essential tool for advanced Excel users** who need greater control over their searches.

Breaking Down INDEX and MATCH

What Does INDEX Do?

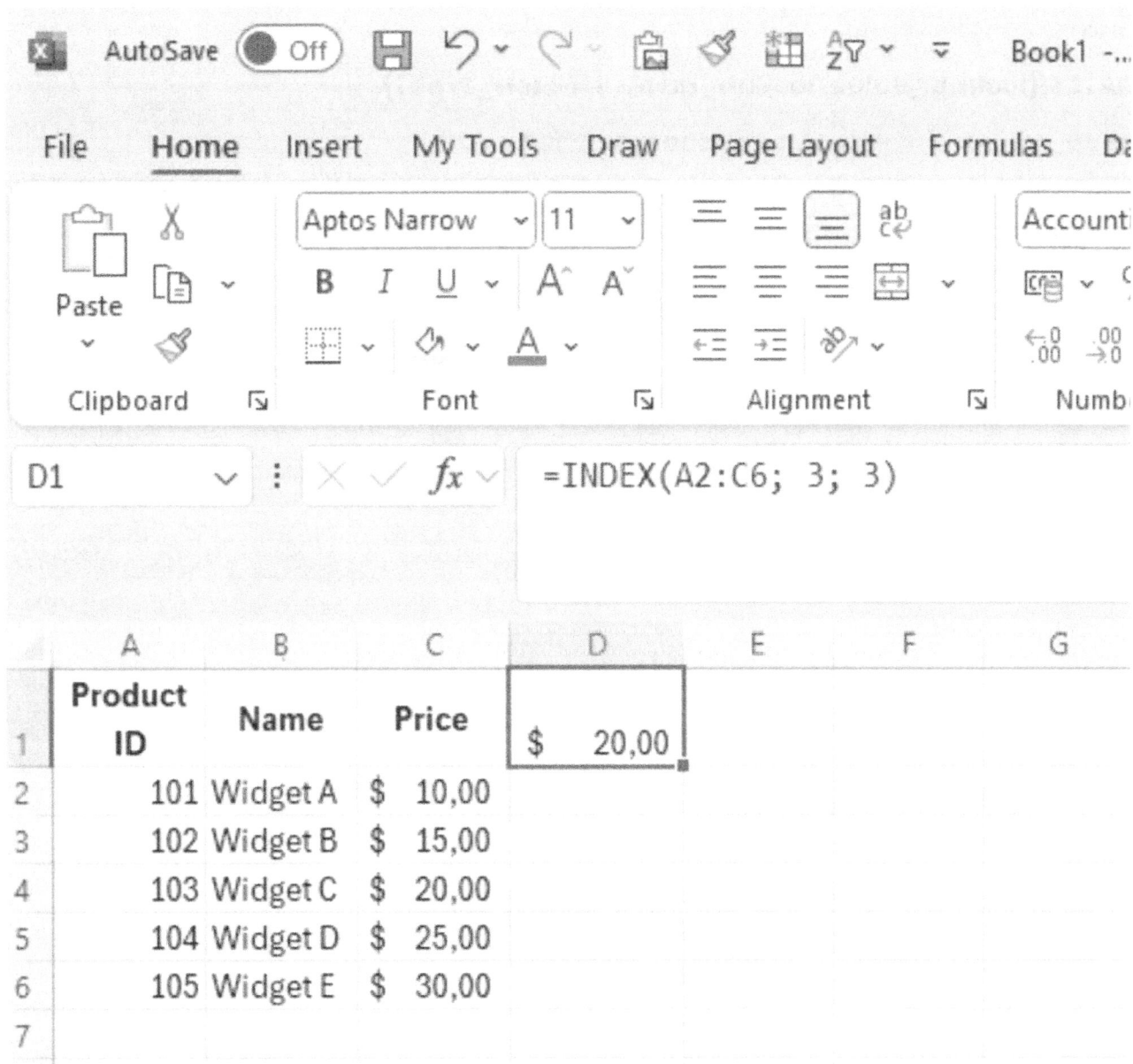

The **INDEX function** retrieves a value from a specified row and column in a dataset. Think of it as an Excel GPS—it finds the exact location of your data and pulls it out for you.

Syntax:

=INDEX(array, row_number, [column_number])

array: The range of data.

- **row_number:** The row within the array where the value is located.
- **column_number (optional):** The column number (only needed for 2D arrays).

What Does MATCH Do?

The **MATCH function** finds the **position** of a value in a column or row. Instead of returning the actual data, it tells you **where** the data is located within the dataset.

Syntax:

=MATCH(lookup_value, lookup_array, [match_type])

lookup_value: The value you're searching for.

- **lookup_array:** The column or row to search in.
- **match_type (optional):** Usually `0` for an exact match.

Combining INDEX and MATCH: A More Powerful Lookup

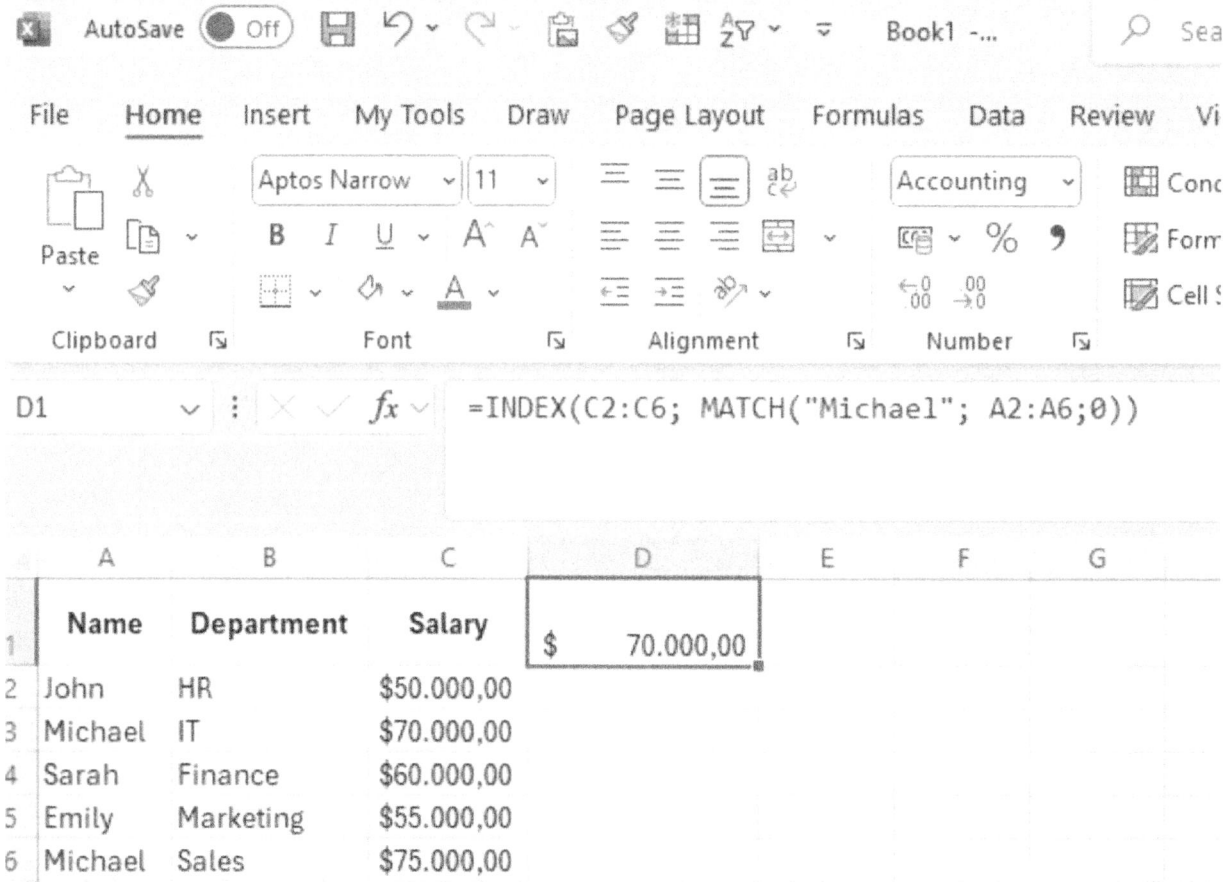

When you **nest MATCH inside INDEX**, you create a **flexible lookup system** that doesn't have the same restrictions as VLOOKUP.

Example: Looking Up an Employee's Salary

Suppose you have an **employee database** where Column A lists names, Column B lists departments, and Column C lists salaries. You want to find the salary of an employee named "Michael."

Formula:

=INDEX(C2:C100, MATCH("Michael", A2:A100, 0))

How it works:

- **MATCH("Michael", A2:A100, 0)** searches for "Michael" in column A and returns his **row number**.
- **INDEX(C2:C100, row_number)** then retrieves the corresponding salary from column C.

This method **solves VLOOKUP's biggest flaw**—allowing lookups in columns to the **left or right** of the search column.

Why INDEX and MATCH Are Superior to VLOOKUP

- **No Left-to-Right Restriction** – You can search any column, even if the lookup column isn't the first one.
- **Faster with Large Datasets** – VLOOKUP scans entire tables, but INDEX and MATCH only search the necessary range, making it **more efficient for large files**.
- **No Hardcoded Column Numbers** – If a column is inserted or deleted, INDEX and MATCH don't break, whereas **VLOOKUP formulas often fail**.
- **Works with Both Vertical and Horizontal Data** – Can search **rows or columns**, unlike VLOOKUP and HLOOKUP, which are restricted to one direction.

By mastering **INDEX and MATCH**, you unlock **greater accuracy, flexibility, and efficiency**, making it the go-to method for **advanced Excel lookups**.

CHAPTER 7

LOGICAL AND MATHEMATICAL FUNCTIONS: SMART CALCULATIONS FOR BUSINESS SUCCESS

Solve complex business problems with elegant formulas that showcase your analytical capabilities to management

IF, AND, OR, and Nested Functions Made Easy

Excel's logical functions—**IF, AND, OR**—are the backbone of decision-making in spreadsheets. These functions allow you to automate calculations, control workflows, and **make Excel "think" for you**. Whether you need to classify data, flag errors, or create custom conditions, mastering these functions will make your spreadsheets **smarter and more dynamic**.

The IF Function: The Foundation of Logical Testing

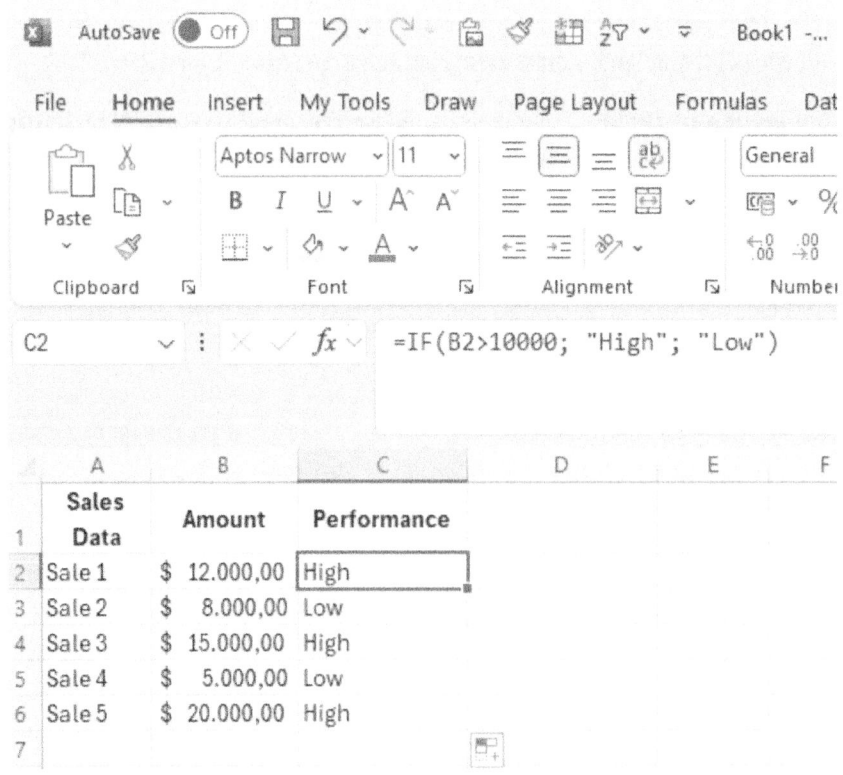

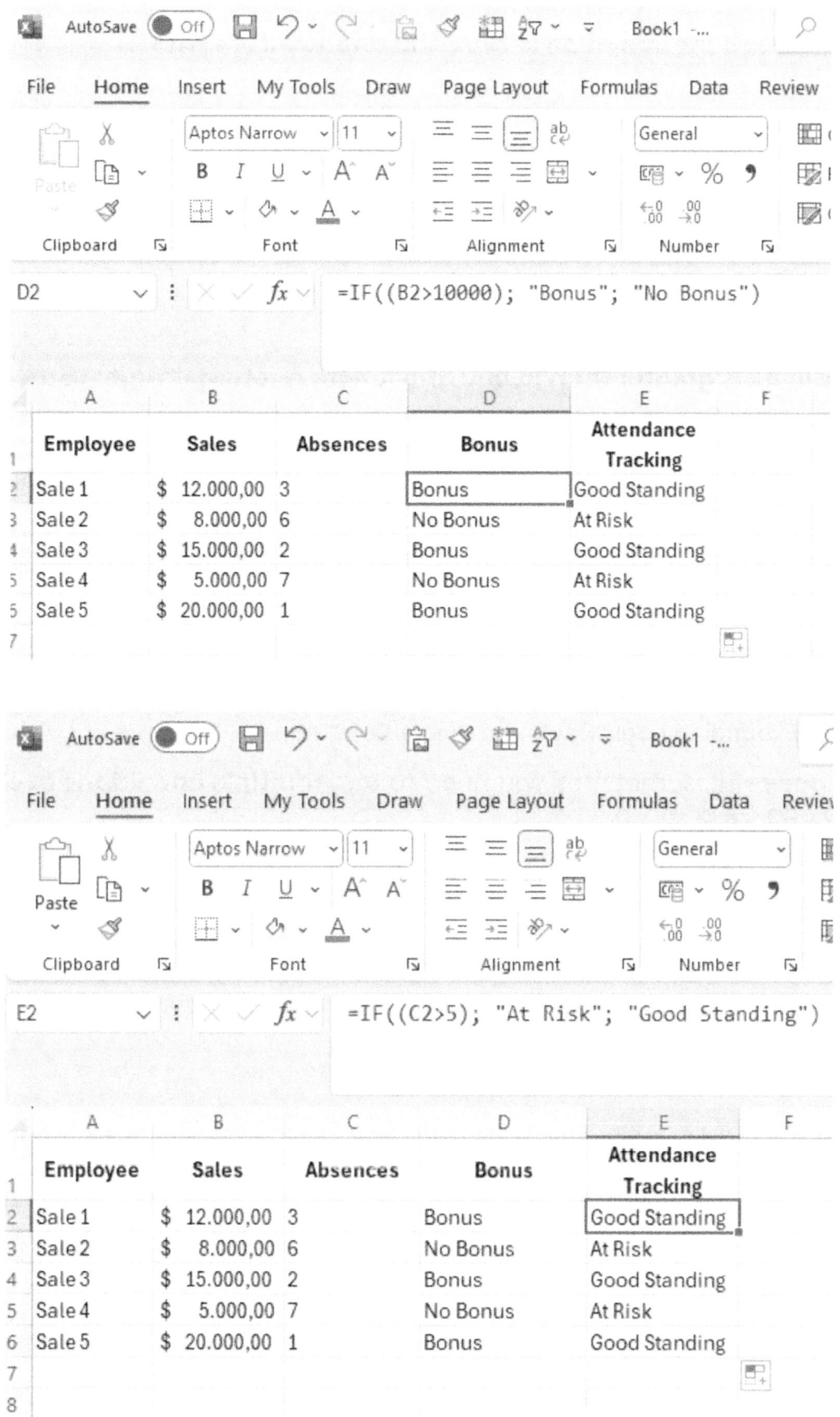

D2   fx   =IF((B2>10000); "Bonus"; "No Bonus")

	A	B	C	D	E
1	Employee	Sales	Absences	Bonus	Attendance Tracking
2	Sale 1	$ 12.000,00	3	Bonus	Good Standing
3	Sale 2	$ 8.000,00	6	No Bonus	At Risk
4	Sale 3	$ 15.000,00	2	Bonus	Good Standing
5	Sale 4	$ 5.000,00	7	No Bonus	At Risk
6	Sale 5	$ 20.000,00	1	Bonus	Good Standing
7					

E2   fx   =IF((C2>5); "At Risk"; "Good Standing")

	A	B	C	D	E	F
1	Employee	Sales	Absences	Bonus	Attendance Tracking	
2	Sale 1	$ 12.000,00	3	Bonus	Good Standing	
3	Sale 2	$ 8.000,00	6	No Bonus	At Risk	
4	Sale 3	$ 15.000,00	2	Bonus	Good Standing	
5	Sale 4	$ 5.000,00	7	No Bonus	At Risk	
6	Sale 5	$ 20.000,00	1	Bonus	Good Standing	
7						
8						

The **IF function** is Excel's most fundamental logical formula. It evaluates a condition and returns **one value if the condition is TRUE and another if it's FALSE**.

Syntax:

=IF(logical_test, value_if_true, value_if_false)

Example: Categorizing Sales Performance

Let's say you have a list of sales figures, and you want to label sales **above $10,000 as "High"** and others as "Low":

=IF(A2>10000, "High", "Low")

If the value in A2 is greater than 10,000, the function returns "High"; otherwise, it returns "Low".

Common Uses for IF

- **Calculating Bonuses** – "If sales exceed the target, give a bonus; otherwise, no bonus."
- **Attendance Tracking** – "If total absences exceed 5, mark as 'At Risk'; otherwise, 'Good Standing'."
- **Error Checking** – "If a cell is blank, display 'Missing Data'; otherwise, show the value."

AND and OR: Expanding Logic Beyond a Single Condition

While **IF is powerful**, sometimes you need to test **multiple conditions at once**. That's where **AND** and **OR** come in.

The AND Function: All Conditions Must Be TRUE

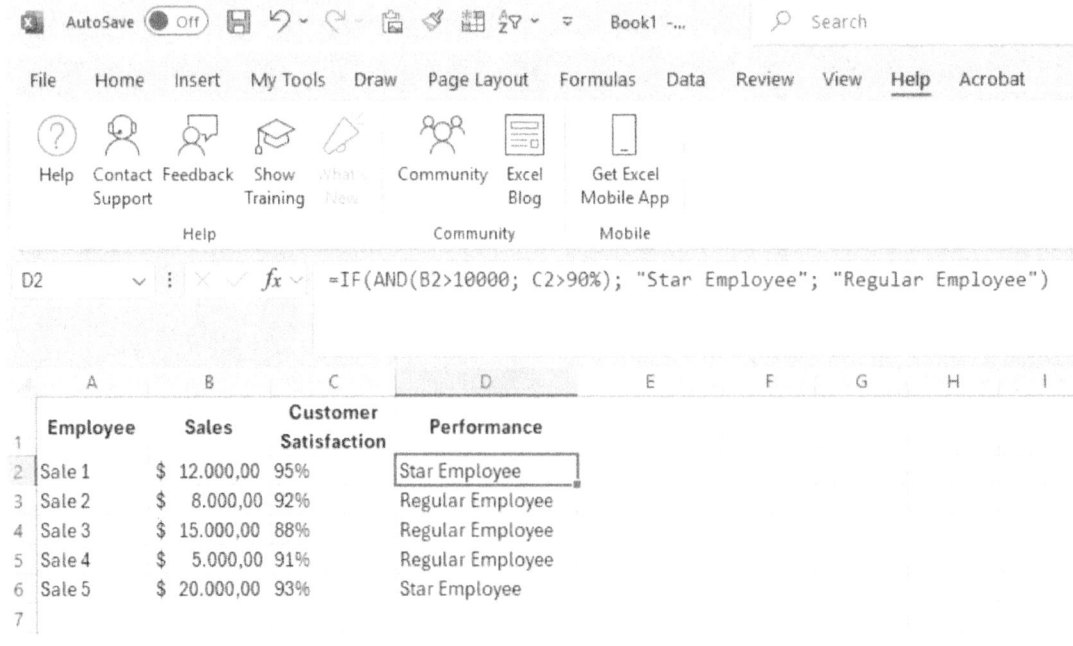

AND checks multiple conditions and **returns TRUE only if all are met**.

Syntax:

=AND(condition1, condition2, condition3, …)

Example: If an employee's sales are above $10,000 AND their customer satisfaction score is over 90%, mark them as "Star Employee":

=IF(AND(A2>10000; B2>90); "Star Employee"; "Regular Employee")

If either condition fails, the formula returns "Regular Employee".

The OR Function: At Least One Condition Must Be TRUE

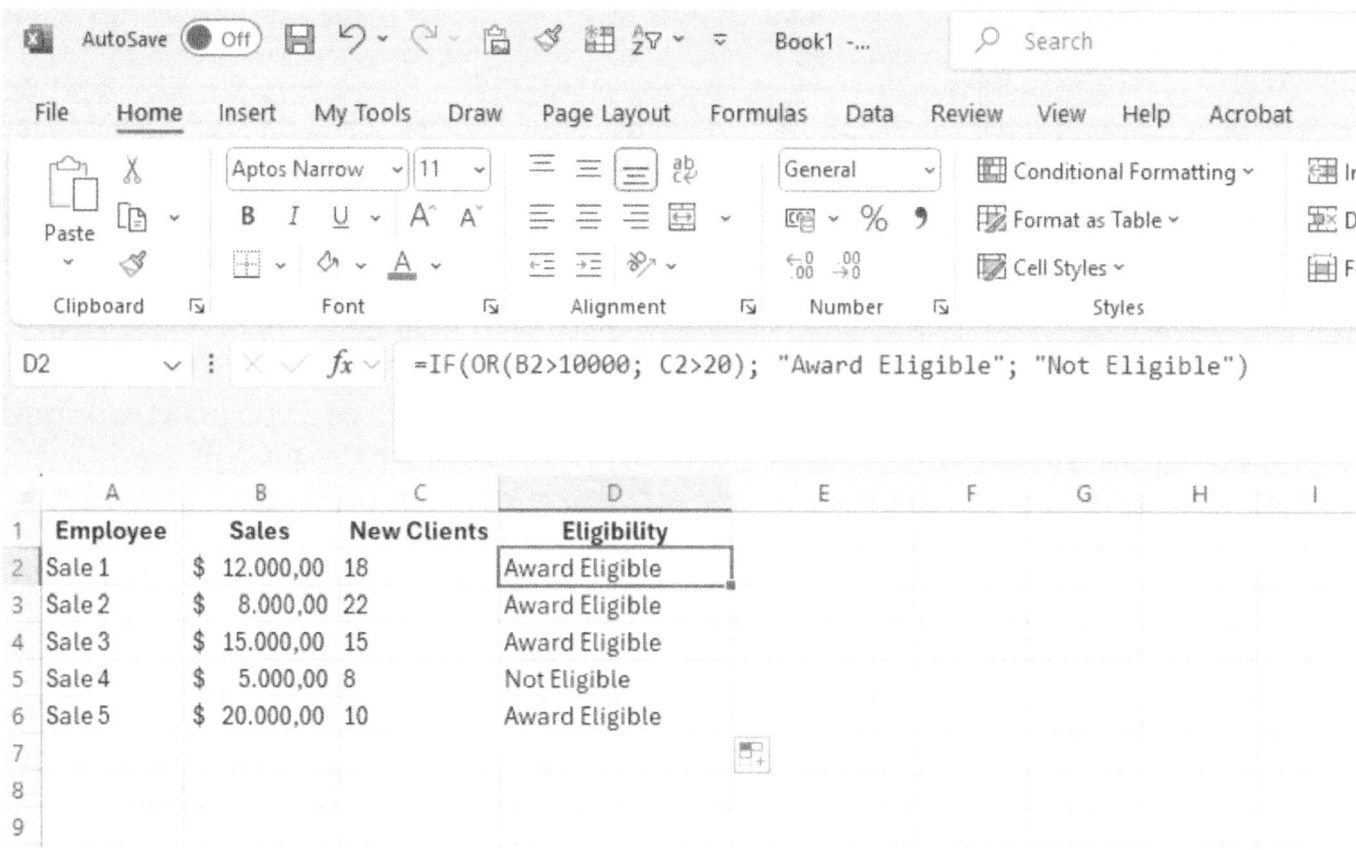

OR is more flexible—it returns **TRUE if at least one condition is met**.

Syntax:

=OR(condition1, condition2, condition3, …)

Example: An employee qualifies for a performance award if they achieve $10,000 in sales OR sign 20 new clients:

=IF(OR(A2>10000; B2>20); "Award Eligible"; "Not Eligible")

Unlike AND, here the employee only needs to meet one of the conditions.

Nesting IF Statements: Handling Multiple Outcomes

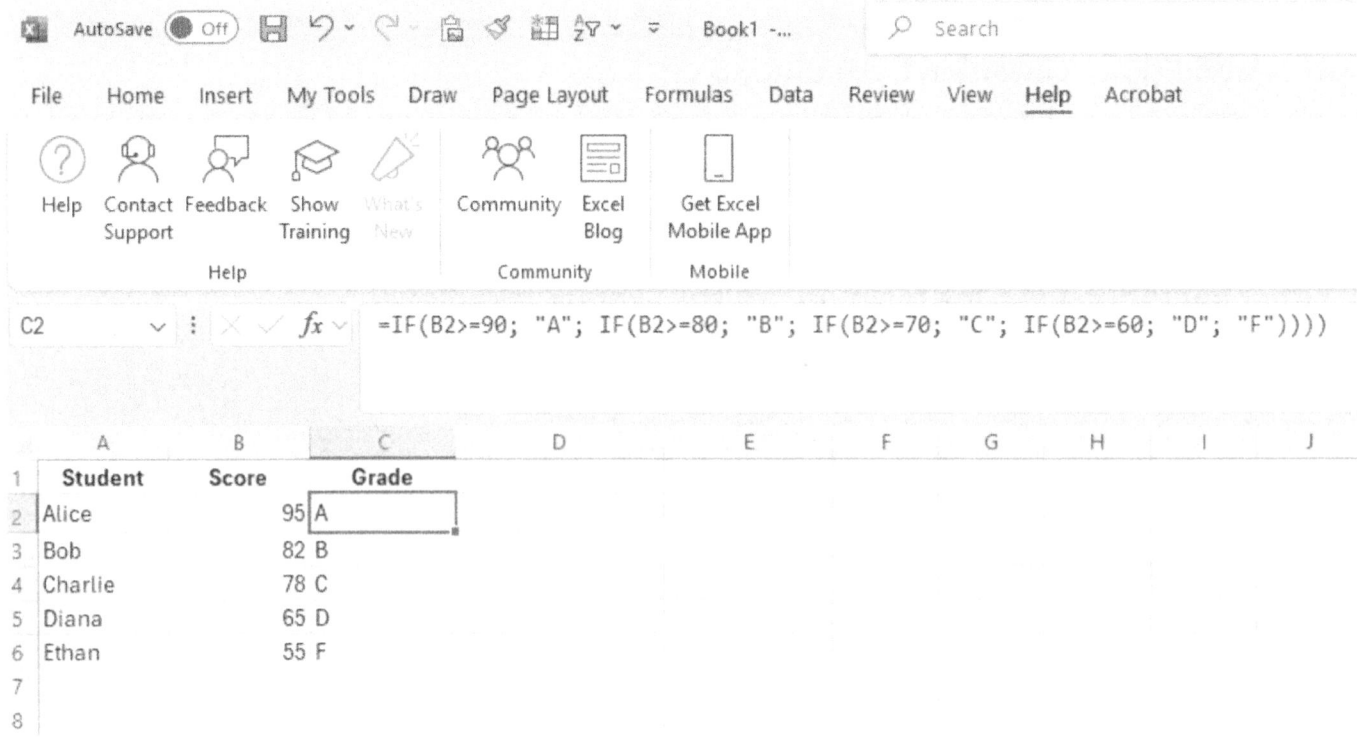

A single IF function only allows for **two possible outcomes**, but what if you need to handle more? **Nesting IF statements** lets you test multiple conditions in sequence.

Example: Grading System

Assigning letter grades based on student scores:

=IF(A2>=90; "A"; IF(A2>=80; "B"; IF(A2>=70; "C"; IF(A2>=60; "D"; "F"))))

This formula checks:

- If the score is **90 or above**, return **"A"**.
- If between **80-89**, return **"B"**.
- If between **70-79**, return **"C"**.
- If between **60-69**, return **"D"**.
- Otherwise, return **"F"**.

Building Smarter, More Dynamic Spreadsheets

By combining **IF, AND, OR, and nested functions**, you can create **highly automated and responsive** Excel sheets. These functions let Excel **make decisions for you**, ensuring **accuracy, efficiency, and better data-driven insights**.

Mastering SUMIF, COUNTIF, and Advanced Calculations

Excel is more than just a place to store numbers—it's a powerful **calculation engine** that helps businesses analyze data efficiently. Whether you're summing sales based on region, counting overdue invoices, or applying advanced filtering in calculations, **SUMIF and COUNTIF** are two of the most **essential conditional functions** you need to master. These functions allow Excel to perform calculations based on specific criteria, reducing the need for manual sorting and filtering.

SUMIF: Adding Values Based on Conditions

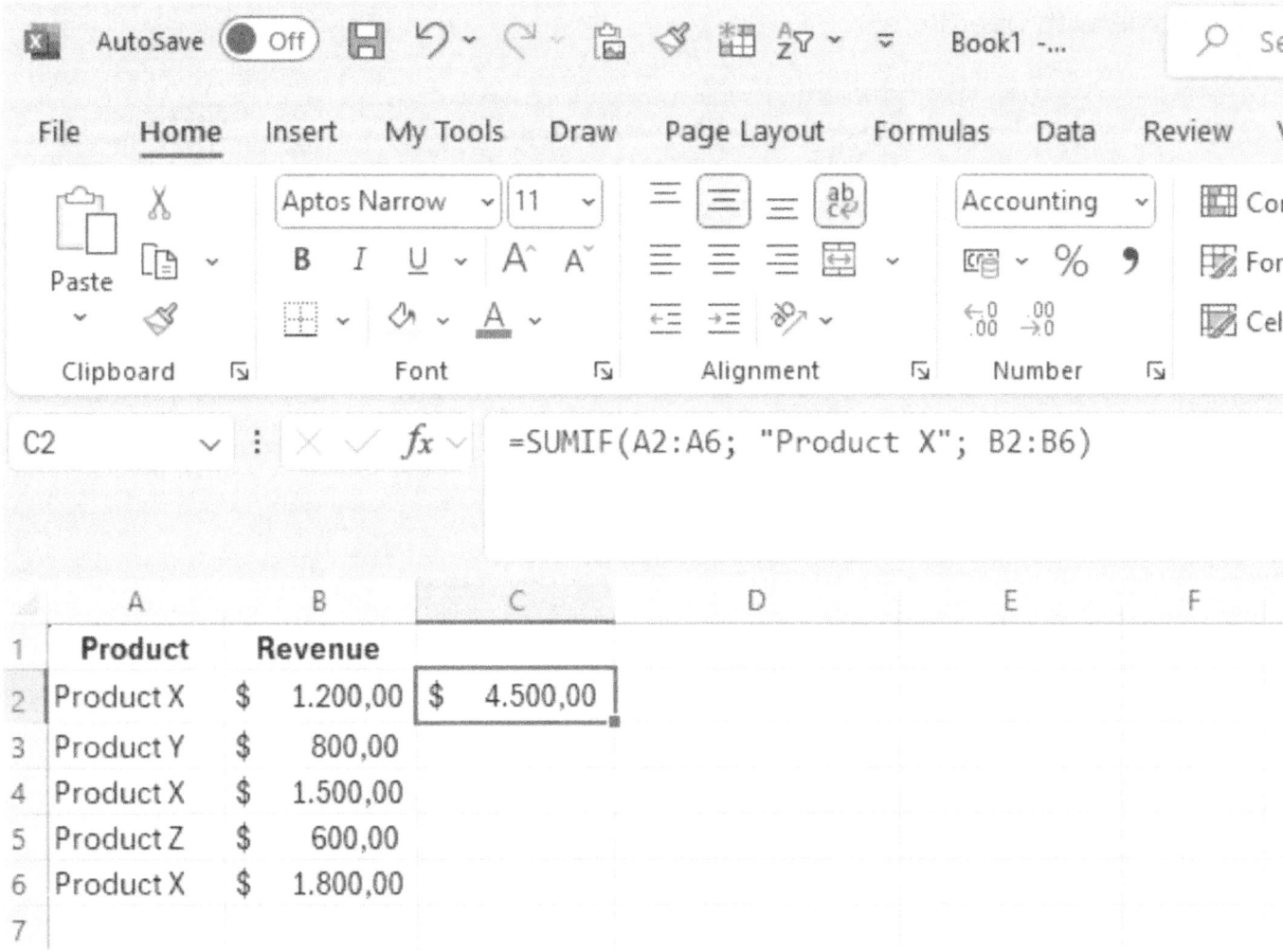

The **SUMIF function** allows you to **sum only the values that meet a specific condition**. Instead of adding up an entire range manually, SUMIF **filters the data** before performing the calculation.

Syntax:

=SUMIF(range, criteria, [sum_range])

range: The column containing the criteria you want to evaluate.

- **criteria:** The condition that must be met for the values to be summed.
- **sum_range (optional):** The column containing the actual numbers to add.

Example: Total Sales for a Specific Product

Imagine you have a sales report where **column A** lists products and **column B** lists revenue. If you want to calculate the total sales for "Product X," you would use:

=SUMIF(A2:A100, "Product X", B2:B100)

This formula searches column A for "Product X" and sums the corresponding values in column B.

Using SUMIF with Operators

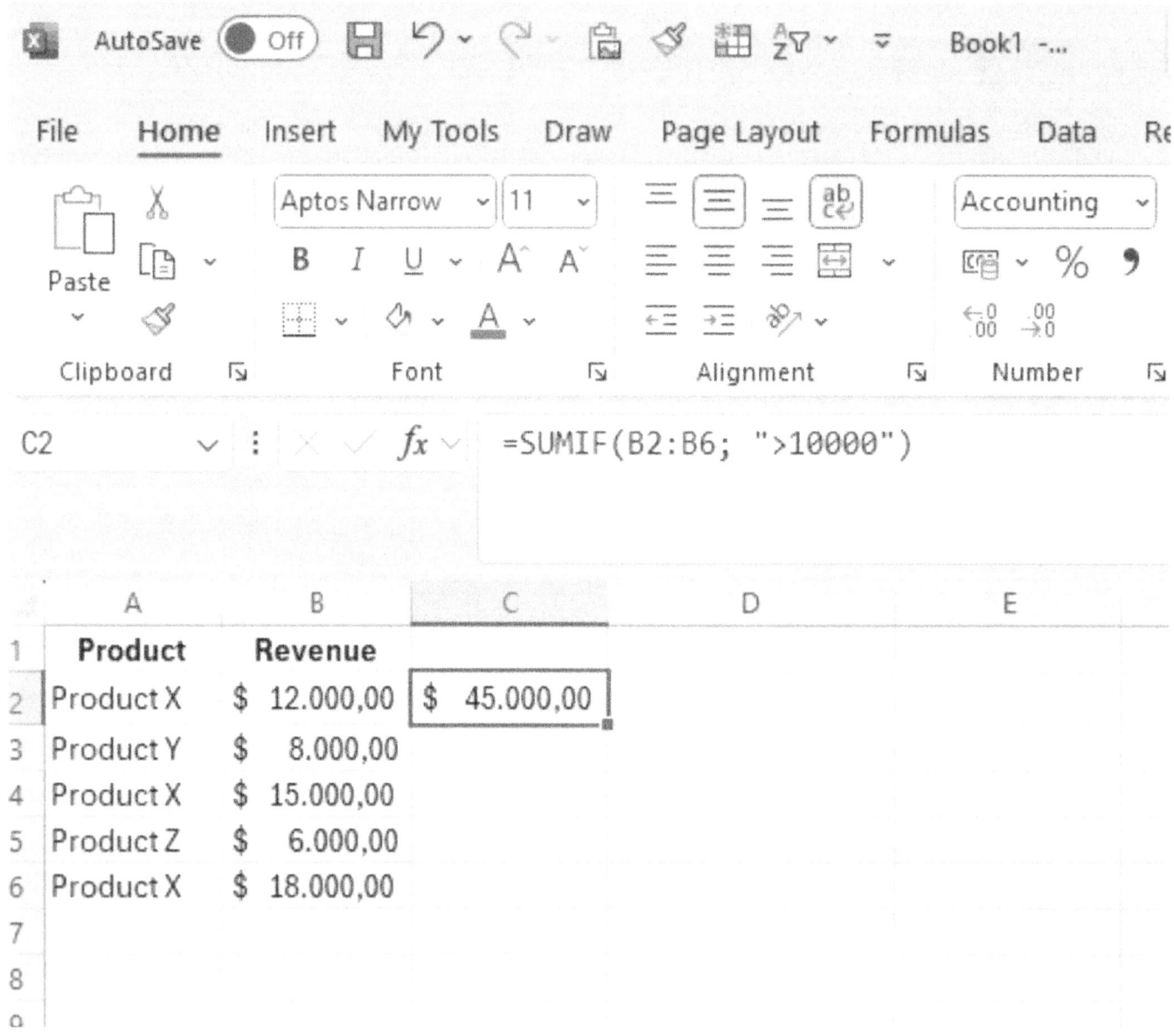

You're not limited to exact matches. You can use **comparison operators** to define your conditions:

- `>1000` (sum values greater than 1000)
- `<=500` (sum values less than or equal to 500)

Example: Summing all sales **greater than $10,000**:

=SUMIF(B2:B100, ">10000")

This formula ignores all values below $10,000, summing only the high-value sales.

COUNTIF: Counting Entries That Meet a Condition

The **COUNTIF function** works similarly to SUMIF, but instead of summing values, it **counts how many times a condition is met**.

Syntax:

=COUNTIF(range, criteria)

range: The column where the criteria will be evaluated.

- **criteria:** The condition that must be met for the count to increase.

Example: Counting Overdue Invoices

If column A contains invoice due dates, and you want to count how many invoices are **overdue** (before today's date), use:

=COUNTIF(A2:A100; "<"&TODAY())

This formula counts how many invoices have due dates earlier than today, helping finance teams track outstanding payments efficiently.

Counting Unique Entries

Need to count how many times a specific customer appears in a dataset?

=COUNTIF(A2:A100; "Customer A")

This formula counts the number of times Customer A appears in column A.

Advanced Conditional Calculations: SUMIFS and COUNTIFS

For even **more complex scenarios**, you can use **SUMIFS and COUNTIFS**—these functions allow you to apply **multiple conditions at once**.

Example: Total Revenue for a Specific Product in a Specific Region

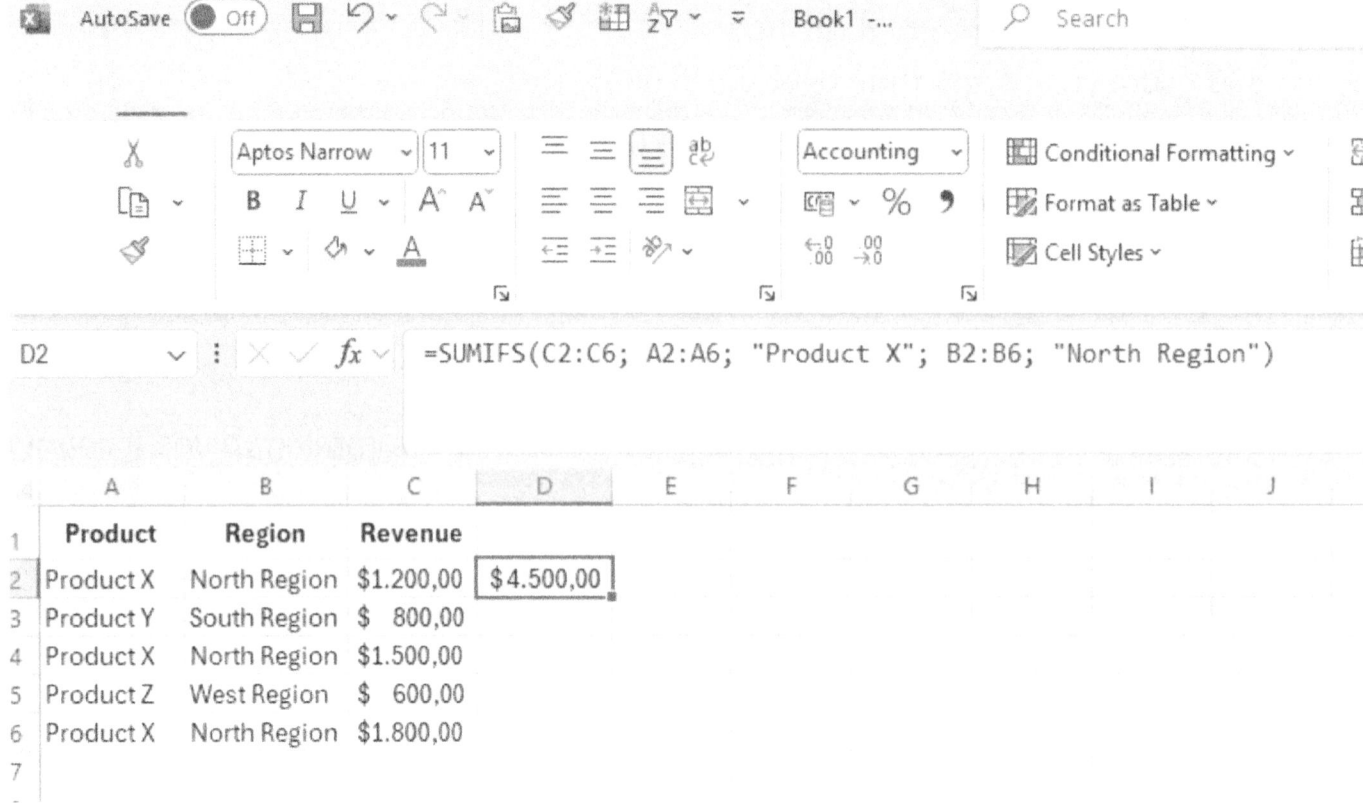

=SUMIFS(C2:C100, A2:A100, "Product X", B2:B100, "North Region")

This formula sums revenue from column C, but only if the product is "Product X" AND the region is "North Region."

Similarly, **COUNTIFS** works for counting based on multiple conditions:

=COUNTIFS(A2:A100, "Completed", B2:B100, "High Priority")

This formula counts the number of completed high-priority tasks, making it invaluable for project tracking.

Why These Functions Matter

By mastering **SUMIF, COUNTIF, and their advanced counterparts**, you can:

- **Eliminate manual filtering and sorting.**
- **Automate data analysis** for business insights.
- **Speed up reporting** and avoid formula errors.

These functions make Excel not just a tool for data entry—but a **powerful assistant in decision-making**.

CHAPTER 8

MACROS AND AUTOMATION: SAVE TIME BY LETTING EXCEL WORK FOR YOU

Automate repetitive weekly tasks that currently take hours, demonstrating your efficiency and technical skills to leadership

Recording and Using Macros Without Programming

If you find yourself **repeating the same tasks in Excel**, such as formatting reports, applying formulas, or copying and pasting data across sheets, you're **wasting valuable time**. Instead of doing these steps manually every day, wouldn't it be great if Excel could do them for you? **That's where Macros come in.**

The best part? **You don't need to know how to program.** Excel's built-in **Macro Recorder** allows you to automate tasks by simply recording your actions. Once recorded, the macro can **replay those steps instantly**, saving **hours of manual work** and reducing human error.

What is a Macro?

A **Macro** is a **set of recorded actions** that Excel can play back whenever needed. Think of it as Excel's **memory button**—you perform a task once, record it, and Excel **remembers exactly what you did** so it can repeat it for you later.

This is **incredibly useful for**:

- **Formatting reports automatically** (applying fonts, colors, borders).
- **Cleaning data** (removing blank rows, standardizing formats).
- **Automating repetitive calculations** (copying formulas, inserting data).
- **Generating reports** (sorting, filtering, and exporting data).

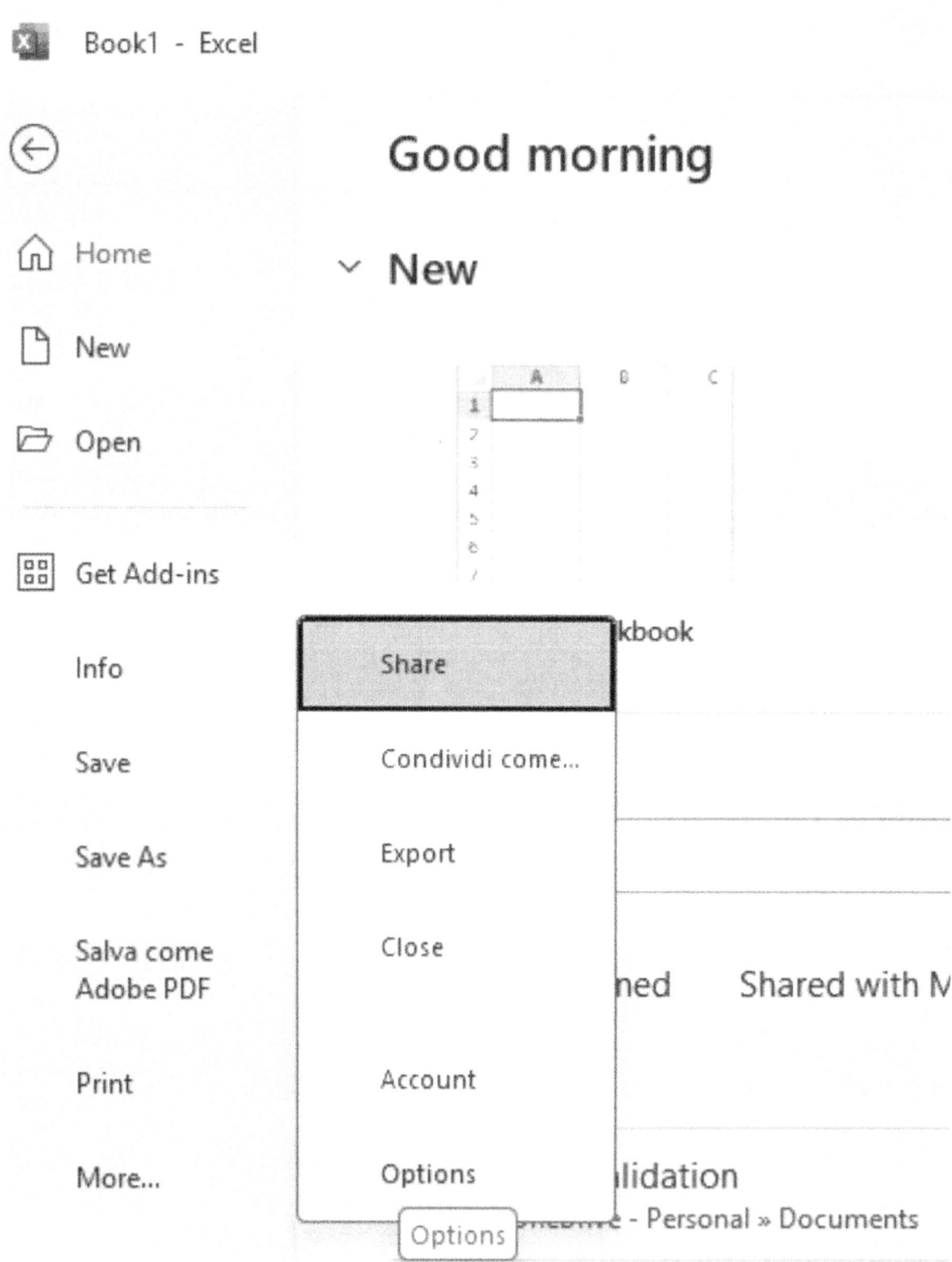

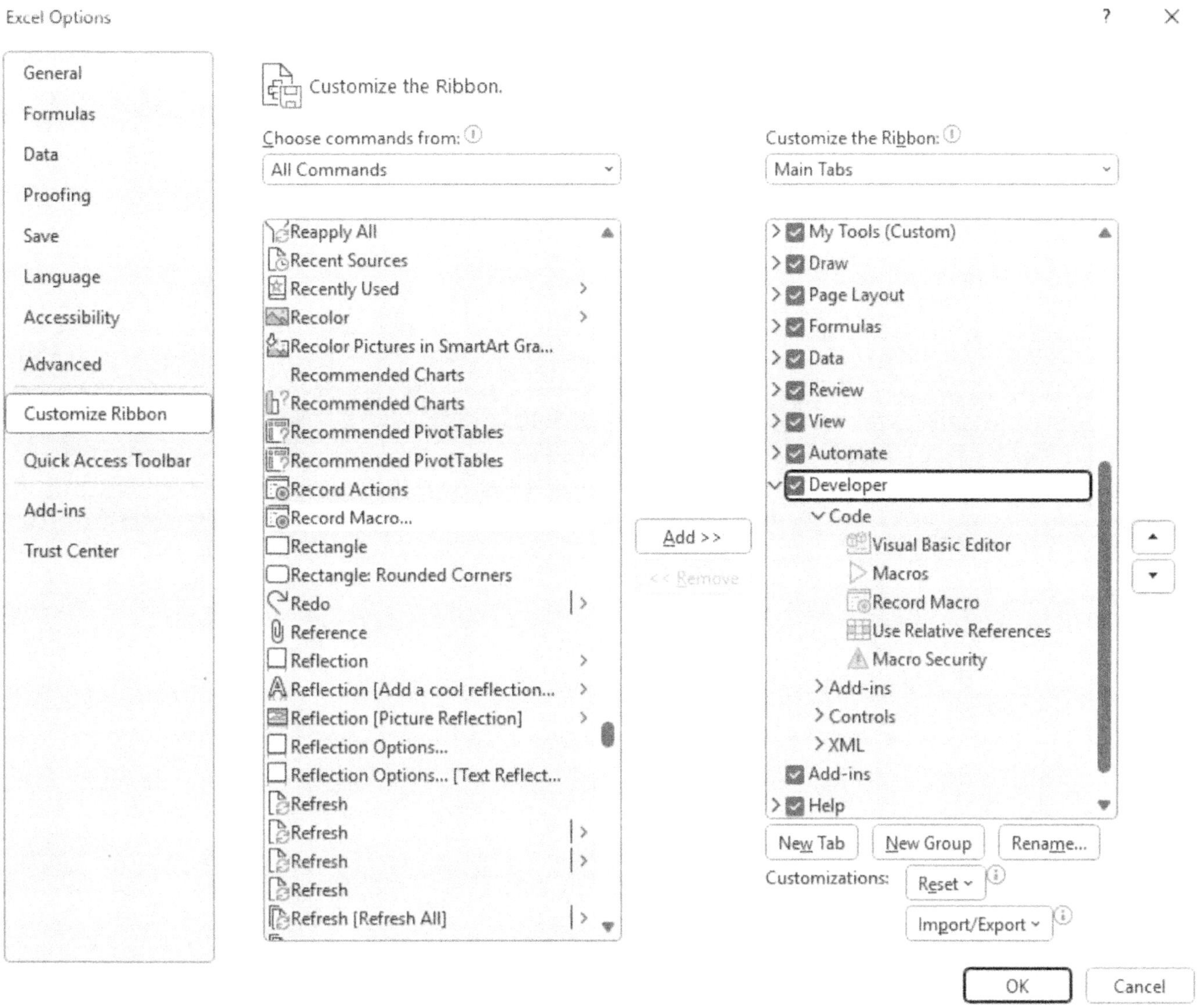

Excel Options

General

Formulas

Data

Proofing

Save

Language

Accessibility

Advanced

Customize Ribbon

Quick Access Toolbar

Add-ins

Trust Center

Customize the Ribbon.

Choose commands from: ⓘ

All Commands ▾

Reapply All
Recent Sources
Recently Used   >
Recolor   >
Recolor Pictures in SmartArt Gra...
    Recommended Charts
Recommended Charts
Recommended PivotTables
Recommended PivotTables
Record Actions
Record Macro...
Rectangle
Rectangle: Rounded Corners
Redo   >
Reference
Reflection   >
Reflection [Add a cool reflection... >
Reflection [Picture Reflection]   >
Reflection Options...
Reflection Options... [Text Reflect...
Refresh
Refresh   >
Refresh   >
Refresh
Refresh [Refresh All]   >

Add >>

<< Remove

Customize the Ribbon: ⓘ

Main Tabs ▾

> ☑ My Tools (Custom)
> ☑ Draw
> ☑ Page Layout
> ☑ Formulas
> ☑ Data
> ☑ Review
> ☑ View
> ☑ Automate
∨ ☑ Developer
    ∨ Code
        Visual Basic Editor
        ▷ Macros
        Record Macro
        Use Relative References
        ⚠ Macro Security
    > Add-ins
    > Controls
    > XML
  ☑ Add-ins
> ☑ Help

New Tab   New Group   Rename...

Customizations: Reset ˅ ⓘ

Import/Export ˅ ⓘ

OK   Cancel

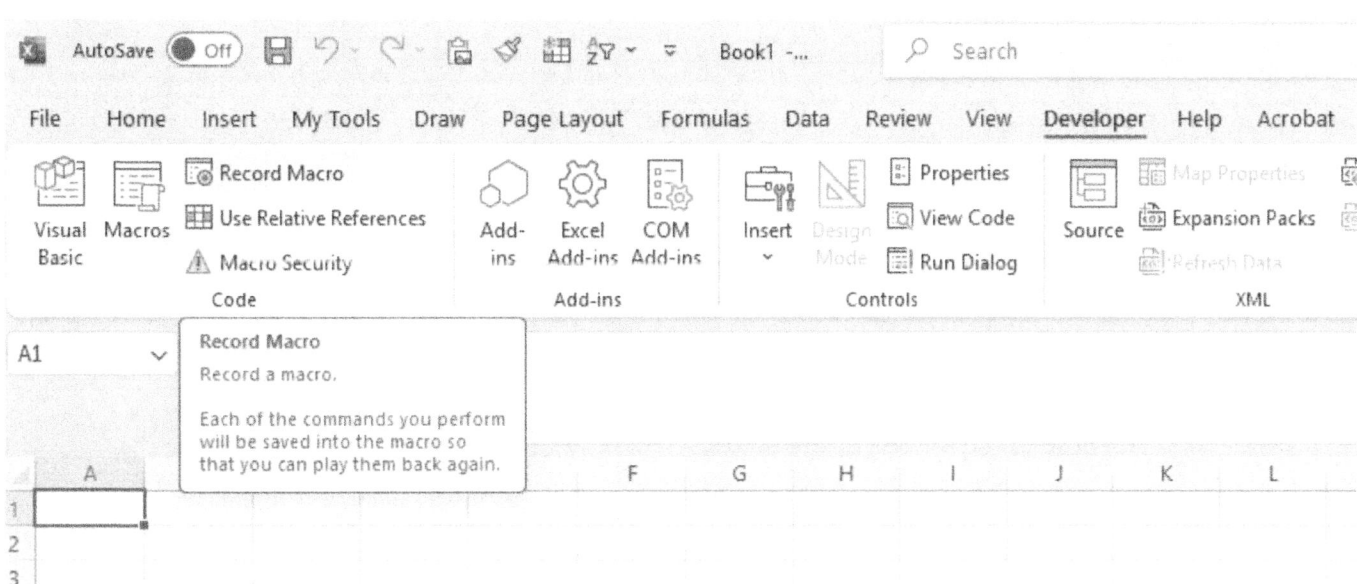

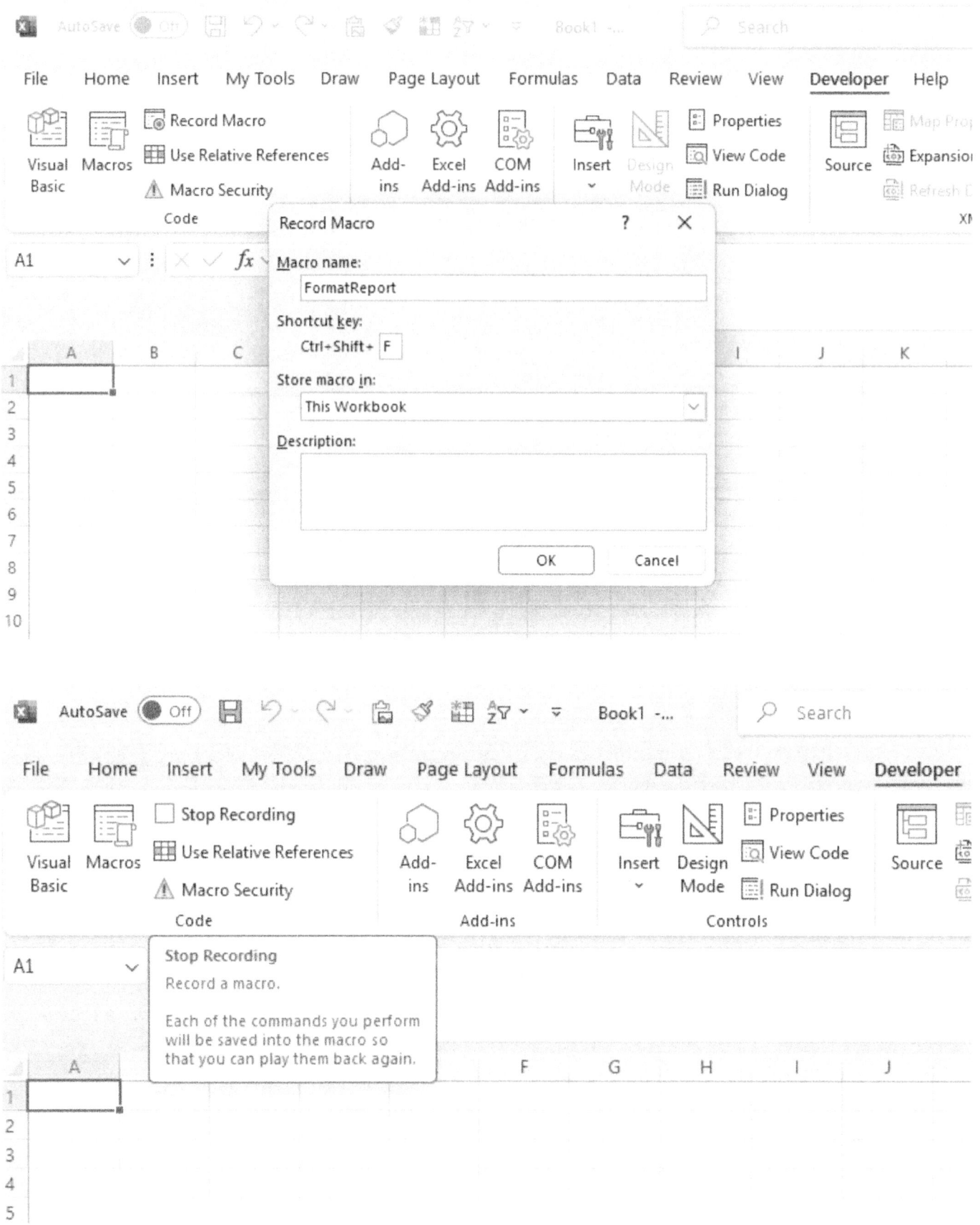

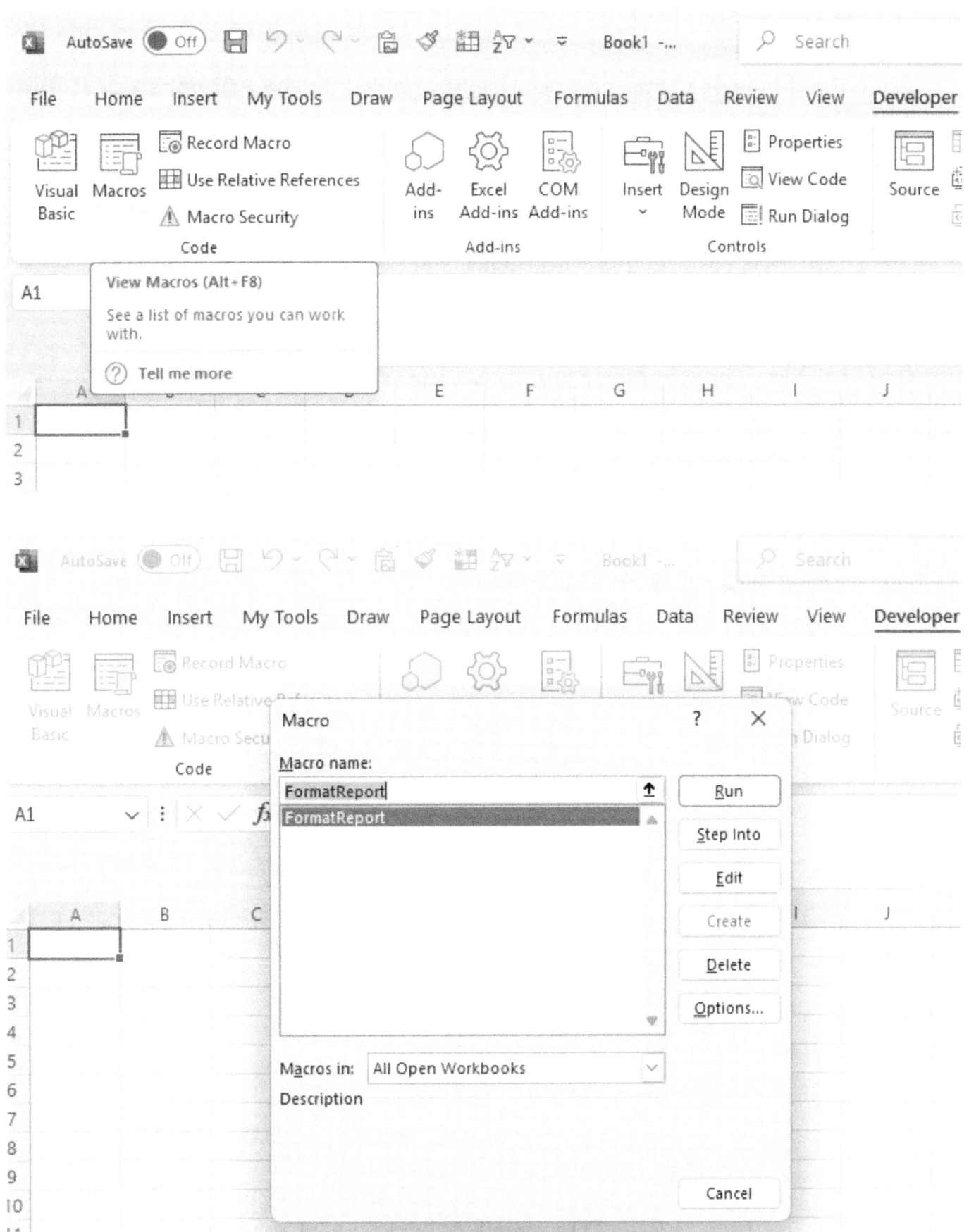

Recording a Macro is as easy as pressing **Record** and going through the motions of your task. Here's how to do it:

1. **Open the Developer Tab** (if it's not visible, enable it in **File > Options > Customize Ribbon**).
2. Click **Record Macro** (found in **Developer > Code** section).
3. In the **Record Macro** dialog box:

- Na**me your Macro (**e.g., "FormatReport").
- Choose where to store it (Th**is Workbook i**s the best choice for beginners).
- Assign a sh**ortcut key (**optional) for quick execution.

4. Click **OK** and start performing the task **as you normally would**.
5. Once finished, click **Stop Recording** (**Developer > Stop Recording**).

Excel has now stored every step you took. To **run the macro**, simply:

- Press the **shortcut key** (if assigned).
- Go to **Developer > Macros**, select your macro, and click **Run**.

Editing and Managing Macros Without Coding

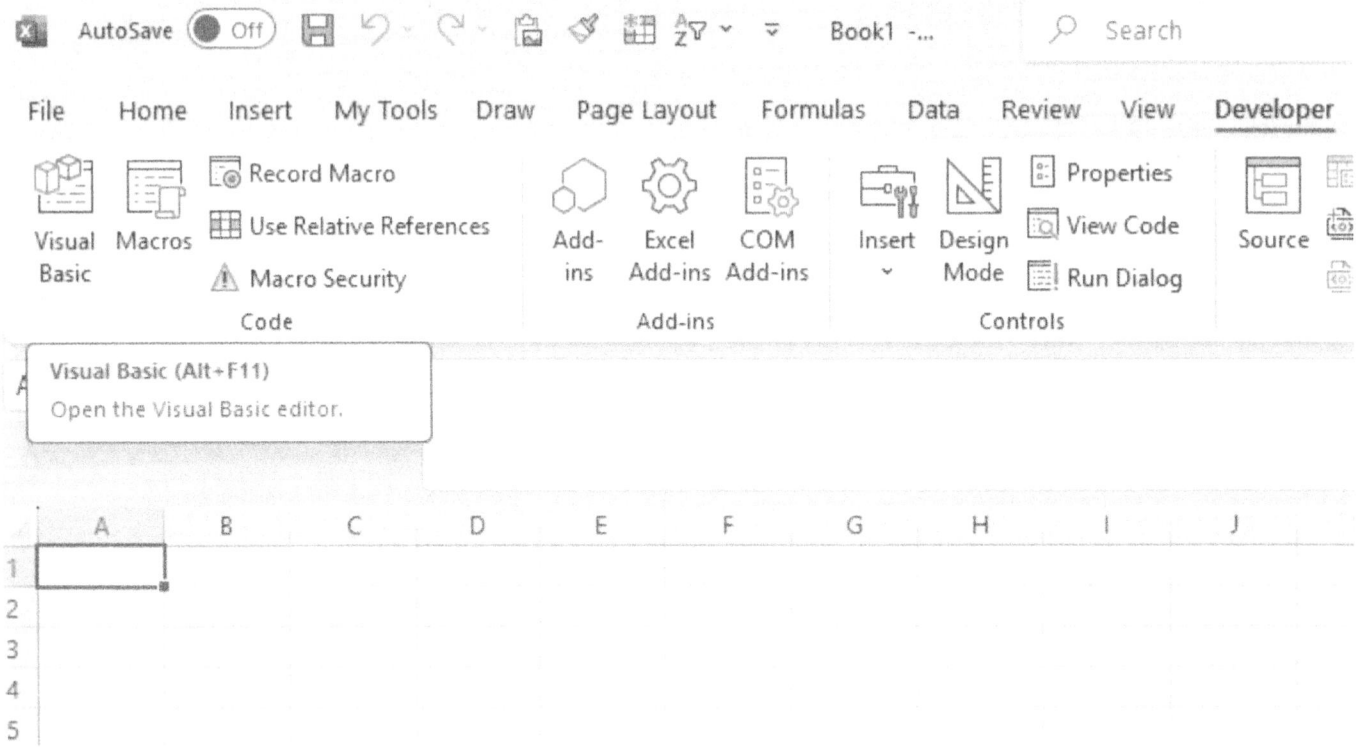

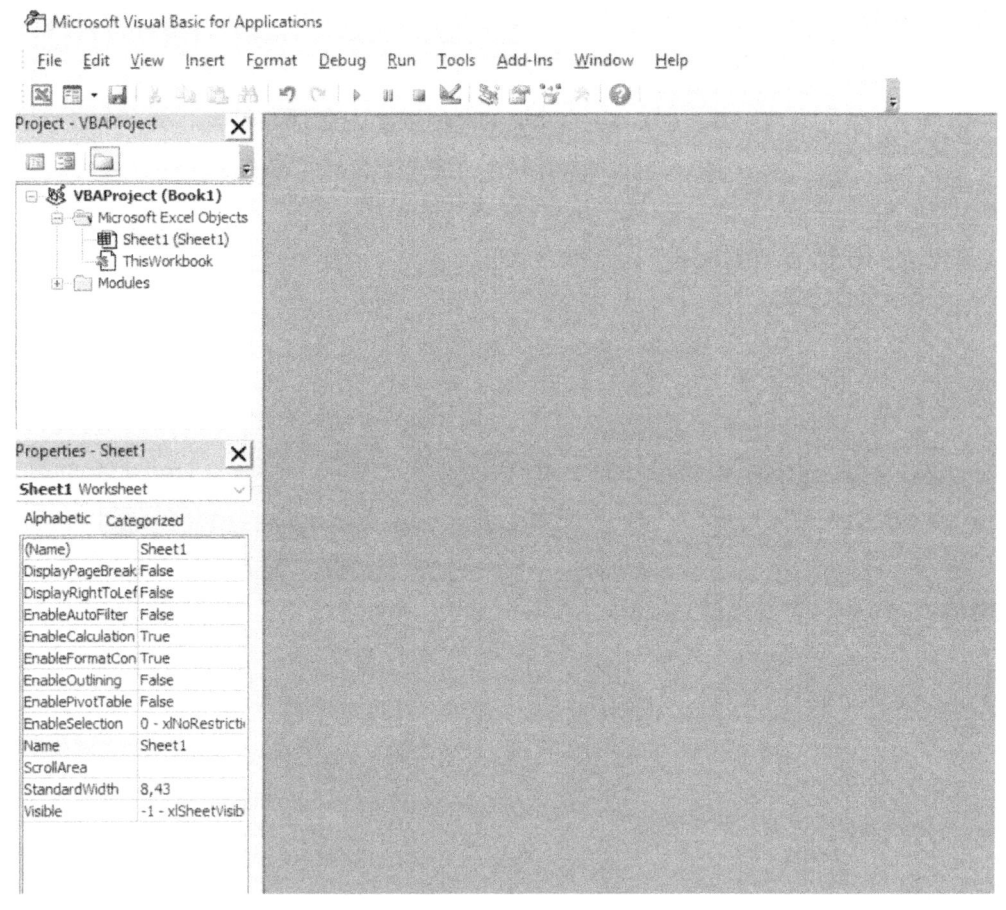

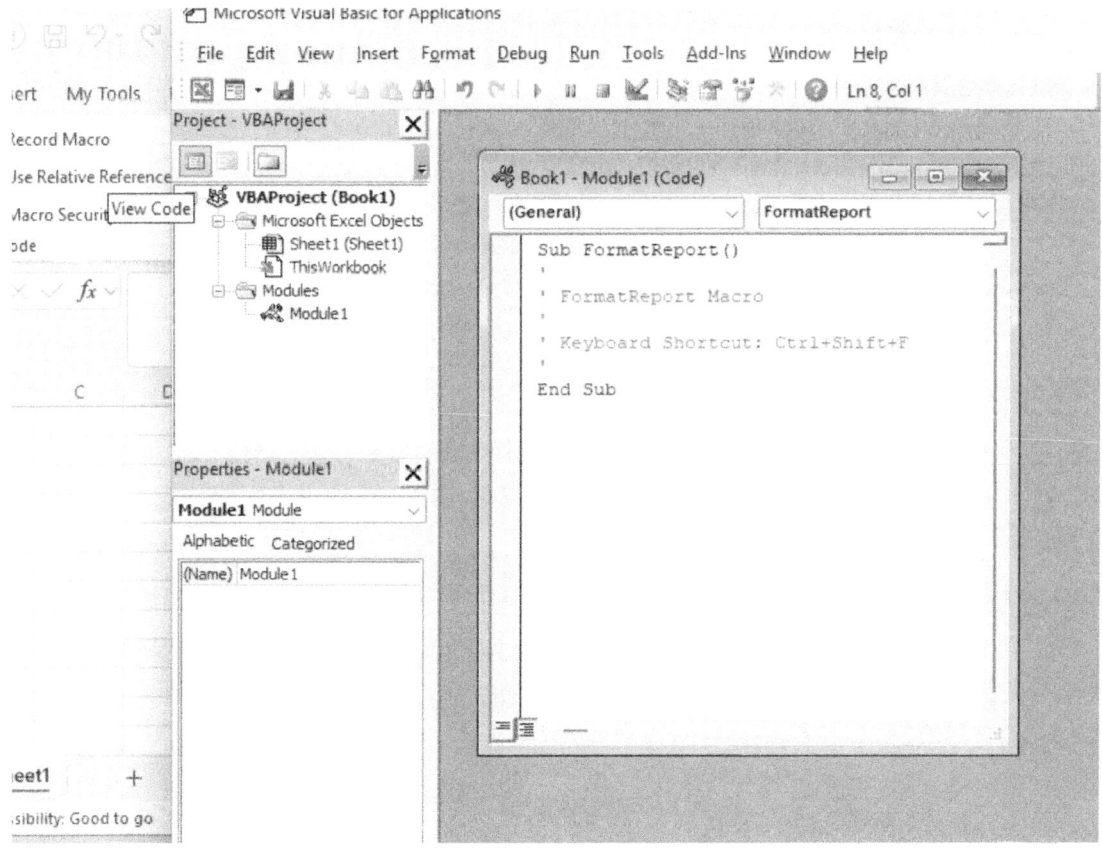

Even though macros are recorded in VBA (Visual Basic for Applications), you **don't need to write or understand VBA** to manage them.

- **To delete a macro:** Go to **Developer > Macros**, select the macro, and click **Delete**.
- **To edit a macro:** Use **Developer > Macros > Edit** (this opens the VBA Editor, but you don't have to modify the code unless necessary).
- **To assign a macro to a button:** Insert a shape or button (`Insert > Shapes`), right-click it, and select **Assign Macro**.

Best Practices for Using Macros

- **Test before saving** – Run the macro on sample data before using it in real reports.
- **Keep backup copies** – Macros **cannot be undone**, so save your file before running one.
- **Use relative references** – If your macro needs to work on different sets of data, use **relative references** instead of absolute cell selections (`Use Relative References` in the Developer tab).

By **leveraging Excel's Macro Recorder**, you can eliminate **time-consuming repetitive work**, allowing you to **focus on analysis rather than manual tasks**.

Introduction to VBA for Automating Repetitive Tasks

If you've ever wished Excel could perform tasks on its own—beyond what Macros can record—then **VBA (Visual Basic for Applications)** is the answer. VBA is **Excel's built-in programming language**, allowing you to create custom automation, manipulate data, and build tools that significantly boost efficiency. While it might sound technical, **learning VBA doesn't require a programming background**. Once you understand its basics, you can automate almost anything in Excel, from generating reports to performing complex calculations with a single click.

Why Use VBA Instead of Macros?

While **recording Macros** is a great way to automate simple tasks, it has limitations. The Macro Recorder **captures every action you take**, meaning it lacks flexibility. VBA, on the other hand, allows you to:

- **Automate repetitive processes** beyond what the Macro Recorder can handle.
- **Create interactive tools** like custom dialog boxes and forms.
- **Perform logic-based automation** (e.g., running specific actions based on conditions).
- **Process large datasets faster** than standard formulas and functions.

Getting Started with VBA in Excel

 Microsoft Visual Basic for Applications

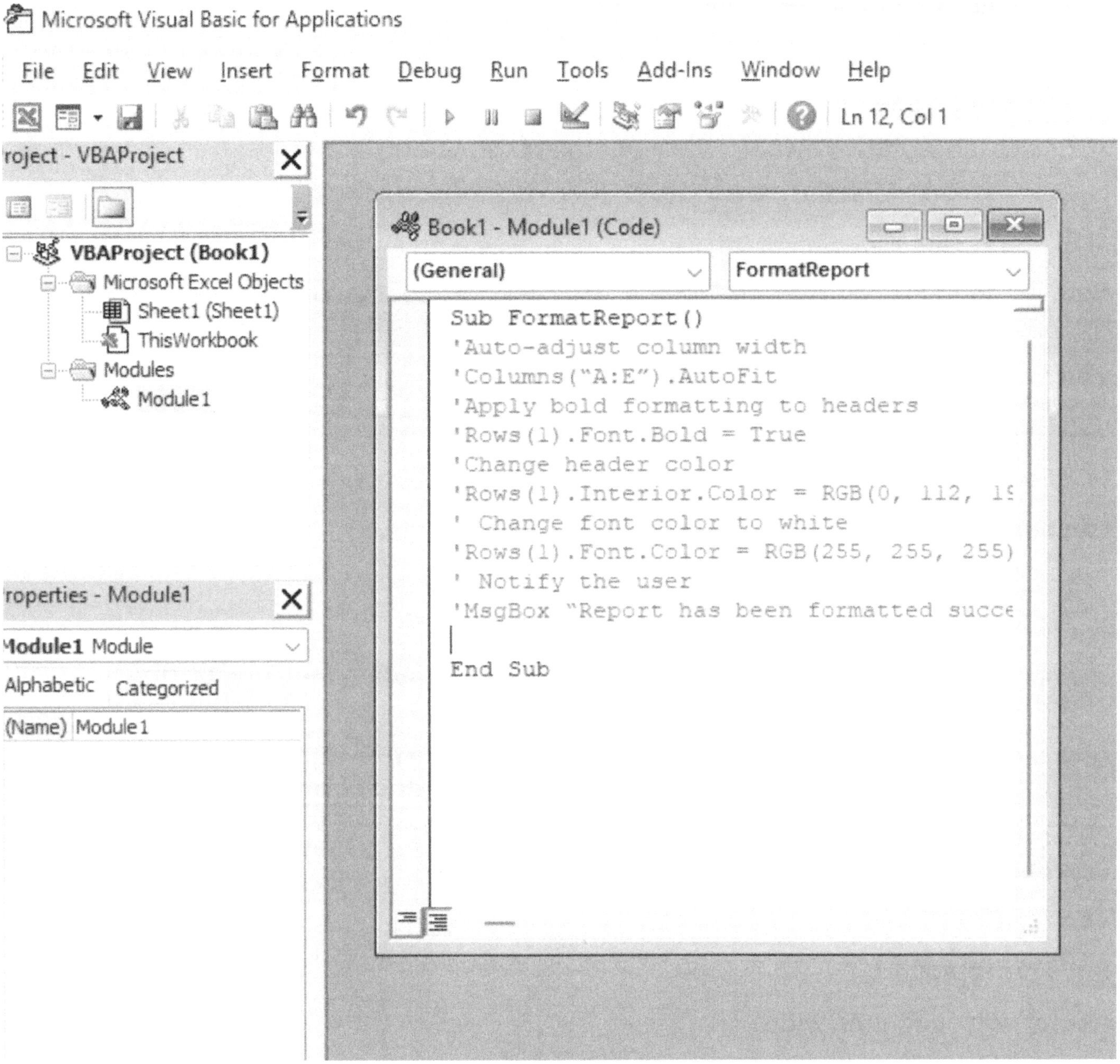

File Edit View Insert Format Debug Run Tools Add-Ins Window Help

Ln 12, Col 1

Project - VBAProject ✕

- **VBAProject (Book1)**
  - Microsoft Excel Objects
    - Sheet1 (Sheet1)
    - ThisWorkbook
  - Modules
    - Module1

Properties - Module1 ✕

Module1 Module

Alphabetic Categorized

(Name) Module1

Book1 - Module1 (Code)

(General) ∨ FormatReport ∨

```vba
Sub FormatReport()
'Auto-adjust column width
'Columns("A:E").AutoFit
'Apply bold formatting to headers
'Rows(1).Font.Bold = True
'Change header color
'Rows(1).Interior.Color = RGB(0, 112, 1?
' Change font color to white
'Rows(1).Font.Color = RGB(255, 255, 255)
' Notify the user
'MsgBox "Report has been formatted succe

End Sub
```

---

1. Opening the VBA Editor

To write VBA code, you need to access the **VBA Editor**, which allows you to create, edit, and run macros.

2. Enable the Developer Tab (if not already visible)

- Go to **File › Options › Customize Ribbon**
- Check **Developer** and click **OK**

3. Open the VBA Editor

- Click **Developer > Visual Basic**, or
- Press **ALT + F11** to open the VBA Editor

4. Insert a New Module (The missing step)

- In the **VBA Editor**, locate the **Project Explorer** (If not visible, press `CTRL + R`)
- Select the **workbook** where you want to add VBA code
- Go to **Insert > Module**—this is where your VBA code will be written

5. Writing Your First VBA Macro

Now, inside the newly inserted **Module**, you can start coding. For example, write the following simple macro:

```vba
Sub HelloWorld()
MsgBox "Hello, VBA!"
End Sub
```

- Press **F5** to run the macro
- A message box with "Hello, VBA!" will appear

By following these steps, you will successfully reach the **coding area** and be able to modify or write VBA macros.

Let's start with a simple VBA script that **automatically formats a report**. Suppose you frequently apply **bold headers, adjust column width, and change font colors**—instead of doing it manually every time, let VBA handle it:

Example: Formatting a Report with VBA

```vba
Sub FormatReport()
' Auto-adjust column width
Columns("A:E").AutoFit
' Apply bold formatting to headers
Rows(1).Font.Bold = True
' Change header color
Rows(1).Interior.Color = RGB(0, 112, 192) ' Excel blue color
' Change font color to white
Rows(1).Font.Color = RGB(255, 255, 255)
' Notify the user
```

MsgBox "Report has been formatted successfully!", vbInformation, "Formatting Complete"

End Sub

This script:

- Adjusts column width for **columns A to E**.
- Applies **bold formatting** to the first row (headers).
- Changes the background color of headers to **blue**.
- Changes the text color to **white** for contrast.
- Displays a **confirmation message** when done.

To run the macro:

1. **Go to Developer > Macros**.
2. Select **FormatReport** and click **Run**.

Automating Tasks Based on Conditions

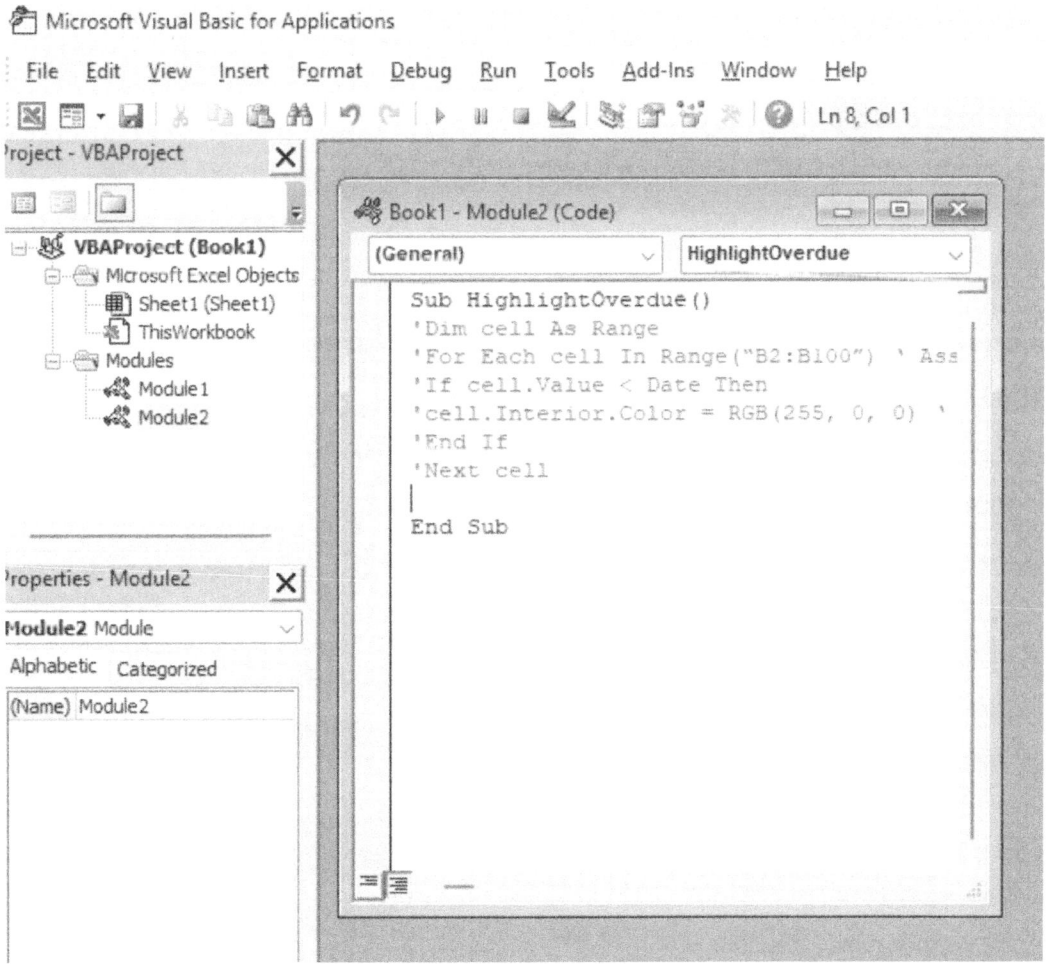

VBA shines when you need **conditional automation**. For example, let's say you manage invoices and want to automatically **highlight overdue invoices** (i.e., dates older than today).

Example: Highlight Overdue Invoices

vba

```
Sub HighlightOverdue()

Dim cell As Range

For Each cell In Range("B2:B100") ' Assuming column B contains due dates

If cell.Value < Date Then

cell.Interior.Color = RGB(255, 0, 0) ' Red for overdue

End If

Next cell

End Sub
```

This script:

- Loops through **column B** (due dates).
- If the date is **before today**, it colors the cell **red**.
- Runs automatically on **100 rows**, but can be adjusted.

Unlocking Excel's Full Automation Potential

VBA allows **customization beyond built-in Excel features**, helping you:

- **Eliminate manual work** by automating recurring tasks.
- **Improve accuracy** by reducing human error in reports and calculations.
- **Create interactive dashboards** with buttons, input boxes, and user forms.

Once you understand the basics, VBA becomes an **indispensable tool** for transforming Excel into a **powerful automation machine**.

PART 4

PIVOT TABLES AND DATA VISUALIZATION – TURNING NUMBERS INTO INSIGHTS

CHAPTER 9

PIVOT TABLES: THE SECRET TO QUICK AND POWERFUL DATA ANALYSIS

Answer complex business questions on the spot during meetings, turning data analysis from a headache into your competitive advantage

Building Your First Pivot Table Step by Step

If you work with large datasets, you know how frustrating it can be to analyze information quickly. Scanning through thousands of rows to find trends, totals, or summaries is time-consuming and prone to error. That's where **Pivot Tables** come in—they allow you to **summarize and analyze large data sets in just a few clicks**.

Pivot Tables might seem intimidating at first, but they are actually **one of the most user-friendly tools in Excel**. Follow this **step-by-step guide**, and you'll be building Pivot Tables like a pro in no time.

Step 1: Prepare Your Data for a Pivot Table

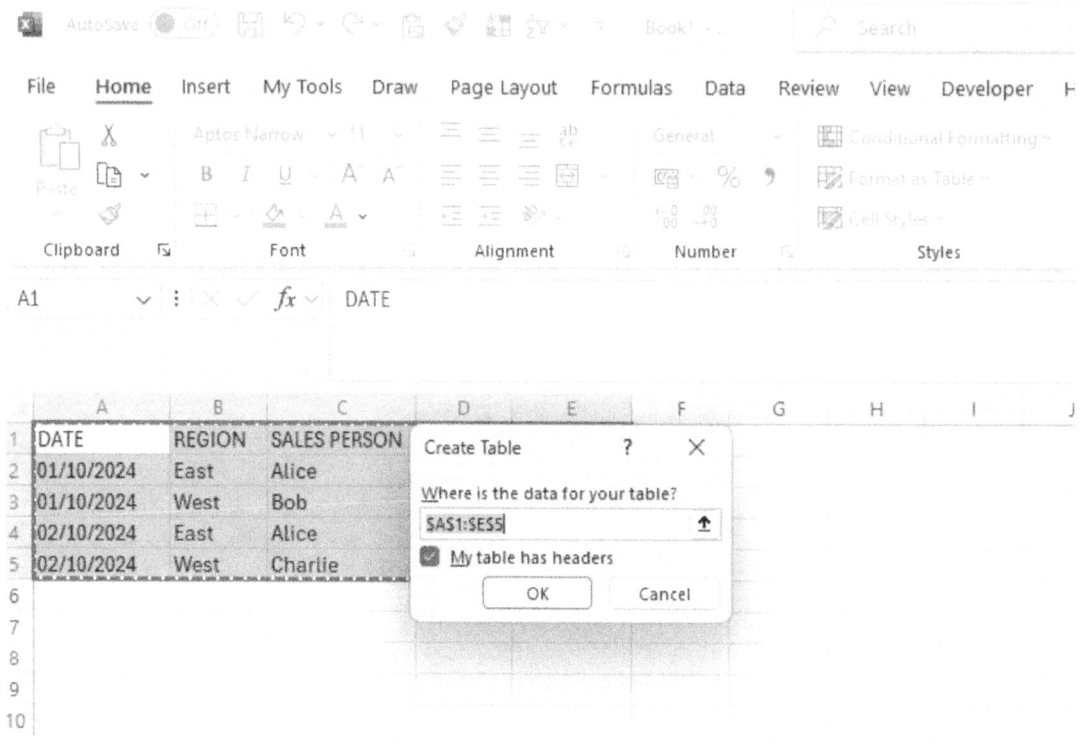

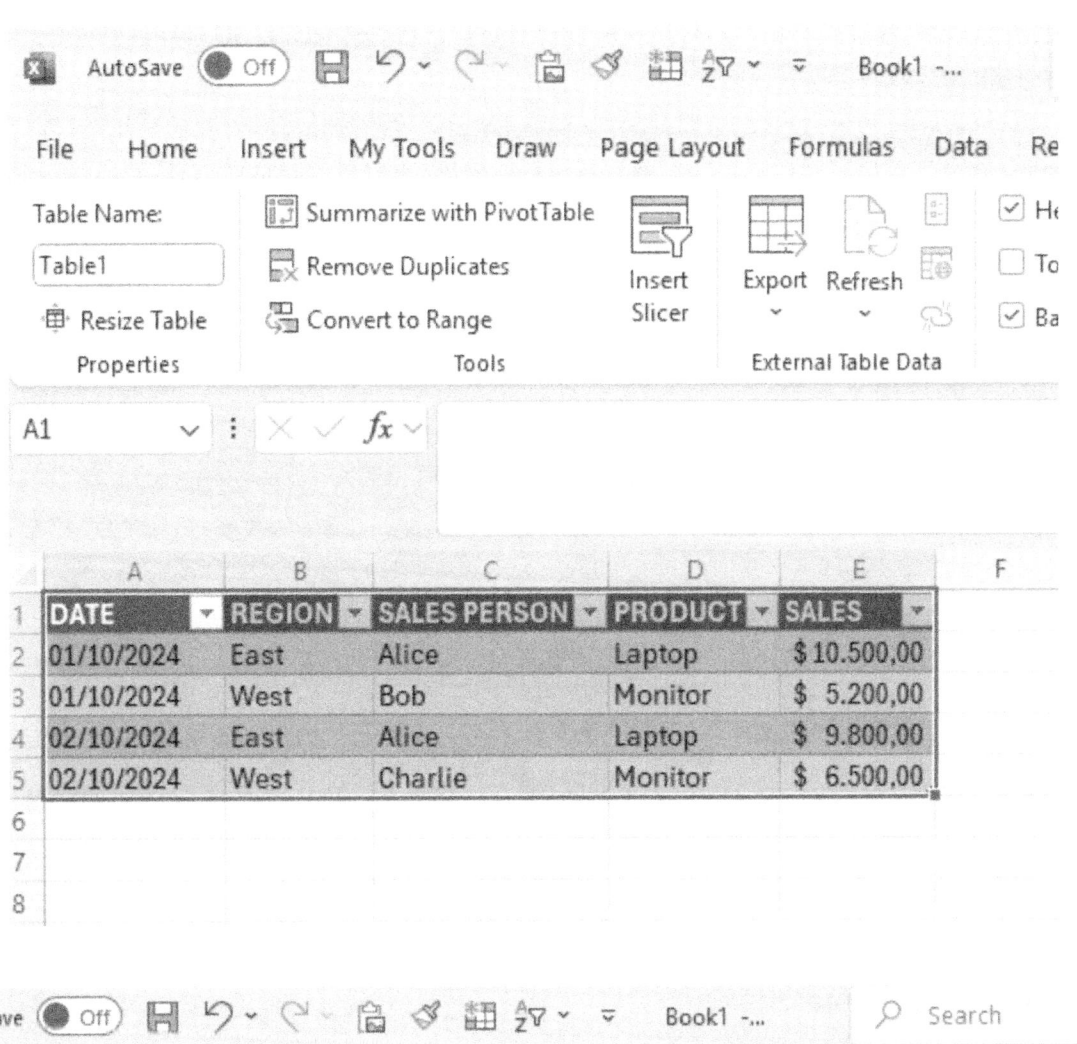

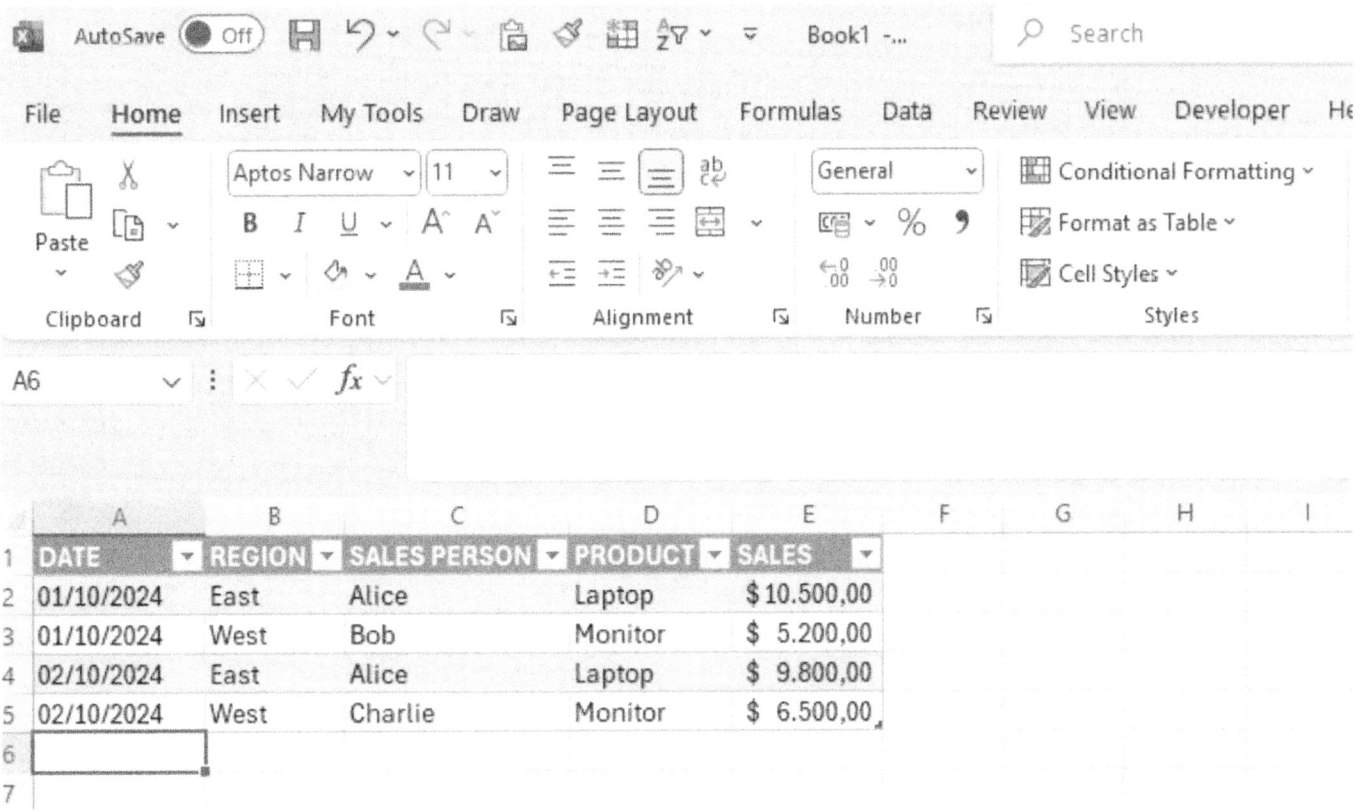

Before creating a Pivot Table, your dataset needs to be **clean and well-structured**. Here's what to check:

- **Ensure column headers are clearly labeled**—these will be used as field names in the Pivot Table.
- **Remove blank rows and duplicate values**—inconsistent data can lead to incorrect calculations.
- **Convert your dataset into a Table (`Ctrl + T`)**—this makes the Pivot Table dynamic, meaning it will automatically include new data.

Example dataset:

DATE	REGION	SALESPERSON	PRODUCT	SALES
01/10/2024	East	Alice	Laptop	10,500
01/10/2024	West	Bob	Monitor	5,200
02/10/2024	East	Alice	Laptop	9,800
02/10/2024	West	Charlie	Monitor	6,500

With data in this format, you're ready to build a Pivot Table.

Step 2: Insert a Pivot Table

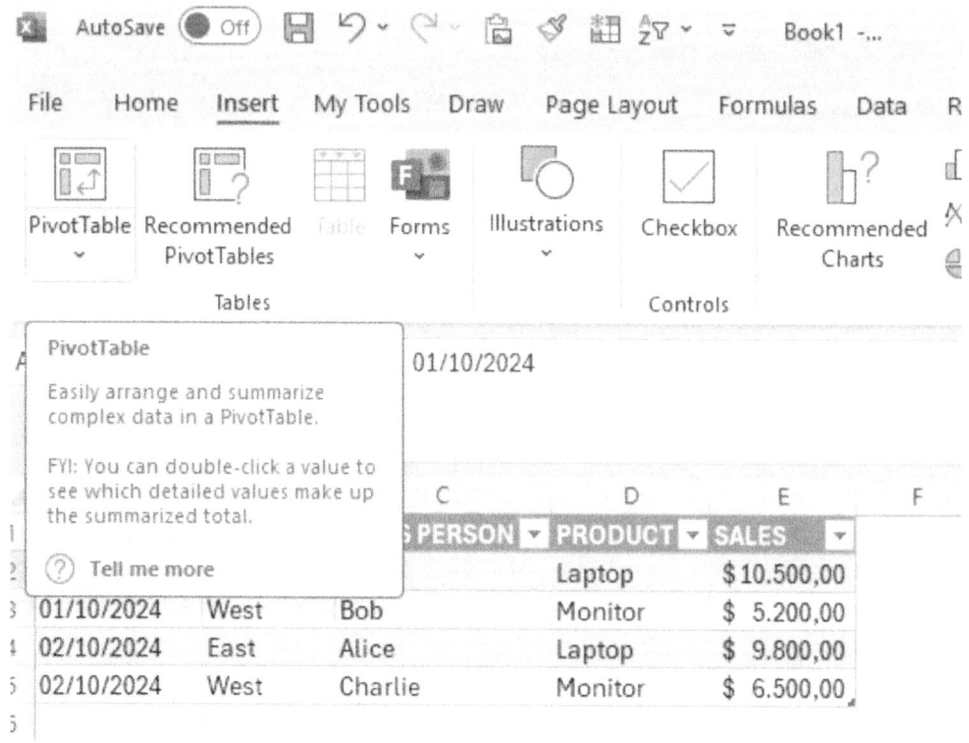

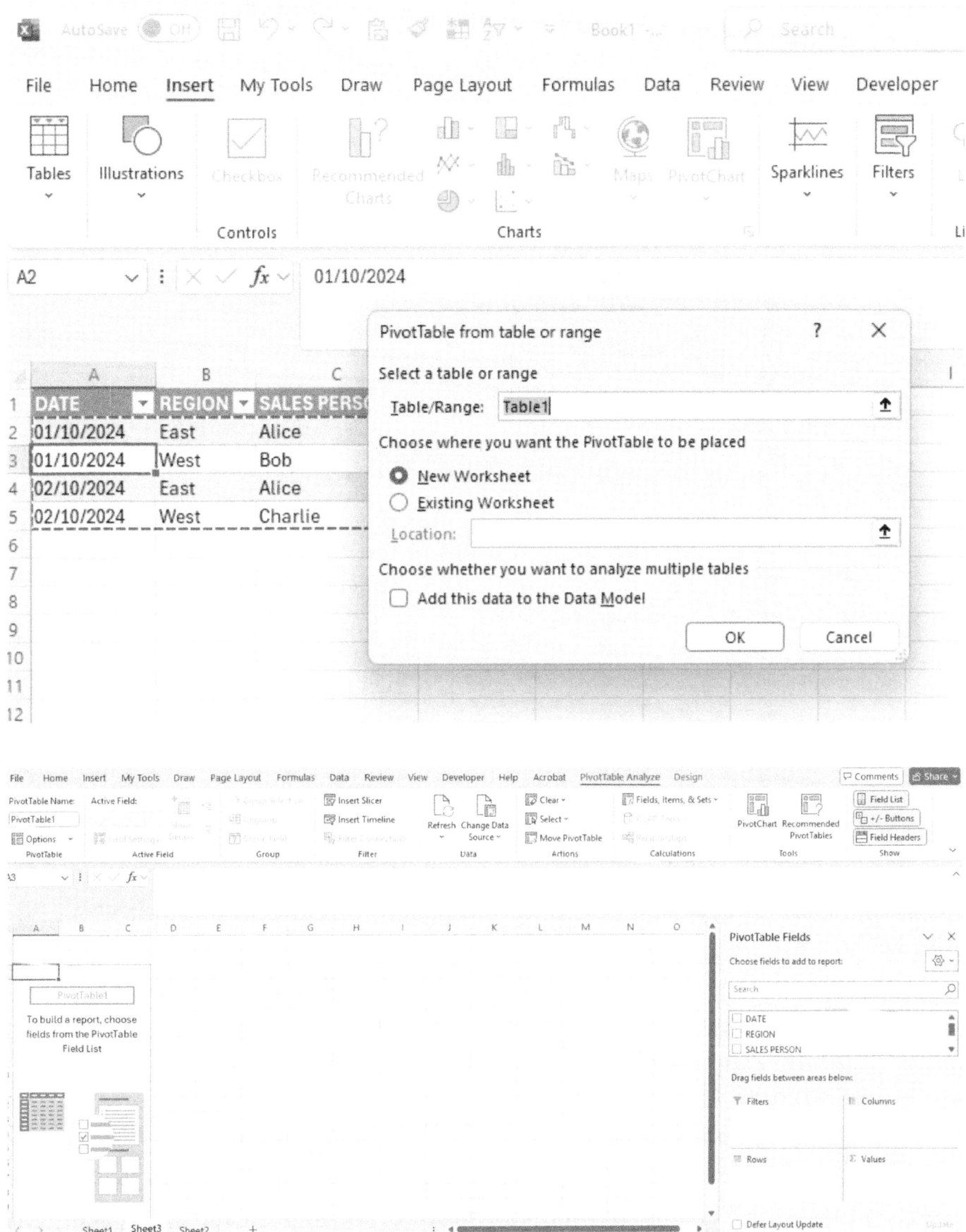

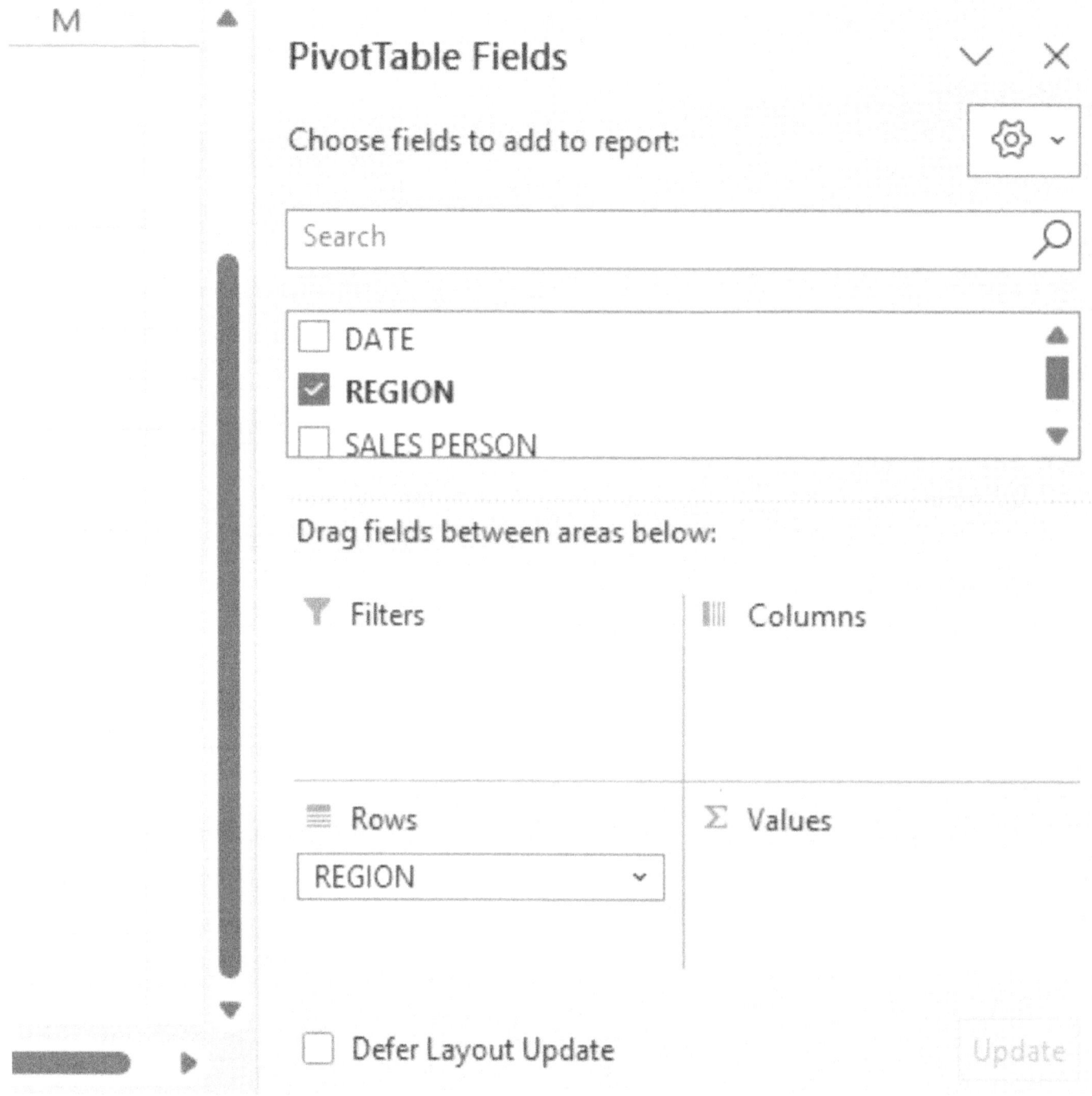

1. **Select your dataset**—click anywhere inside the table.
2. Go to **Insert > Pivot Table**.
3. In the **Create PivotTable** dialog box:

- Ch**oose where to place the Pivot Table—s**elect New **Worksheet f**or a clean workspace.
- En**sure "Use this range" is correct—E**xcel should automatically detect your data.

4. Click **OK**—Excel will create a blank Pivot Table and open the **PivotTable Fields Pane** on the right.

Step 3: Add Fields to the Pivot Table

Now comes the fun part—**dragging and dropping fields to build your summary**. The PivotTable Fields Pane contains four areas:

- **Rows** – Categories for analysis (e.g., Salesperson, Region).
- **Columns** – Additional breakdowns (e.g., Product categories).
- **Values** – The numbers you want to calculate (e.g., Total Sales).
- **Filters** – Optional filters to refine results (e.g., Show only "East" region).

Example: Analyzing Sales by Salesperson

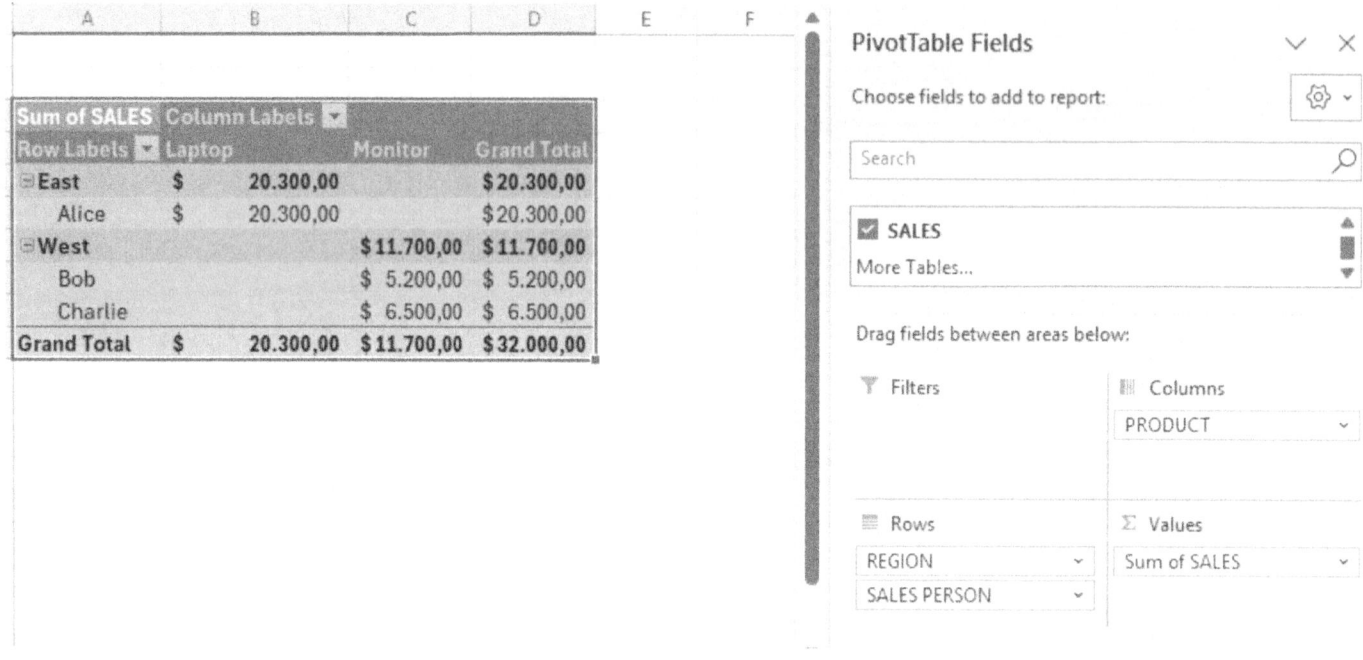

To create a summary of total sales by salesperson:

1. Drag **Salesperson** into the **Rows** area.
2. Drag **Sales** into the **Values** area—Excel will automatically sum the sales figures.

Your Pivot Table will now display:

SALESPERSON	SUM OF SALES
Alice	20,300
Bob	5,200
Charlie	6,500

Step 4: Format and Customize the Pivot Table

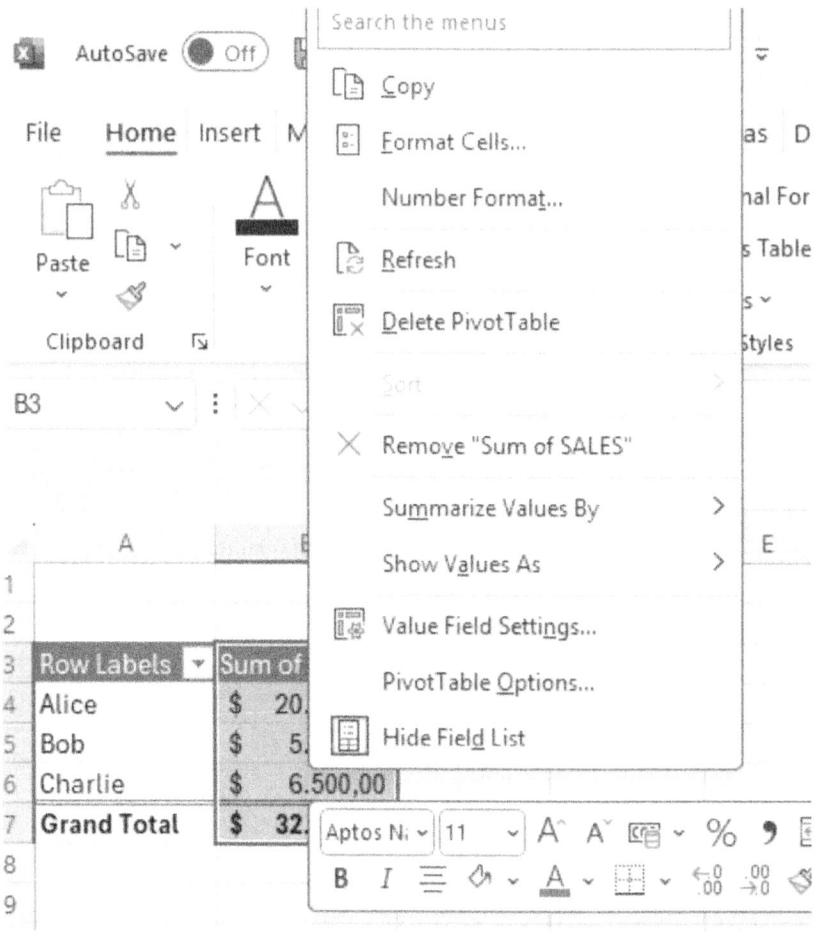

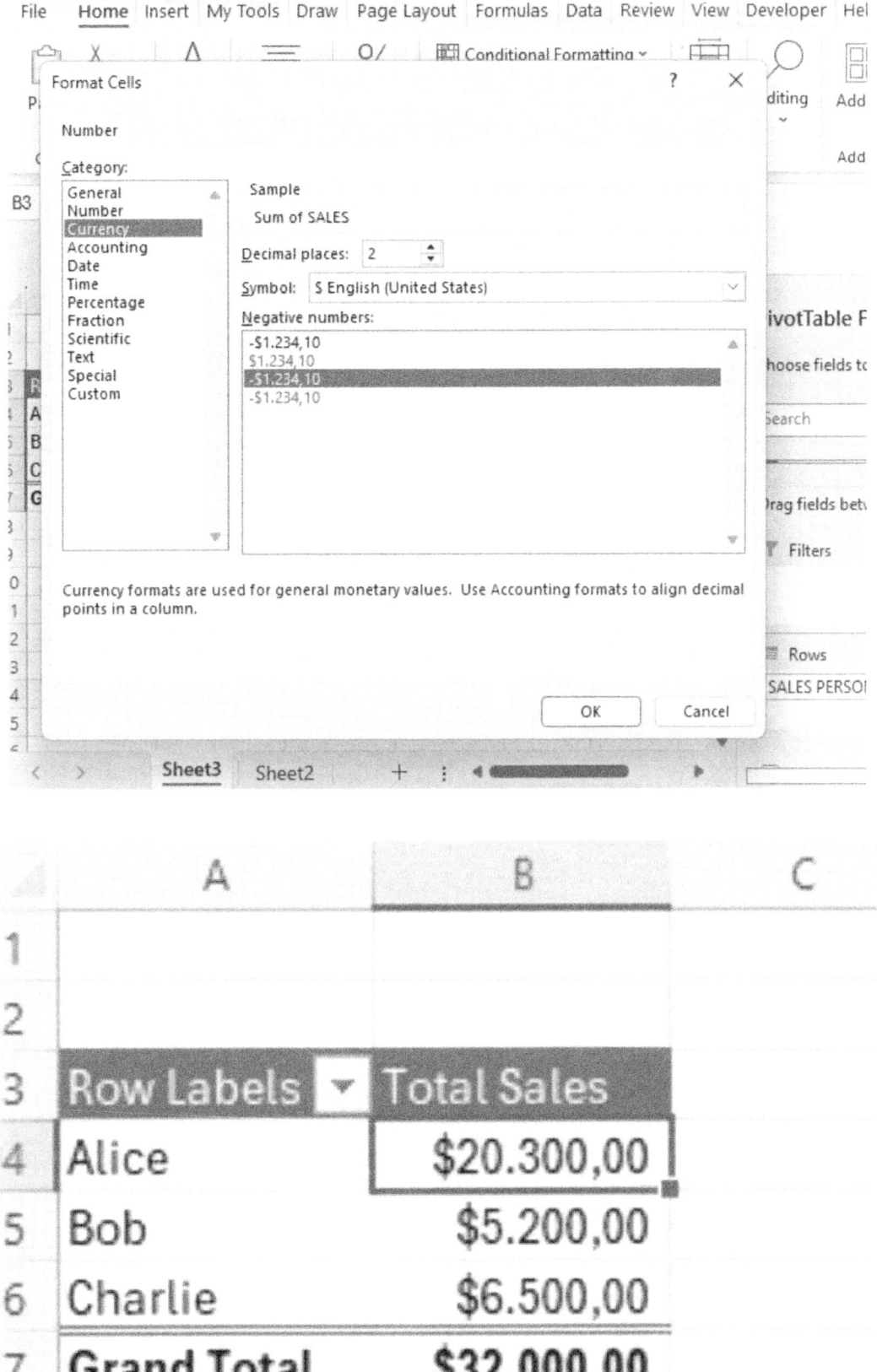

A raw Pivot Table is powerful, but let's make it **more readable and polished**.

- **Apply a Pivot Table Style**—click inside the table, go to **PivotTable Design > Styles**, and choose a professional look.

- **Change the Number Format**—right-click on **Sum of Sales > Number Format**, and set it to **Currency** or **Comma Style** for clarity.

- **Rename Fields**—double-click on "Sum of Sales" and change it to "Total Sales" for better readability.

Step 5: Refresh and Update the Pivot Table

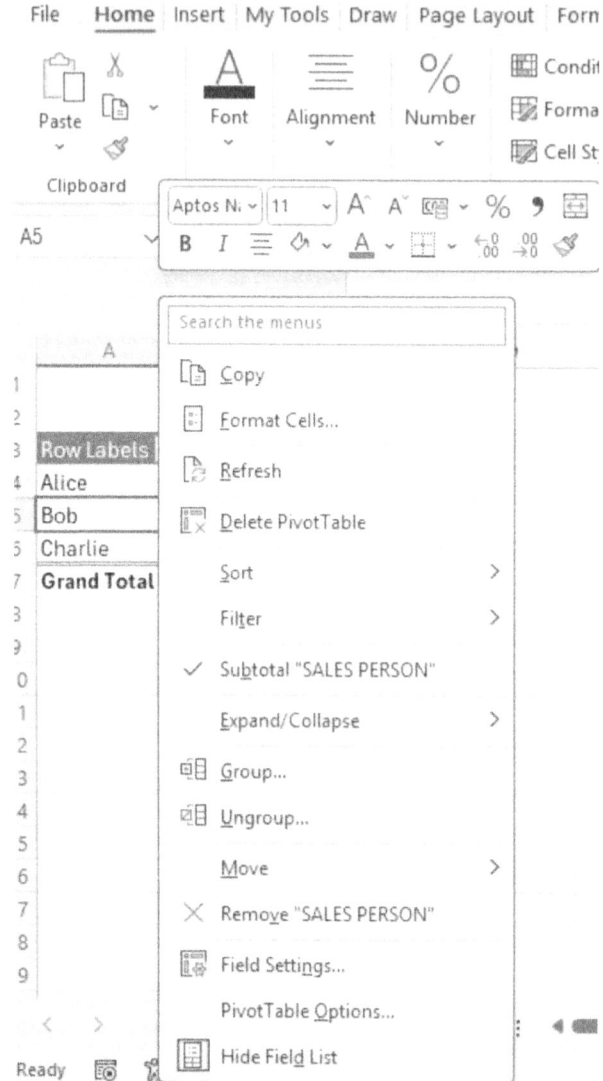

Pivot Tables don't automatically update when new data is added—so it's important to **refresh them**:

- Right-click anywhere inside the Pivot Table and select **Refresh**.

- If your dataset grows, go to **PivotTable Analyze > Change Data Source** to expand the range.

Pivot Tables: A Game-Changer for Data Analysis

By following these steps, you can **quickly summarize large datasets, identify trends, and generate instant insights**, making Pivot Tables an essential tool for efficient data analysis.

Filtering, Sorting, and Grouping for Better Insights

Pivot Tables are powerful on their own, but to truly **unlock their full potential**, you need to master **filtering, sorting, and grouping**. These tools allow you to refine your data, uncover hidden trends, and make your analysis more actionable. Instead of scanning through overwhelming datasets, you can quickly **zoom in on the most relevant information** with just a few clicks.

Filtering: Focusing on What Matters

When working with large datasets, not all data is immediately relevant. Filtering in Pivot Tables allows you to **isolate specific categories, time periods, or values**, making it easier to focus on key insights.

Applying a Pivot Table Filter

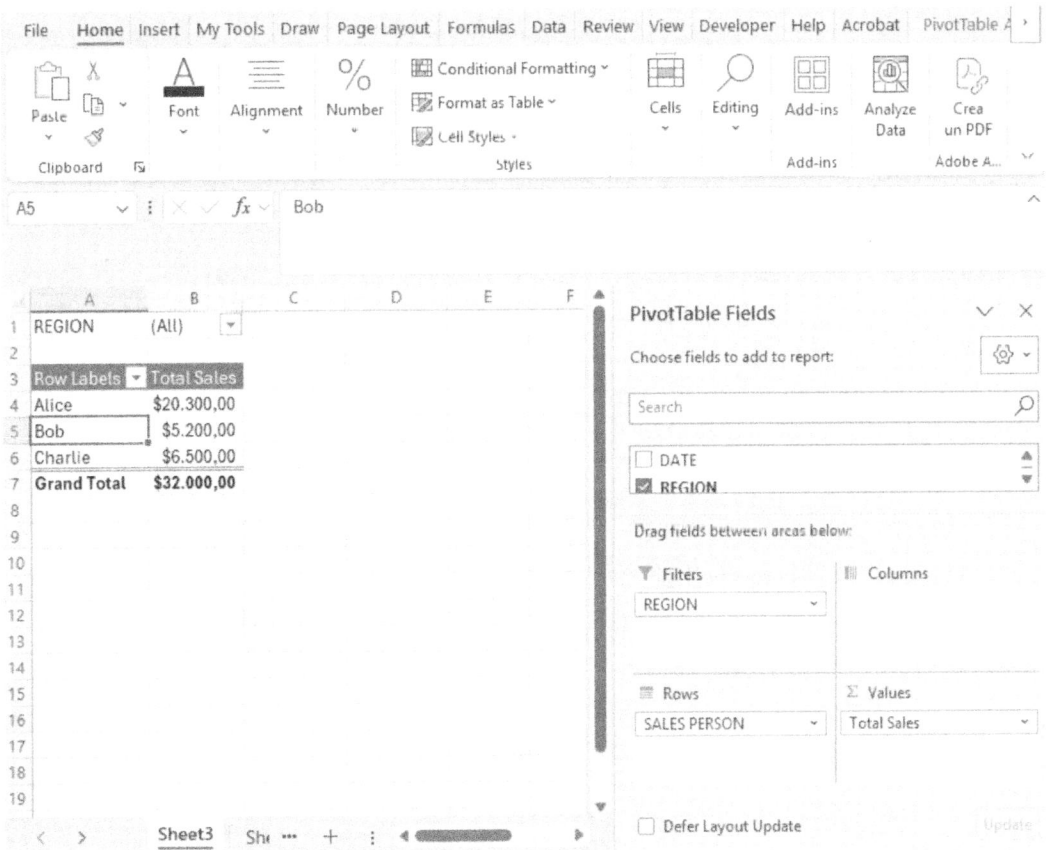

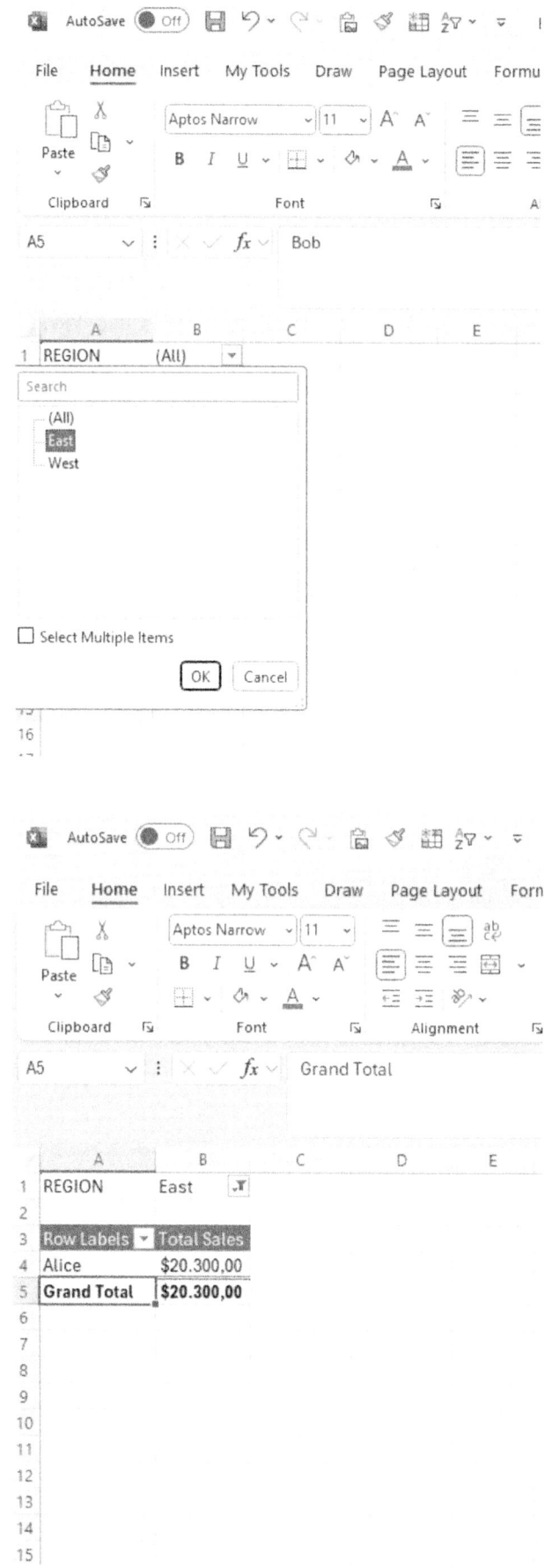

1. Click anywhere inside your **Pivot Table** to activate the **PivotTable Fields Pane**.
2. Drag a field (e.g., "Region" or "Product") into the **Filters** section.
3. A new **drop-down filter** will appear above your Pivot Table.
4. Click the drop-down and select the criteria you want to display (e.g., show only "East" region sales).

Using Value Filters for Advanced Filtering

Beyond basic category filters, you can **filter based on numerical values** to display only **top-performing results**.

- **To show only the top 10 sales transactions:**

1. Click the drop-down arrow on the **Sales** column.
2. Select **Value Filters > Top 10**.
3. Set the filter to **Top 10 items by Total Sales**.

This instantly displays the highest-performing sales transactions, **saving you hours of manual searching**.

Sorting: Organizing Data for Faster Insights

Sorting is essential when you need to **rank items by performance** or **analyze trends over time**. Pivot Tables allow you to **sort data dynamically**, making it easier to spot patterns.

Sorting In Ascending or Descending Order

- **To sort Total Sales from highest to lowest:**

1. Click on **any value** inside the Pivot Table (e.g., a total sales figure).
2. Go to **PivotTable Analyze > Sort & Filter > Sort Largest to Smallest**.

Excel will instantly **rearrange** your Pivot Table, placing the highest values at the top. This is particularly useful for **ranking sales reps, products, or departments** by performance.

Grouping: Simplifying Large Datasets

Grouping is one of the most **underrated features** of Pivot Tables. It allows you to **combine related data points** for better analysis. Instead of looking at a long list of dates or transaction details, you can **group data into months, quarters, or categories** to make it more digestible.

Grouping Dates into Months, Quarters, or Years

If you have sales data spanning multiple dates, analyzing it day by day can be overwhelming. To simplify:

1. Right-click on any date inside the **Pivot Table**.
2. Select **Group**.
3. Choose how you want to group the data (e.g., **Months, Quarters, Years**).

Now, your report will **automatically summarize sales trends over time**, making it easier to identify **seasonal trends and peak periods**.

Grouping Categories for Easier Analysis

Suppose your Pivot Table includes a long list of **product names**, but you want to **group them into broader categories** like "Electronics" or "Office Supplies."

1. Select multiple items inside the **Pivot Table** (e.g., all electronic products).
2. Right-click and choose **Group**.
3. Rename the new grouped category (e.g., "Electronics").

Now, instead of dozens of individual product entries, your Pivot Table will **display summarized totals by category**, making it far more readable.

Combining Filters, Sorting, and Grouping for Powerful Insights

By using **filtering, sorting, and grouping together**, you can create **focused, insightful reports** that highlight exactly what you need to know.

- **Filter** to focus on specific **regions or products**.
- **Sort** to quickly rank **best-selling items**.
- **Group** to summarize **trends over time** or **categorize products**.

These techniques make **large datasets instantly manageable**, allowing you to **find answers in seconds instead of hours**.

CHAPTER 10

ADVANCED PIVOT TABLE STRATEGIES: MULTIDIMENSIONAL ANALYSIS

Discover hidden trends and patterns others miss, positioning
yourself as the analytical problem-solver your team needs

Adding Calculated Fields and Advanced Filtering Techniques

Pivot Tables already make it easy to analyze large datasets, but their true power lies in **customizing calculations and applying advanced filters** to extract meaningful insights. **Calculated Fields** allow you to perform additional computations directly within the Pivot Table—without modifying the original data. Meanwhile, **Advanced Filtering Techniques** help refine reports so you can focus on the most relevant data. Let's explore how these features can help you **unlock deeper insights with minimal effort**.

Adding Calculated Fields: Customizing Pivot Table Analysis

Sometimes, the built-in summarization options (Sum, Average, Count) aren't enough. **Calculated Fields** allow you to create new fields that apply formulas to existing data, letting you **add custom metrics without altering the original dataset**.

How to Create a Calculated Field

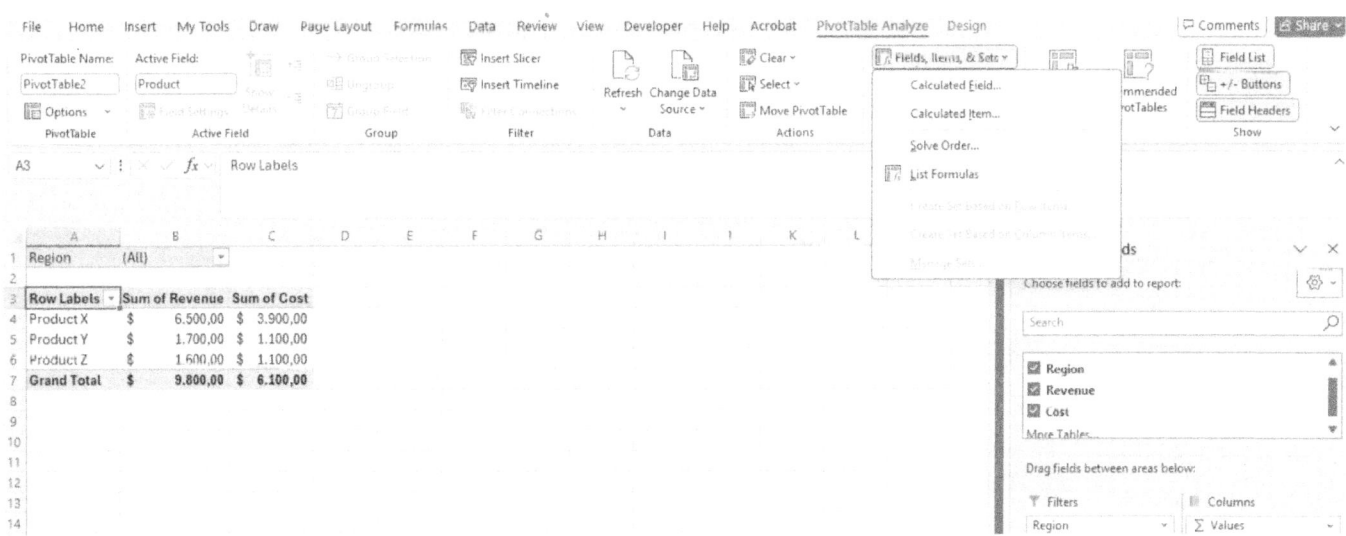

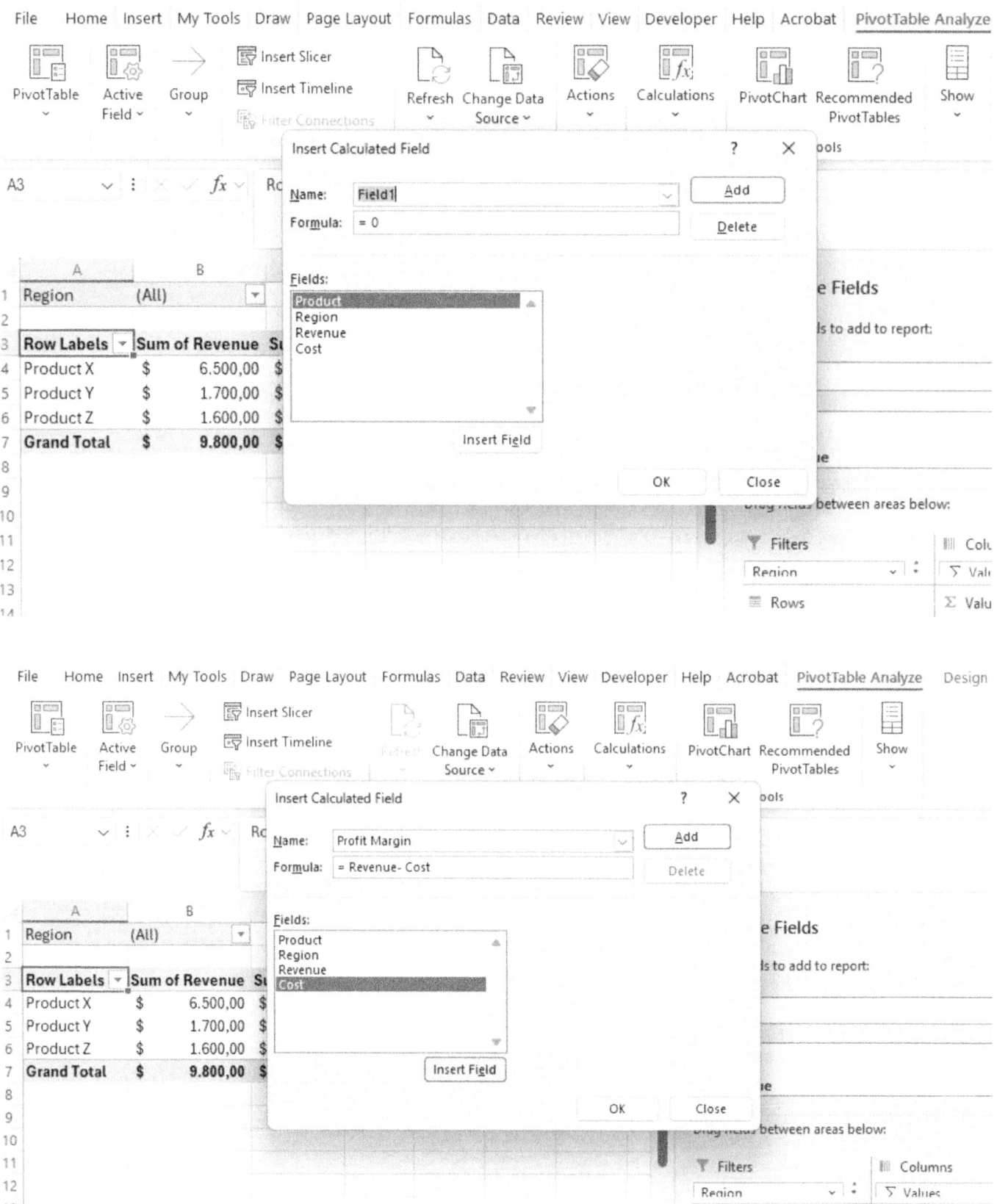

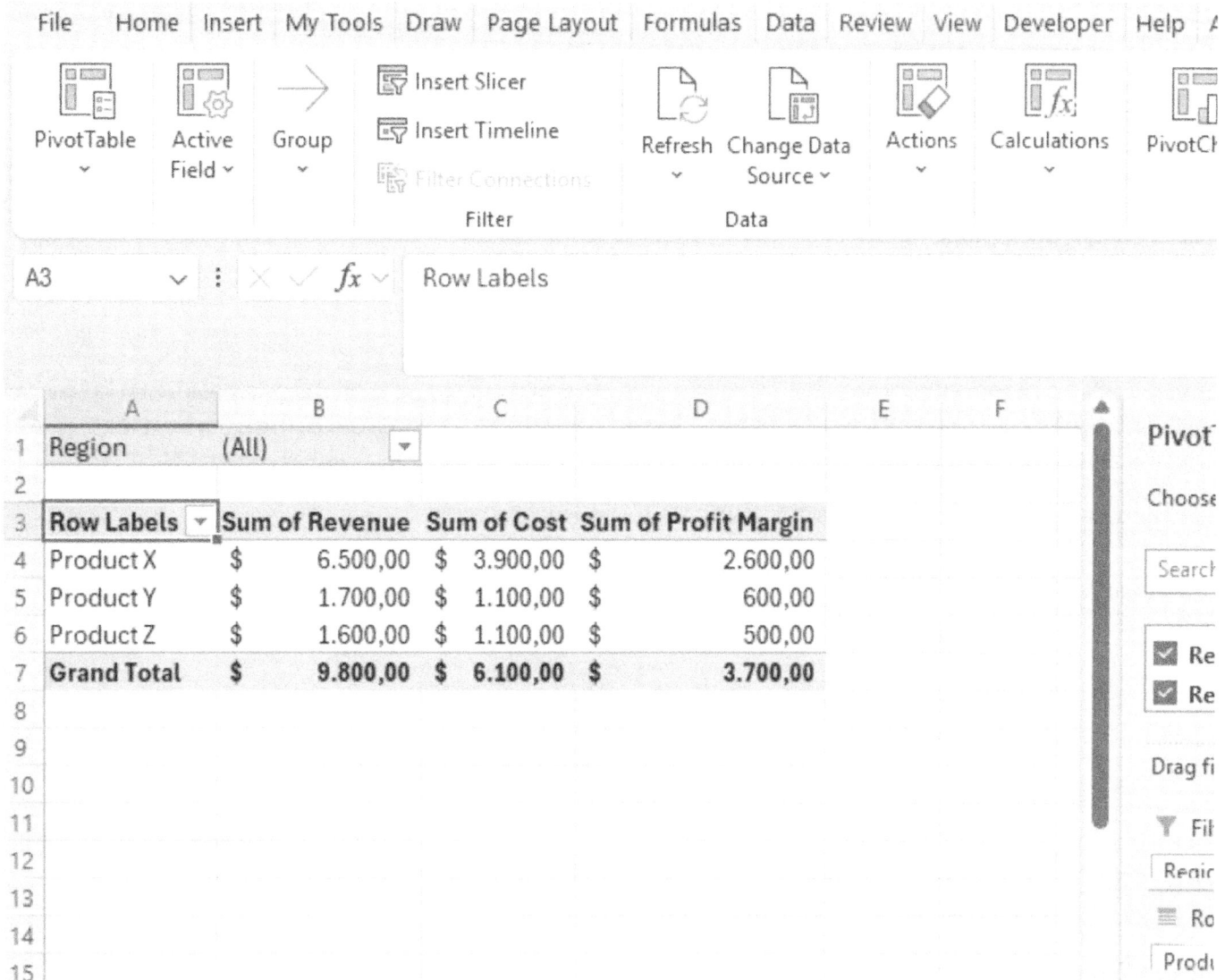

1. Click anywhere inside your Pivot Table.
2. Go to **PivotTable Analyze > Fields, Items & Sets > Calculated Field**.
3. In the **Insert Calculated Field** dialog box:

   » Enter a Fi**eld Name (**e.g., "Profit Margin").
   » In the **Formula b**ox, write your custom formula using field names.
   » **Example:** If your dataset contains `Revenue` and `Cost`, you can calculate Profit as:
   = Revenue - Cost

4. Click **OK**—Excel will add the new field to the Pivot Table as if it were part of the original dataset.

Now, whenever data updates, **Excel will automatically recalculate this field**, eliminating the need for manual adjustments.

Example: Calculating Profit Margins in a Sales Report

If you want to analyze **profit margins across different product categories**, you can add a Calculated Field:

= (Revenue - Cost) / Revenue

This will display the profit percentage for each product, allowing you to quickly identify high-margin items.

Using Advanced Filtering Techniques: Focusing on Key Data

Pivot Tables generate powerful summaries, but **not all data points are relevant at once**. Advanced filters help focus on **specific trends, outliers, or performance indicators**, making reports more actionable.

1. Filtering by Value: Showing Top or Bottom Performers

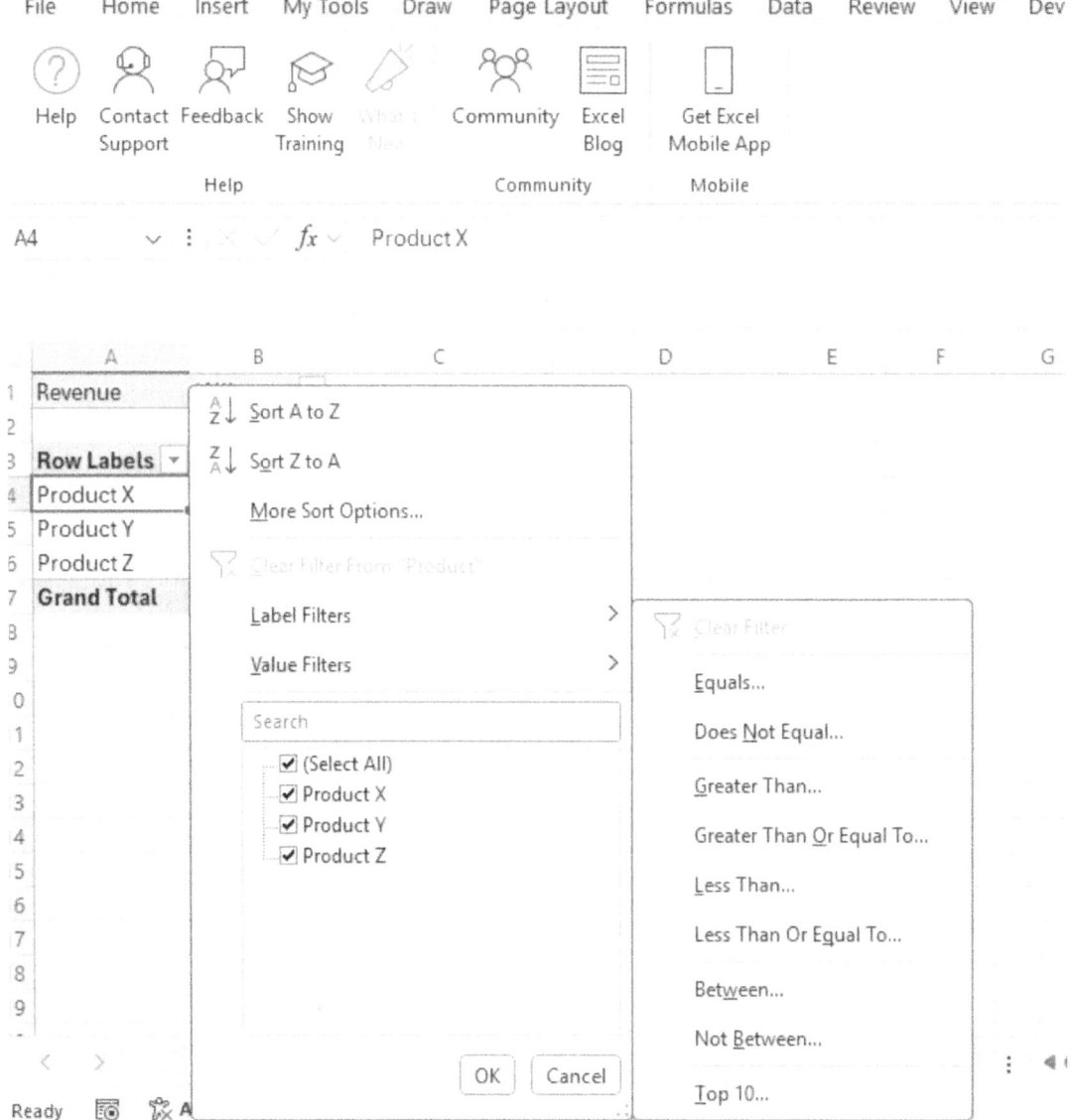

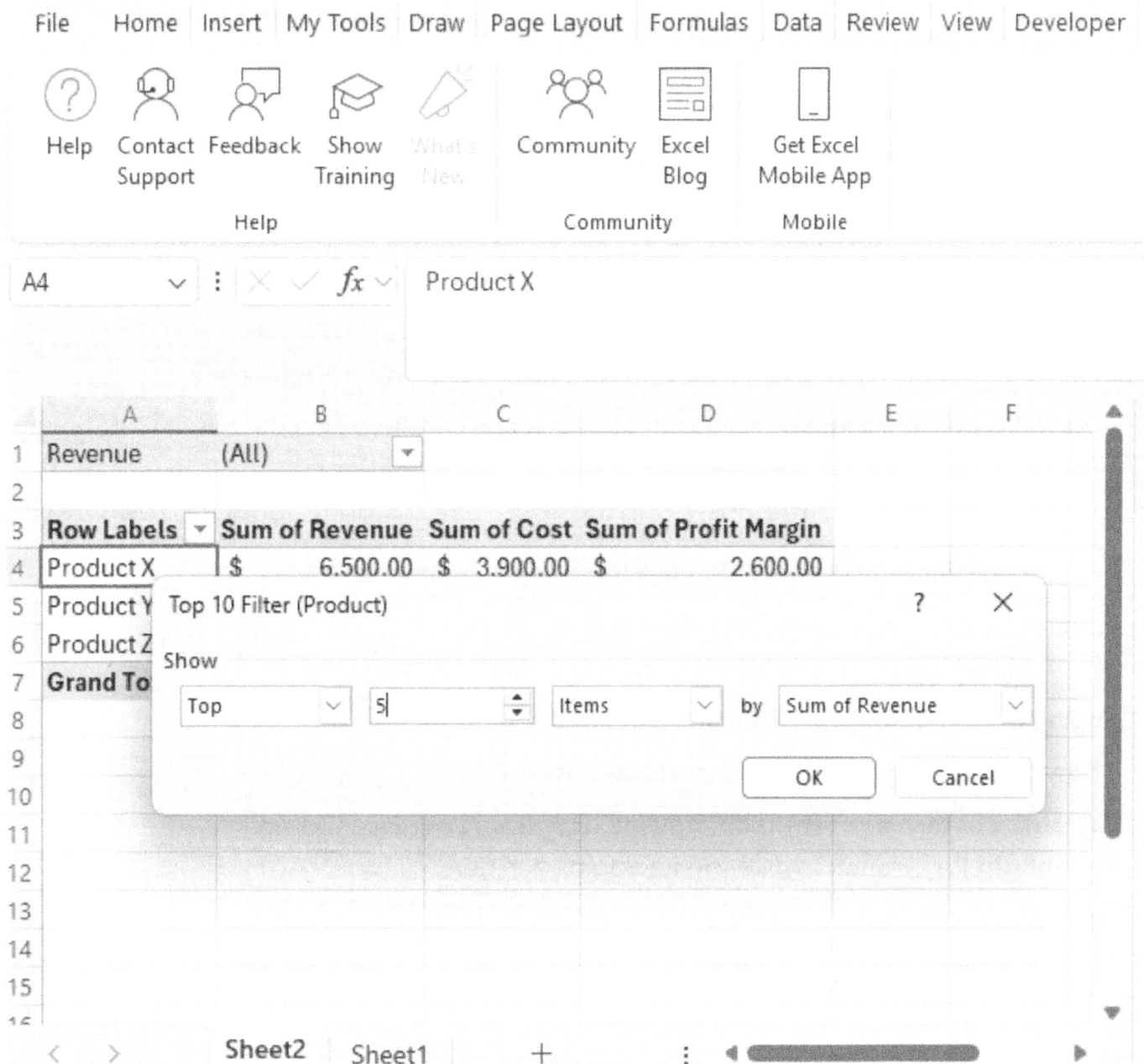

Instead of manually scanning through a long list of entries, you can **filter for the highest or lowest values** automatically.

- **Example: Show only the Top 5 sales regions**

1. Click the drop-down arrow in the Pivot Table column containing sales values.
2. Select **Value Filters > Top 10**.
3. Change "10" to "5" and select **Sum of Sales**.
4. Click **OK**—Excel will now show only the top five regions by total sales.

This method is great for **identifying key contributors** to revenue without unnecessary clutter.

2. Using Report Filters for Dynamic Analysis

Report Filters allow you to **switch views instantly** without rebuilding the Pivot Table.

- Drag **Region** or **Salesperson** into the **Filters** area.
- Use the drop-down menu at the top of the Pivot Table to **toggle between different views**.

For example, if you want to analyze **only West Coast sales**, simply select "West" from the filter list, and Excel will dynamically update the table.

3. Filtering with Slicers: A More Visual Approach

Slicers are an interactive way to **filter Pivot Table data with a single click**.

- Go to **PivotTable Analyze › Insert Slicer** and select a field (e.g., "Product Category").
- Excel will add a **button-based filter panel** to your worksheet.
- Click a category (e.g., "Laptops"), and the Pivot Table instantly updates to display only that category's data.

This is especially useful for **presentations and dashboards**, where users need to quickly switch between different views of the data.

Bringing It All Together: Smarter Data Analysis

By **combining Calculated Fields and Advanced Filtering**, you can:

- **Create custom performance metrics** directly in your Pivot Table.
- **Highlight key trends** by filtering for top performers.
- **Enhance reporting flexibility** with dynamic filtering tools like Slicers.

These techniques **turn basic Pivot Tables into a powerful decision-making tool**, ensuring you extract the most valuable insights from your data.

Using Pivot Charts to Bring Your Data to Life

Numbers in a Pivot Table can tell a story, but **visualizing that data** makes it significantly easier to understand trends, spot patterns, and make informed decisions. Pivot Charts transform **static tables into dynamic, interactive visual reports**, allowing you to analyze data at a glance. Whether you need to showcase monthly sales performance, compare product categories, or break down financial data, Pivot Charts **turn raw numbers into compelling visuals** that can drive business decisions.

What is a Pivot Chart?

A **Pivot Chart** is a **graphical representation of a Pivot Table**. Unlike standard Excel charts, Pivot Charts are **dynamic**—they update automatically when the underlying Pivot Table changes. This means you can **filter, sort, and group data visually**, making them an essential tool for financial reports, executive summaries, and business dashboards.

Pivot Charts help you:

- **Compare sales trends over time** (e.g., monthly revenue growth).
- **Analyze performance by category** (e.g., which product generates the most profit).
- **Identify patterns quickly** (e.g., seasonality in customer demand).

How to Create a Pivot Chart

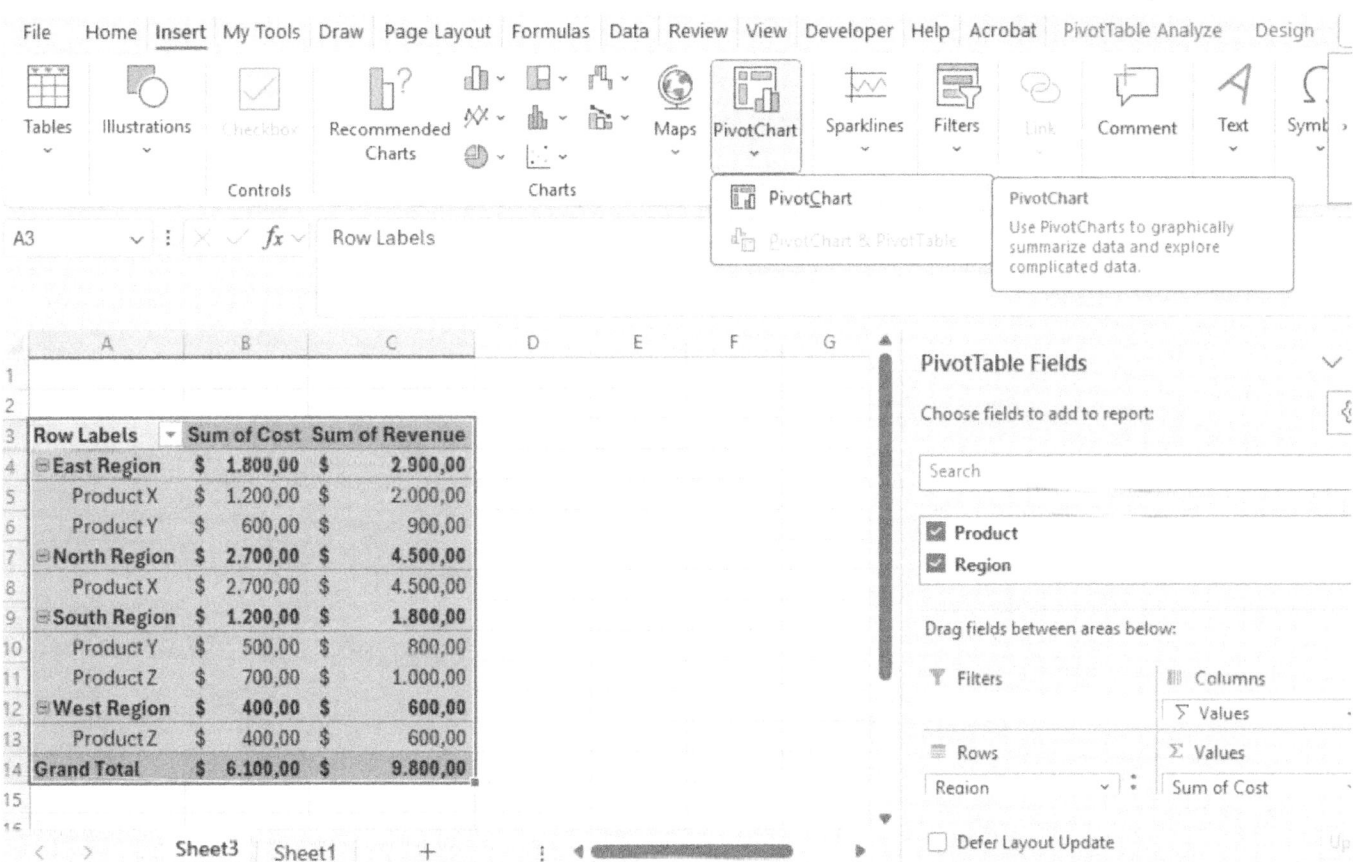

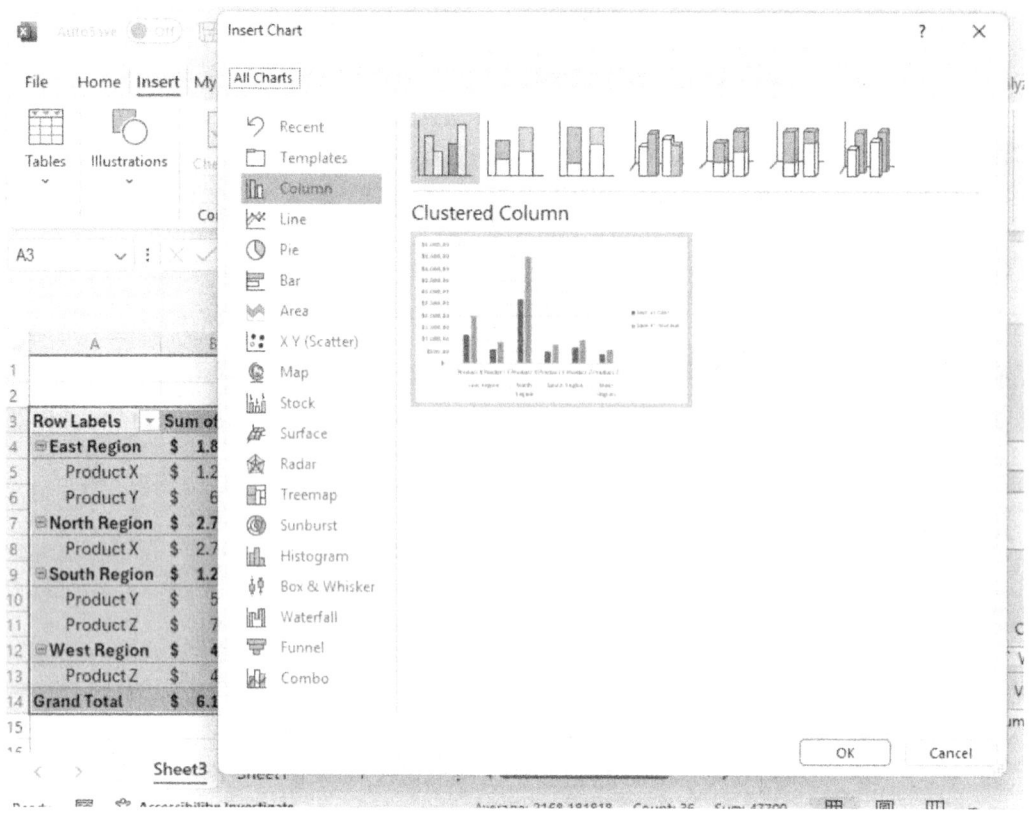

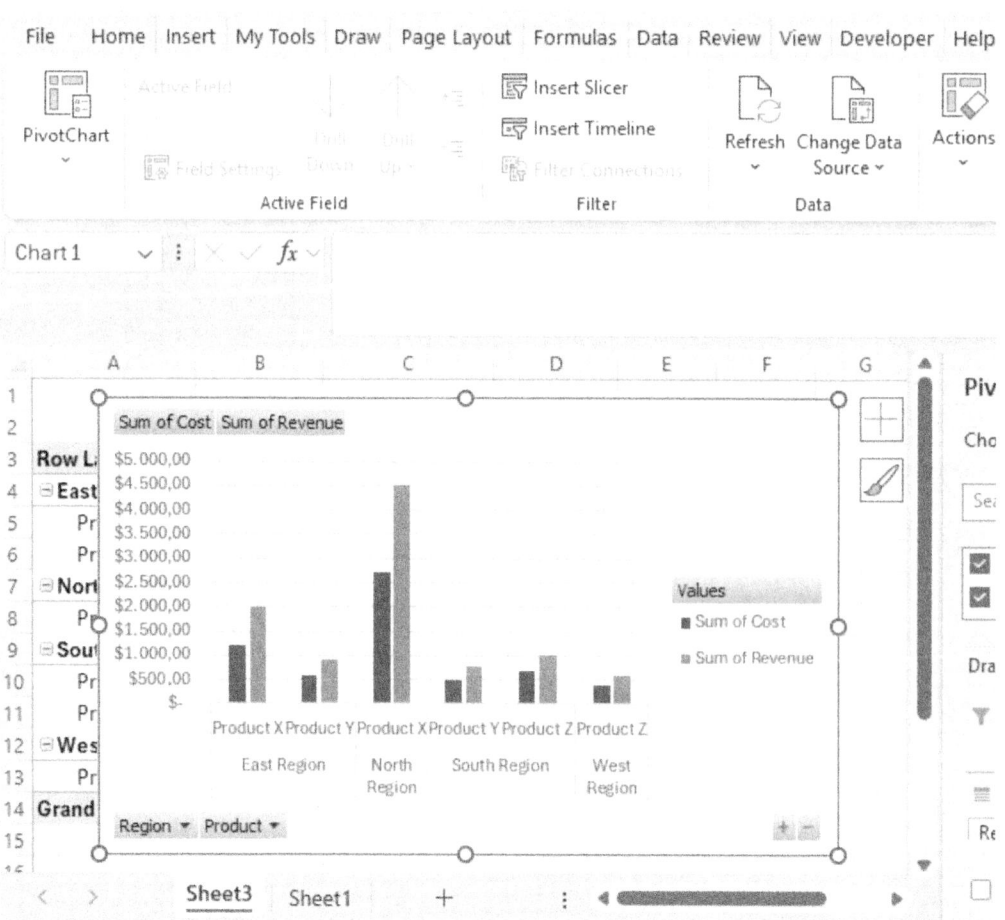

1. **Select Your Pivot Table** – Click anywhere inside your existing Pivot Table.
2. Go to **Insert › Pivot Chart**.
3. Choose the **chart type** (Excel recommends the best options based on your data).
4. Click **OK**—your Pivot Chart will appear, linked directly to your Pivot Table.

The best part? **Whenever you update the Pivot Table, the Pivot Chart updates automatically**—no need to manually adjust the chart each time new data is added.

Choosing the Right Pivot Chart for Your Data

Not all charts are created equal—choosing the right **chart type** ensures that your data is interpreted correctly.

1. Column Chart: Best for Comparing Categories

Ideal for **side-by-side comparisons**, column charts help visualize **which product, salesperson, or region is performing the best**.

- **Example:** Comparing total revenue across different product categories.

2. Line Chart: Best for Trends Over Time

Use a **line chart** to track changes over a period (e.g., sales growth per month).

- **Example:** Analyzing how customer purchases fluctuate throughout the year.

3. Pie Chart: Best for Market Share Breakdown

A **pie chart** is effective for displaying **percentages or proportions**.

- **Example:** Showing how much each sales region contributes to total revenue.

4. Stacked Bar Chart: Best for Comparing Subcategories

When you need to **break down multiple variables**, stacked bar charts provide a clear view of **how different elements contribute to a whole**.

- **Example:** Comparing sales of multiple product categories across different regions.

Customizing a Pivot Chart for Maximum Impact

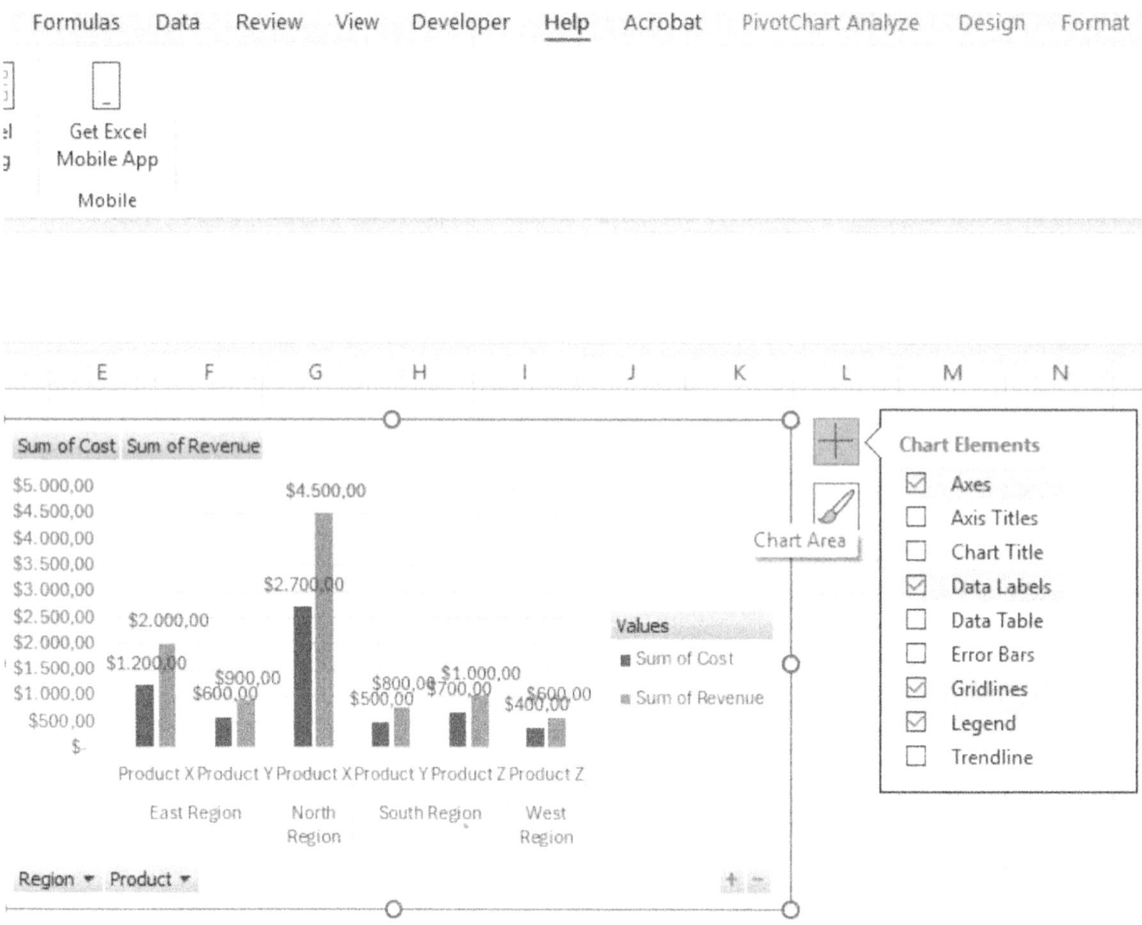

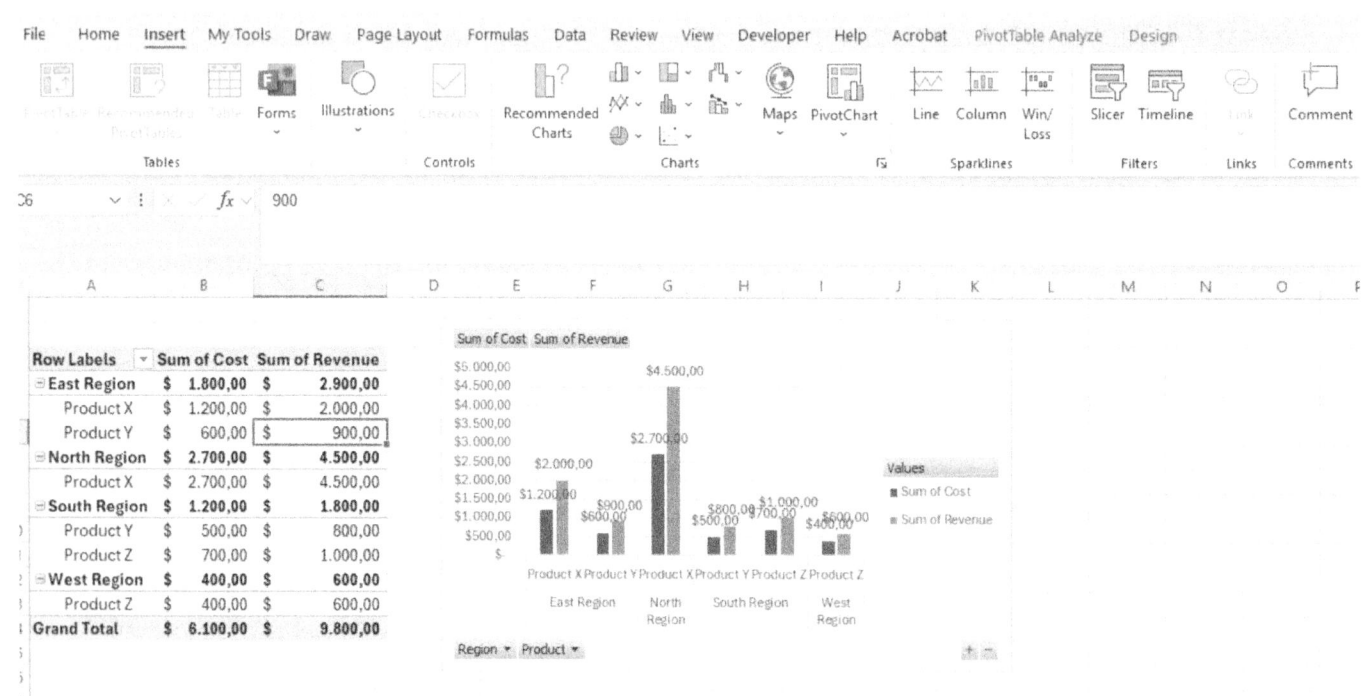

Once your Pivot Chart is created, take a few extra steps to make it **clear, readable, and visually engaging**:

- **Add Data Labels** – Display exact values on the chart for easy interpretation (**Chart Elements > Data Labels**).
- **Modify Chart Styles** – Use pre-set styles in **Chart Design** to enhance readability.
- **Apply Filters via Slicers** – Add **interactive filters** to let users dynamically switch views (**Insert > Slicer**).

Why Pivot Charts Are Essential for Business Analysis

A well-designed Pivot Chart can **reveal insights that a raw table cannot**. By transforming numbers into visuals, you ensure that your data **tells a story**—whether you're presenting to executives, tracking team performance, or forecasting trends. With **Pivot Charts, decision-making becomes faster, clearer, and more data-driven**.

CHAPTER 11

DASHBOARDS AND INTERACTIVE REPORTS: PRESENTING DATA LIKE A PRO

Build impressive, interactive dashboards that update automatically and make you stand out in presentations

Designing Engaging Dashboards with Key Metrics

A well-designed **Excel dashboard** is more than just a collection of charts and tables—it's a **powerful storytelling tool** that allows users to grasp key business insights at a glance. Whether you're tracking financial performance, monitoring sales trends, or managing project progress, a **clear, engaging dashboard** ensures that data is **both accessible and actionable**.

Creating a dashboard isn't just about adding visuals—it's about selecting the **right key metrics**, designing for **clarity**, and ensuring that the **layout enhances decision-making**.

Choosing the Right Key Metrics

Before building your dashboard, **you must define which metrics matter most**. Over-loading a dashboard with too many data points makes it overwhelming and ineffective. Instead, focus on:

- **KPIs (Key Performance Indicators)** – Metrics that reflect the business's overall success (e.g., revenue growth, customer retention, sales conversions).
- **Operational Metrics** – Day-to-day data that supports decision-making (e.g., orders processed, inventory levels, productivity rates).
- **Comparative Metrics** – Year-over-year trends, regional comparisons, or benchmarks against industry standards.

Example: Sales Performance Dashboard Metrics

For a dashboard tracking **sales performance**, the most relevant metrics might include:

- **Total Revenue** (overall sales performance).
- **Revenue by Region** (geographical trends).
- **Top-Selling Products** (which items generate the most sales).
- **Sales Growth Rate** (month-over-month or year-over-year progress).
- **Conversion Rate** (percentage of leads turning into sales).

Laying Out the Dashboard for Maximum Clarity

The **layout of a dashboard** plays a crucial role in how quickly and effectively users can interpret the data. A cluttered, poorly structured dashboard can make even the most useful metrics difficult to understand.

Best Practices for Layout Design

- **Follow a Logical Flow** – Arrange elements **from high-level summaries to detailed breakdowns**. Start with KPIs, then move into supporting data.
- **Use White Space Effectively** – Avoid overcrowding; leave enough space between charts and tables for readability.
- **Align Visuals Properly** – Keep charts and tables aligned for a **clean, professional look**.
- **Group Related Information** – Place similar data points near each other (e.g., put sales revenue and cost side by side for quick margin analysis).

Example: A Well-Structured Sales Dashboard Layout

SECTION	CONTENT
Header	Title, Report Date, Filters (e.g., select time period, region)
Top KPIs	Total Sales, Revenue Growth, Conversion Rate
Main Analysis	Bar chart (Sales by Region), Line Chart (Monthly Sales Trend)
Detailed Breakdown	Table (Top 10 Products), Pie Chart (Revenue Share by Category)

Using Visuals That Enhance, Not Overwhelm

The goal of a dashboard is **clarity**—visuals should enhance understanding, not create confusion.

Choosing the Right Chart for Each Metric

- **Line Charts** – Best for tracking trends over time (e.g., monthly revenue).
- **Bar Charts** – Ideal for comparing categories (e.g., sales by region).
- **Pie Charts** – Useful for showing proportions (e.g., revenue distribution by product type).
- **KPI Cards** – Large, bold number displays for key figures (e.g., total revenue).

Making the Dashboard Interactive

A static dashboard provides insights, but an **interactive dashboard empowers users** to explore the data in real-time.

Adding Interactive Features

- **Slicers** – Allow users to filter data by category, date, or region.
- **Drop-Down Menus** – Let users switch between different time frames (e.g., monthly vs. yearly sales).
- **Dynamic Charts** – Use formulas and Pivot Tables to update visualizations based on selections.

By applying these principles, you can design **engaging, data-driven dashboards** that help users make faster, better decisions based on clear, actionable insights.

Adding Interactive Filters and Dynamic Visualizations

A well-designed dashboard **doesn't just display data—it allows users to explore it**. By incorporating **interactive filters and dynamic visualizations**, you give users the power to customize their view, focus on key insights, and analyze data in real time. Instead of static charts that only tell one story, interactive dashboards let users **ask their own questions and get instant answers**.

Excel provides several powerful tools for making dashboards **more flexible and user-friendly**, including **Slicers, Timelines, and dynamic charts**. Let's explore how to integrate these elements effectively.

Using Slicers for Instant Filtering

Slicers are one of the easiest ways to add **interactive filters** to your dashboard. Unlike standard drop-down filters, Slicers provide **visual buttons** that users can click to filter data instantly.

How to Add a Slicer to Your Dashboard

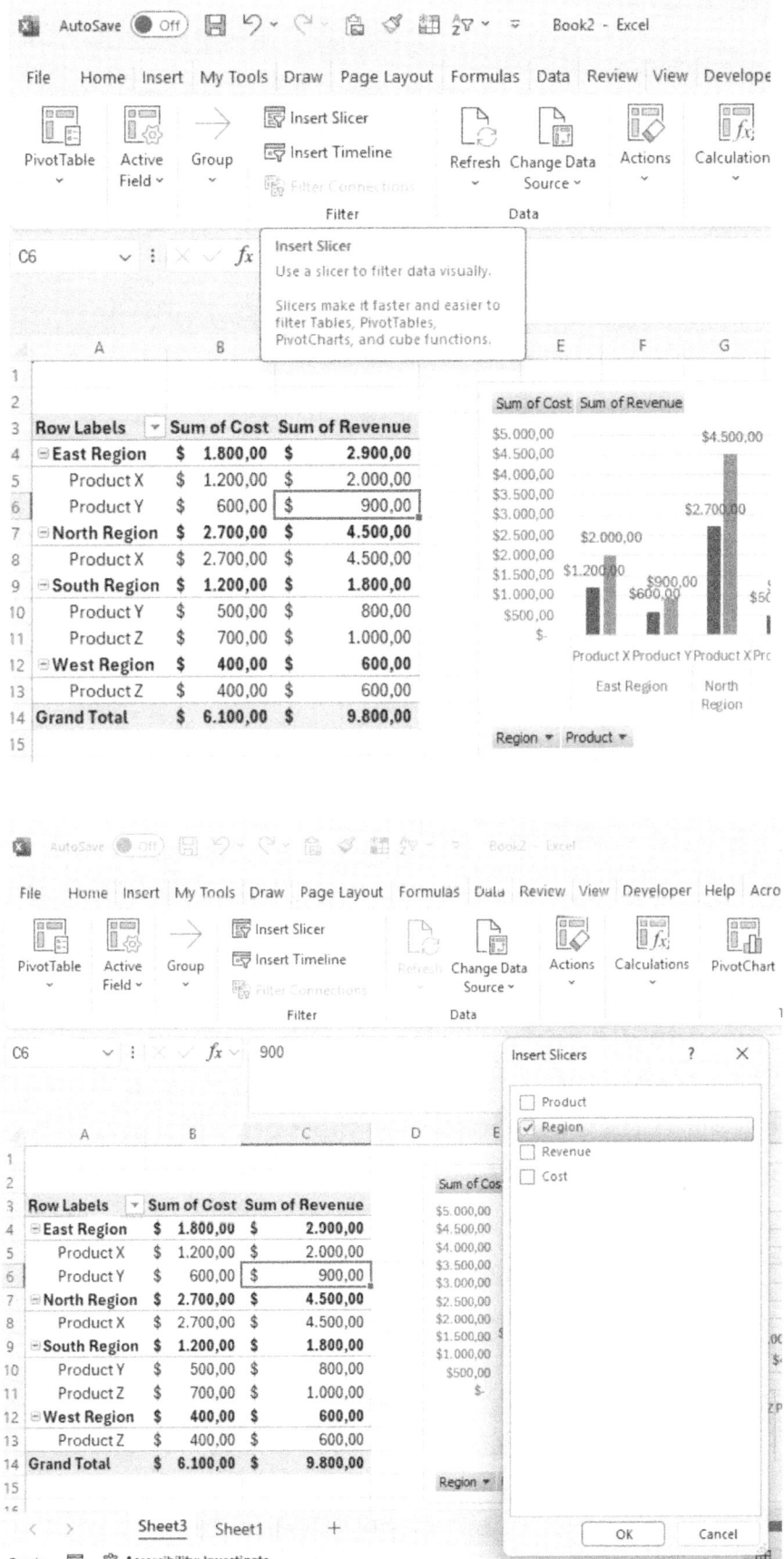

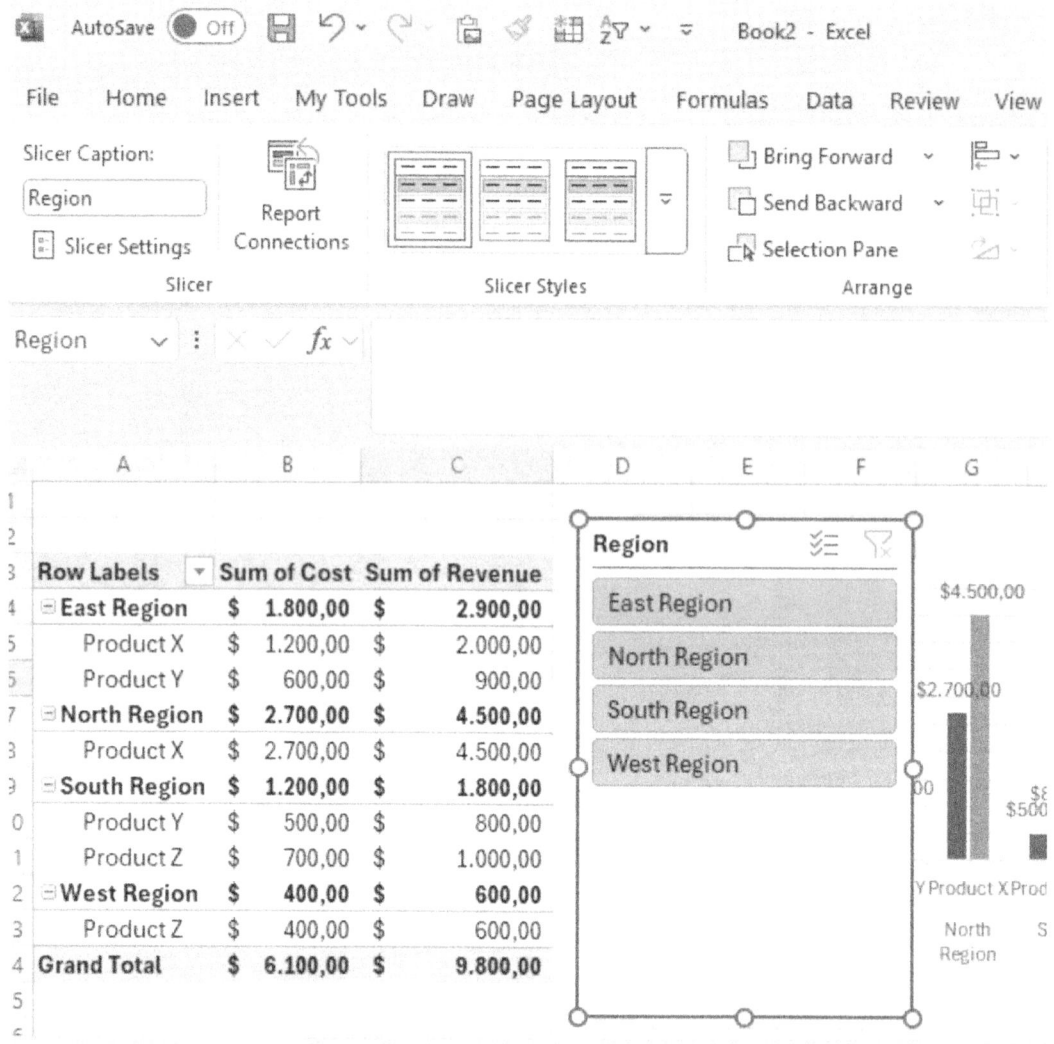

1. Click anywhere inside your **Pivot Table**.
2. Go to **PivotTable Analyze › Insert Slicer**.
3. Choose the field you want to filter (e.g., "Region" or "Product Category").
4. Click **OK**—Excel will insert a **button-based filter panel** on your worksheet.
5. Resize and position the Slicer within your dashboard for easy access.

Now, when a user clicks a button on the Slicer (e.g., "West Region"), all connected charts and tables **update instantly** to show only that subset of data.

Best Practices for Slicers

- **Use Slicers for categorical data** (e.g., regions, sales reps, product types).
- **Format them for readability**—adjust column width, font size, and color coding to enhance visibility.
- **Connect multiple Pivot Tables**—go to **Report Connections** to link the Slicer to multiple elements at once.

Adding Timelines for Date-Based Analysis

For **time-based data**, Timelines are even better than Slicers. A Timeline lets users filter data dynamically by **days, months, quarters, or years** with a simple scroll bar.

How to Add a Timeline

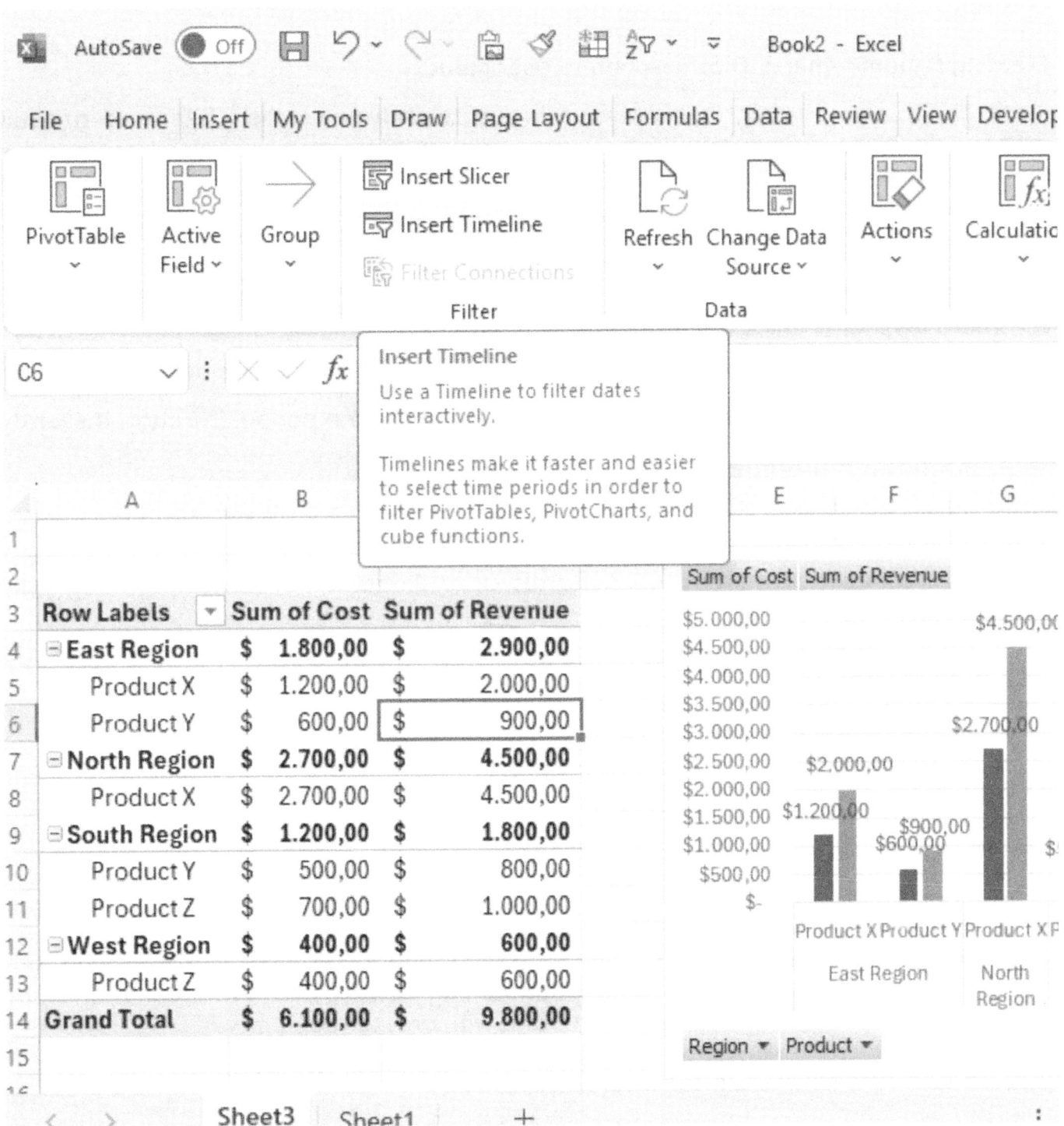

1. Click inside your **Pivot Table**.

2. Go to **PivotTable Analyze > Insert Timeline**.
3. Select a **date field** (e.g., "Order Date").
4. Click **OK**, then position the Timeline in your dashboard.

Users can now **drag the Timeline slider** to select a specific time range, instantly updating the data displayed in charts and tables.

Creating Dynamic Charts That Respond to User Input

Static charts provide insights, but **dynamic charts change as users filter and interact with the dashboard**. By linking Pivot Charts to Slicers and Timelines, you can create **real-time visualizations** that adapt to user selections.

Steps to Make a Pivot Chart Interactive

1. **Create a Pivot Chart** from an existing Pivot Table (**Insert > Pivot Chart**).
2. **Insert a Slicer or Timeline** to allow users to filter the dataset.
3. **Connect the Pivot Chart to the Slicer** via the **Report Connections** option.

Now, when a user selects a different product, region, or time period, the chart **instantly updates** to reflect only the filtered data.

Enhancing Visual Impact with Conditional Formatting

To make your dashboard even **more dynamic**, apply **Conditional Formatting** to highlight trends and outliers.

- Use **color scales** to show **performance variations** (e.g., red for low sales, green for high sales).
- Apply **data bars** to compare values within a table visually.
- Use **icon sets** (e.g., arrows or warning signs) to indicate **growth or decline**.

Why Interactive Dashboards Matter

An interactive dashboard isn't just a reporting tool—it's an **exploration tool**. By incorporating **filters, slicers, timelines, and dynamic charts**, you create an environment where users can **drill down into the data, test scenarios, and extract insights instantly**. This makes your dashboards **not only visually compelling but also highly functional**, ensuring that data-driven decisions happen faster and with greater accuracy.

PART 5
ADVANCED STRATEGIES – BECOMING A TRUE EXCEL EXPERT

CHAPTER 12

BUSINESS ANALYSIS AND FORECASTING: PREDICT THE FUTURE WITH EXCEL

Deliver credible forecasts and projections that help management make confident strategic decisions

Trend Analysis and Market Forecasting Tools

Understanding **past trends** is the key to predicting **future outcomes**, and Excel provides powerful tools for **trend analysis and market forecasting**. Whether you're a financial analyst predicting revenue growth, a business owner estimating future sales, or a project manager planning for resource allocation, **Excel's built-in forecasting functions** can help you make **data-driven decisions** with confidence.

Let's explore how to leverage Excel's trend analysis and forecasting tools to gain **valuable insights into future performance**.

Identifying Trends with Moving Averages

A **moving average** is one of the simplest ways to **identify trends** in your data. It smooths out fluctuations, helping you **spot patterns** that might otherwise be hidden in raw numbers.

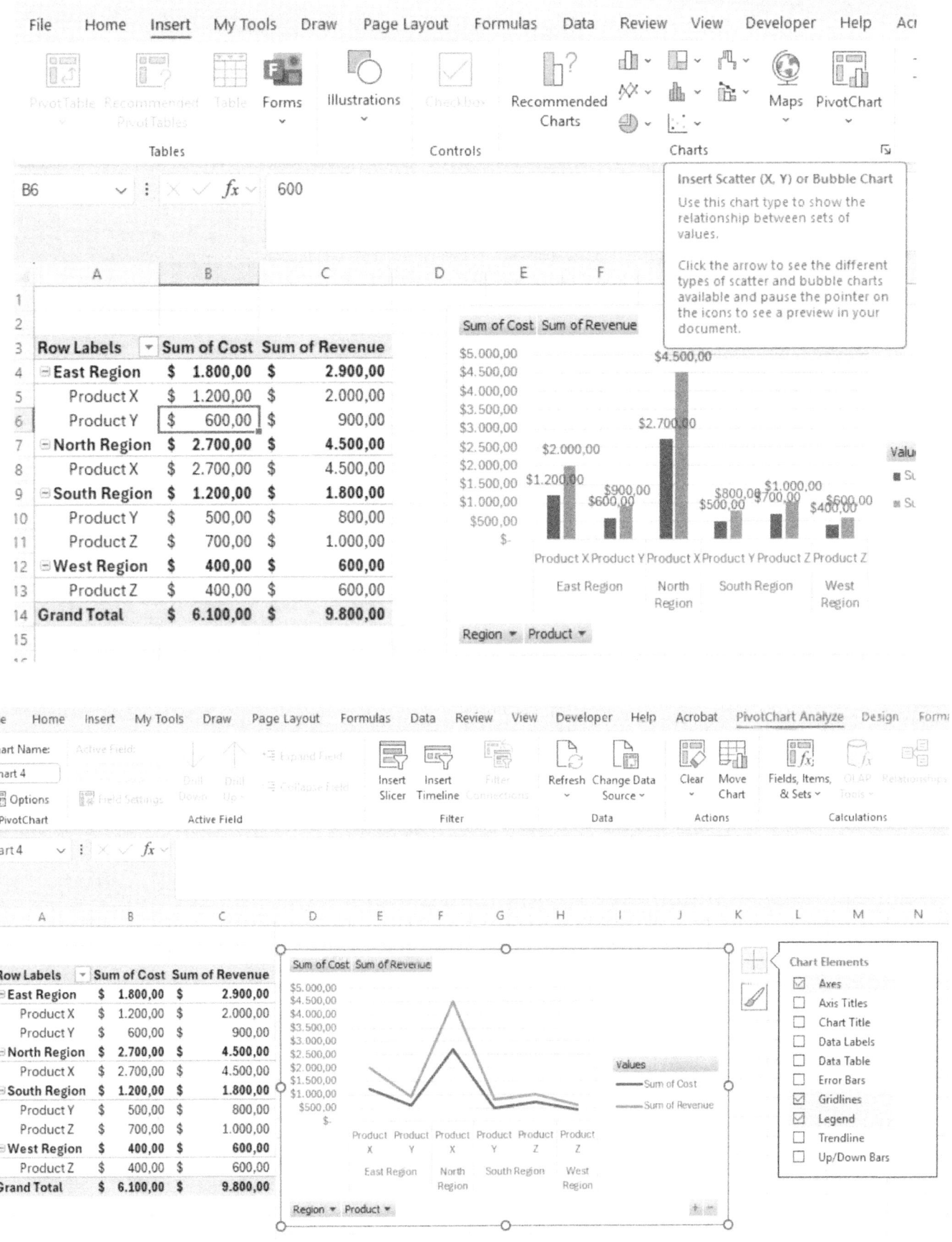

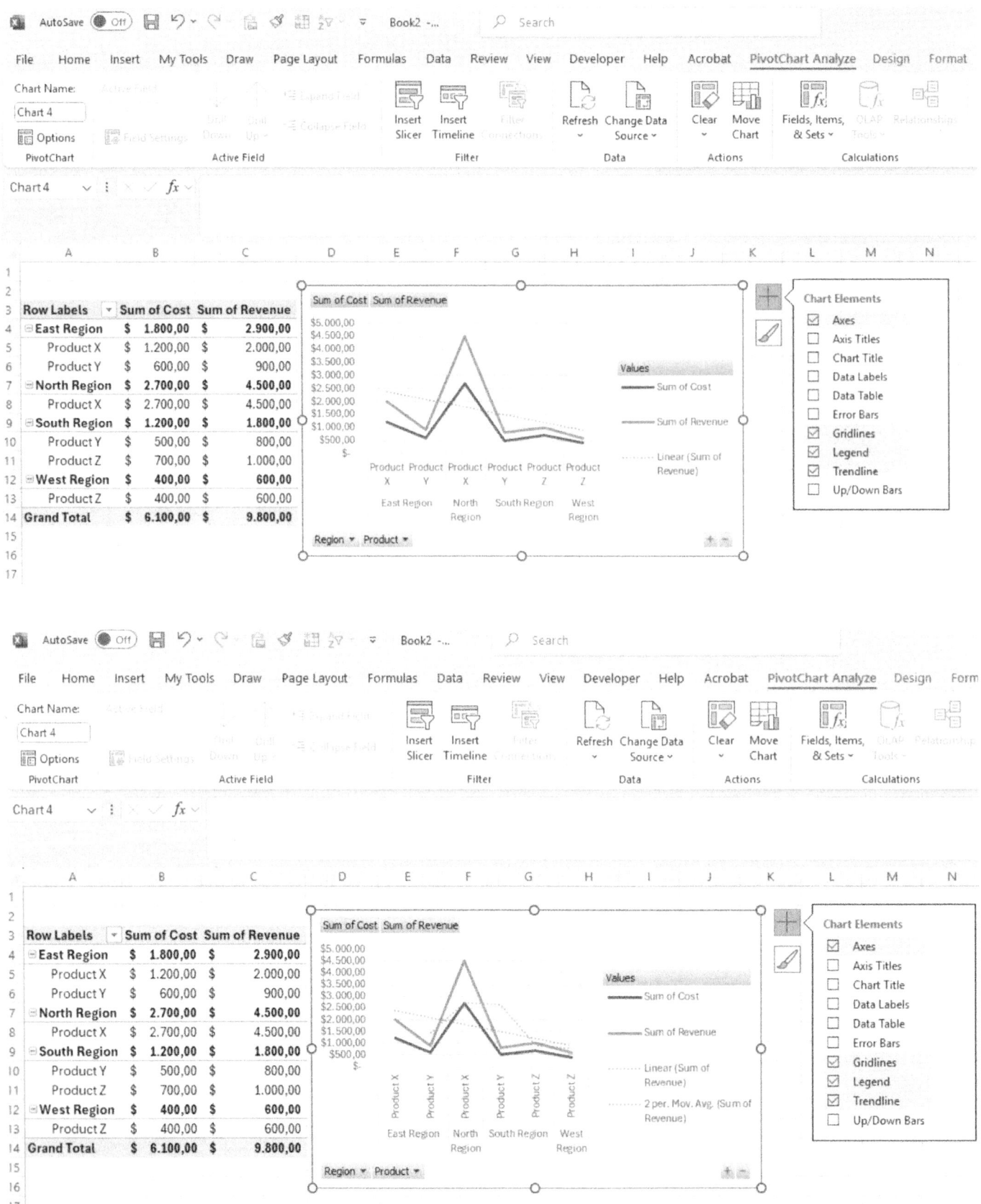

1. Select your **dataset** (e.g., monthly sales data).
2. Go to **Insert › Chart › Line Chart** to visualize the trend.
3. Click on the **chart line**, then select **Chart Elements › Trendline › Moving Average**.
4. In the **Format Trendline** panel, set the **period** (e.g., a 3-month moving average for quarterly trends).

Example: Spotting Revenue Trends

Suppose your company's monthly sales fluctuate due to **seasonality**. A **6-month moving average** helps reveal whether your revenue is **truly growing over time** or just experiencing **short-term spikes**.

Forecasting Future Trends with Excel's FORECAST Function

Excel's **FORECAST.LINEAR** function uses **regression analysis** to predict future values based on historical data. This is especially useful for **sales forecasting, demand planning, or financial projections**.

How to Use FORECAST.LINEAR

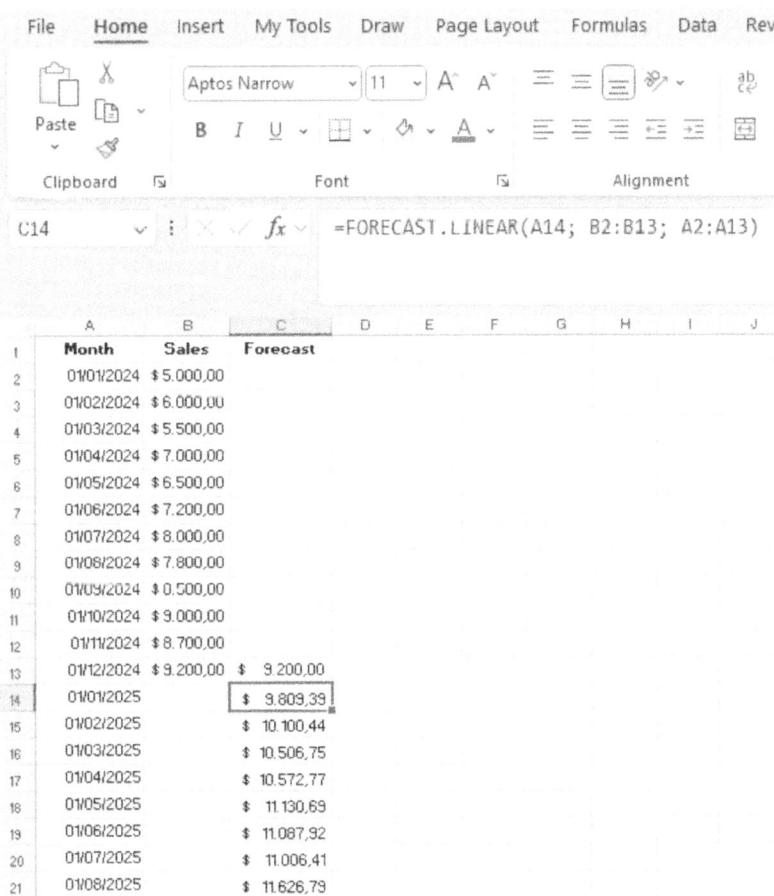

1. Identify your dataset with **historical values** (e.g., sales figures from the past 12 months).

2. Select an empty cell where you want the **forecasted value** to appear.
3. Use the formula:

=FORECAST.LINEAR(target_x, known_y's, known_x's)

target_x: The future period you want to predict (e.g., month 13).

- **known_y's:** The historical data (e.g., past sales figures).
- **known_x's:** The time period associated with the data.

Example: Forecasting Next Month's Sales

If you have monthly sales data from the past year, you can use **FORECAST.LINEAR** to estimate **next month's revenue**. This helps with **inventory planning, budgeting, and setting realistic goals**.

Using Excel's Built-in Forecasting Tool

For more advanced forecasting, Excel includes a **Forecast Sheet** feature that automates trend projections.

Steps to Create a Forecast Sheet

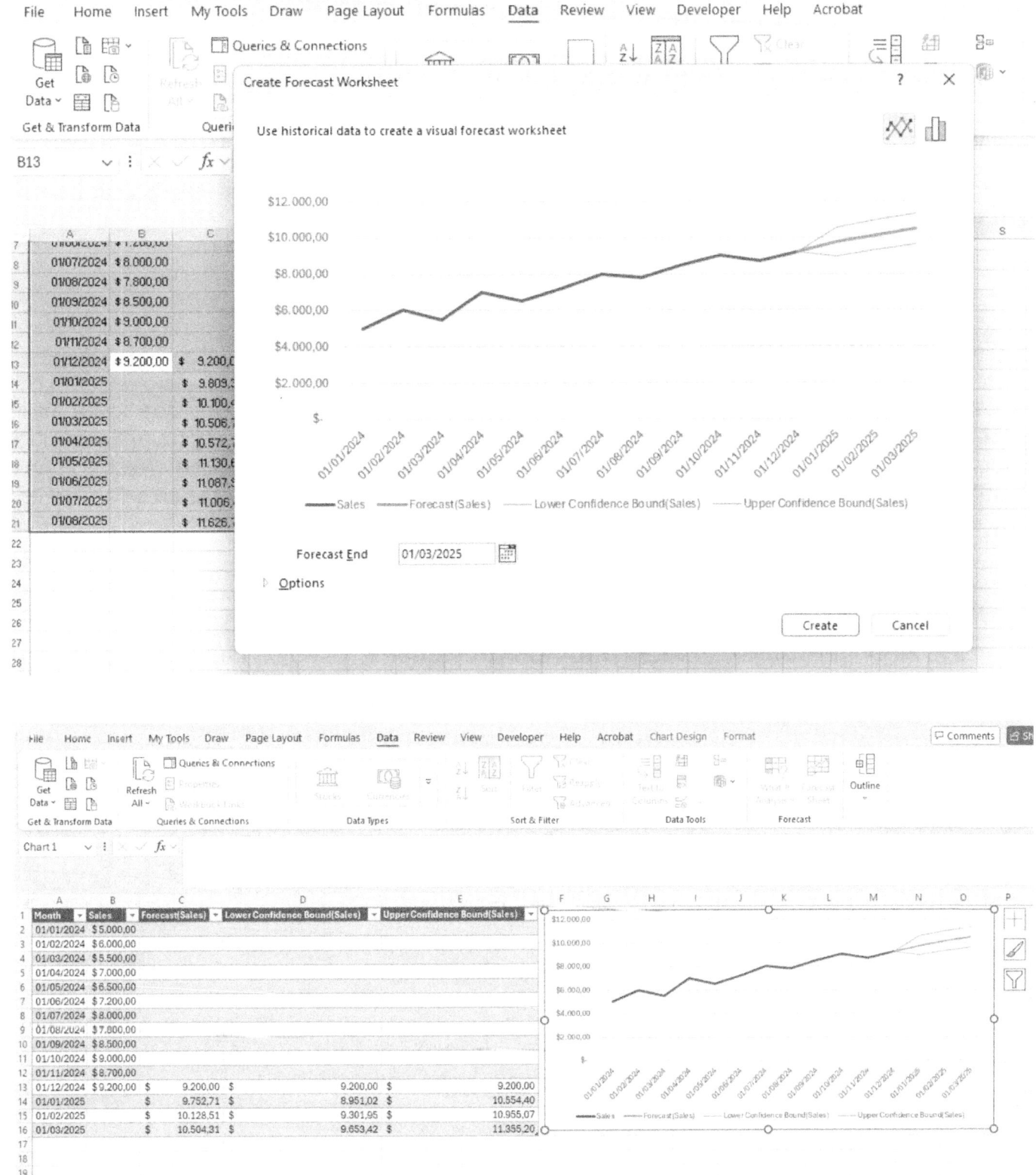

1. Select your dataset (date in one column, values in another).
2. Go to **Data > Forecast Sheet**.
3. Choose a **forecast end date** and adjust confidence intervals.
4. Click **Create**—Excel generates a forecasted trendline with **upper and lower confidence limits**.

This tool is especially useful for **business planning**, allowing you to **visually predict market trends** and **prepare for potential fluctuations**.

Scenario Planning and Sensitivity Analysis for Smarter Decisions

Uncertainty is a constant in business, and making decisions without considering multiple potential outcomes can be risky. **Scenario planning** and **sensitivity analysis** are essential tools that allow you to test different assumptions, anticipate risks, and make informed decisions. By using these Excel techniques, you can analyze **"what-if" scenarios**, adjust key inputs, and understand how various factors affect your results.

What is Scenario Planning?

Scenario planning involves **creating multiple projections** based on different possible future conditions. Instead of relying on a single forecast, you prepare for **best-case, worst-case, and most likely scenarios**, allowing you to be ready for unexpected challenges.

Example: Forecasting Revenue for Different Economic Conditions

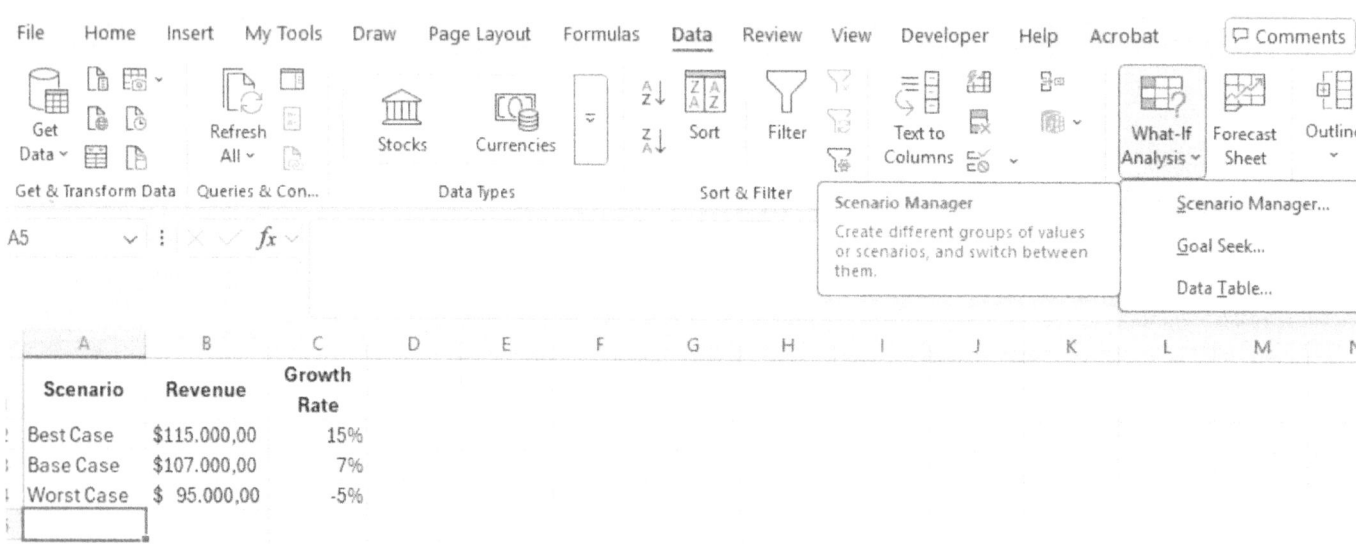

Scenario	Revenue	Growth Rate
Best Case	$115.000,00	15%
Base Case	$107.000,00	7%
Worst Case	$ 95.000,00	-5%

Imagine you're forecasting **next year's revenue** for your company. Instead of assuming a single growth rate, you can create three different scenarios:

- **Best Case:** The market grows faster than expected, leading to a 15% revenue increase.
- **Worst Case:** A recession causes a 5% decline in revenue.
- **Base Case:** The market remains stable, leading to a 7% revenue increase.

By modeling all three scenarios in Excel, you can **compare the financial impact of each** and adjust your strategy accordingly.

How to Create Scenario Planning in Excel

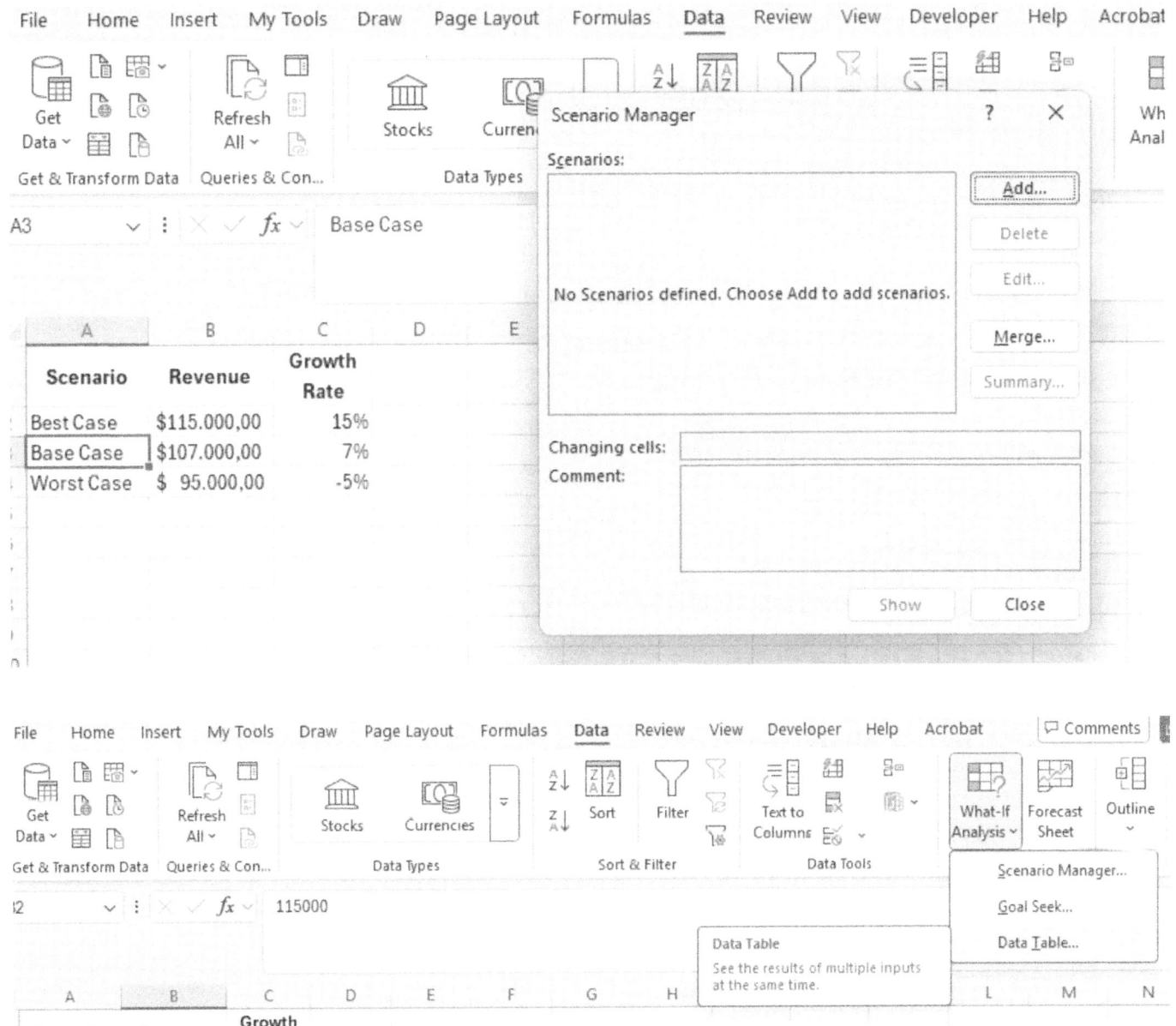

1. Go to **Data > What-If Analysis > Scenario Manager**.

2. Click **Add** to create a new scenario (e.g., "Best Case").
3. Define the **input variables** that will change (e.g., sales growth rate).
4. Repeat for **multiple scenarios** (Worst Case, Base Case).
5. Click **Show** to switch between scenarios and see the impact on your financial model.

Using Sensitivity Analysis to Test Key Variables

While scenario planning explores different possible futures, **sensitivity analysis** examines how a single **input variable affects your results**. This helps you determine which factors have the **biggest impact on your outcomes**.

Example: How Interest Rates Impact Profitability

Suppose you are analyzing the profitability of an investment. You might want to see how **changing interest rates** affect your projected profit. By using **sensitivity analysis**, you can test different rates (e.g., 3%, 5%, 7%) and see how each impacts your **bottom line**.

How to Perform Sensitivity Analysis with Data Tables

1. Set up your financial model with an **input cell** (e.g., interest rate).
2. Go to **Data > What-If Analysis > Data Table**.
3. Choose **one-variable or two-variable analysis** based on how many factors you want to test.
4. Excel will generate a **dynamic table** showing the results for different input values.

Why These Tools Matter

By integrating **scenario planning and sensitivity analysis**, you can:

- **Prepare for uncertainty** and make informed business decisions.
- **Identify critical risk factors** that impact profitability.
- **Develop strategic plans** based on multiple possible outcomes.

These Excel techniques are **indispensable** for business professionals who need to make **data-driven decisions in an unpredictable world**.

CHAPTER 13

REPORTING AND DATA STORYTELLING: MAKE AN IMPACT WITH YOUR INSIGHTS

Transform raw data into compelling narratives that resonate with decision-makers and showcase your strategic thinking

How to Build Executive-Ready Reports

In a fast-paced business environment, executives don't have time to sift through complex spreadsheets or dense data tables. They need **clear, concise, and actionable insights**—reports that provide the right information, in the right format, at the right time. An **executive-ready report** isn't just a collection of numbers; it's a **strategic tool for decision-making**.

So, how do you transform raw data into a polished, professional report that **captures attention and drives action**? It starts with **clarity, relevance, and impact**.

1. Understand the Audience and Purpose

Tailoring Executive Reports: Audience, Purpose & Format

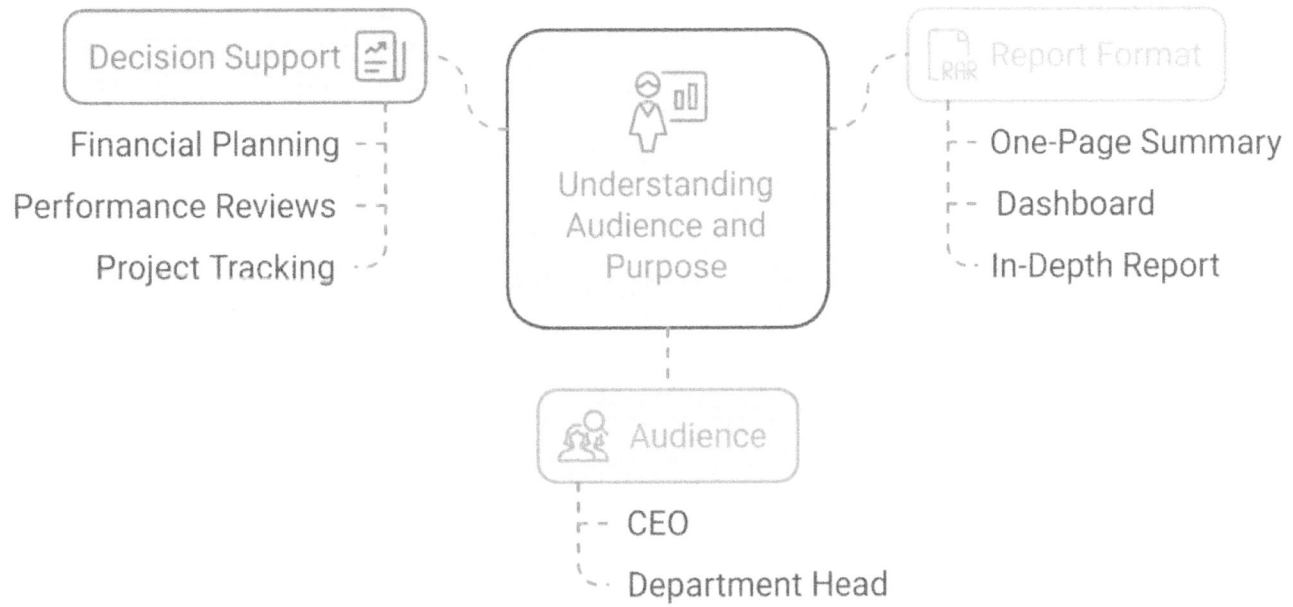

Before creating a report, ask yourself:

- **Who will read this?** A CEO may need **high-level insights**, while a department head may require **operational details**.
- **What decisions will this report support?** Financial planning, performance reviews, or project tracking?
- **What's the ideal format?** A one-page summary, dashboard, or in-depth report?

Example: A Sales Performance Report

A CEO might only need a **monthly revenue summary**, whereas a sales manager may require **regional breakdowns, product performance data, and sales rep achievements**.

2.   Structure the Report for Maximum Clarity

A well-structured report **guides the reader's attention** to the most important insights first.

The Ideal Executive Report Flow:

- **Headline Summary** – A short section highlighting the key takeaway (e.g., "Revenue Increased by 12% This Quarter").
- **Key Metrics & KPIs** – The most important figures, displayed clearly (e.g., revenue, profit margins, customer growth).
- **Visual Representations** – Charts and tables to make data **digestible at a glance**.
- **Brief Analysis & Insights** – A few bullet points explaining **what the numbers mean and why they matter**.
- **Recommended Actions** – Clear, actionable next steps based on the data.

3.   Use Visuals to Tell the Story

Executives process visual data **60,000 times faster than text**, making **charts, graphs, and dashboards** essential for effective reports.

Choosing the Right Visualization:

- **Bar Charts** – Compare performance across departments, products, or regions.
- **Line Charts** – Show trends over time (e.g., revenue growth, customer acquisition).
- **Pie Charts** – Illustrate proportions (e.g., sales by product category).
- **Heat Maps** – Highlight areas of concern (e.g., sales performance by region).

Best Practices for Data Visualization:

- **Keep it simple.** Avoid cluttered charts—focus on the **key takeaway**.
- **Use consistent colors.** Stick to **one color scheme** to maintain professionalism.
- **Label everything.** Ensure axes, legends, and data points are **clearly labeled**.

4. Make the Report Dynamic and Interactive

Static reports are useful, but **interactive reports empower executives to explore data on demand**.

How to Add Interactivity in Excel:

- **Use Pivot Tables & Slicers** – Allow executives to filter data by region, time period, or department.
- **Incorporate Drop-Down Menus** – Let users toggle between different data views.
- **Create a Summary Dashboard** – Combine key metrics, charts, and insights in one interactive sheet.

5. Keep It Concise and Actionable

Executives don't need **every detail**—they need the **right details**. A well-crafted report should:

- **Fit on one page whenever possible.**
- **Use bullet points** instead of long paragraphs.
- **Highlight critical insights upfront** (avoid burying key findings in data tables).

By structuring reports strategically, using clear visuals, and **keeping insights concise yet powerful**, you ensure that your reports **don't just inform—they drive decisions**.

Data Storytelling: Transforming Numbers into a Compelling Narrative

Raw data alone doesn't inspire action—**stories do. Data storytelling** is the art of translating numbers into **clear, compelling narratives** that inform, persuade, and drive decisions. Whether you're presenting financial performance, customer trends, or market forecasts, the key is to **go beyond the spreadsheet** and tell a story that resonates with your audience.

An effective **data-driven story** doesn't just show facts; it **explains the why behind the numbers** and connects them to real-world impact.

Great data storytelling follows a structure that makes insights easy to understand. Every compelling report or presentation consists of three essential parts:

1. The Setup: Establishing Context

Before diving into charts and figures, **set the stage** for your audience. Ask yourself:

- **What's the problem or opportunity?** (e.g., "Our customer churn rate has increased by 15% over the last quarter.")
- **Who is impacted?** (e.g., "Our sales team is struggling to retain repeat customers.")
- **Why does this matter?** (e.g., "If we don't address this, our revenue will decline by 10% this year.")

A well-defined **setup** ensures your audience understands **why they should care** before seeing the data.

2. The Data: Presenting the Evidence

Once you've established the problem or opportunity, support it with **clear, visualized data**. This is where Excel's **charts, Pivot Tables, and dashboards** come into play.

To make data **more digestible**:

- **Use comparative visuals** (e.g., a bar chart showing churn rate over time).
- **Highlight key numbers** (e.g., bold or color-code the most important figures).

- **Keep it simple** (avoid overloading charts with unnecessary details).

3. The Conclusion: Driving Action

Numbers without **actionable insights** are meaningless. The final piece of data storytelling is answering:

- **What do we do next?** (e.g., "We need to improve customer engagement strategies.")
- **What are the potential solutions?** (e.g., "Increasing personalized follow-ups could improve retention by 20%.")
- **What's the expected outcome?** (e.g., "This could add $1.5M in revenue over the next year.")

This step is **critical**—data should lead to a **decision or strategy**, not just sit in a report.

Best Practices for Creating a Narrative with Data

- **Avoid "data dumping"** – Don't overload your audience with numbers; focus on key insights.
- **Use real-world analogies** – Relating data to familiar concepts makes it easier to grasp (e.g., "Losing 15% of customers is like losing one out of every seven buyers at checkout.").
- **Incorporate storytelling visuals** – Use **annotated charts** to guide the audience's focus to the most relevant points.
- **Tailor the narrative to your audience** – Executives want **high-level summaries**, while analysts may need **granular details**.

By combining **strategic storytelling with clear data visualization**, you ensure that your reports don't just **inform**—they **persuade and inspire action**.

KPI TRACKING AND PERFORMANCE METRICS: MEASURING SUCCESS WITH EXCEL

Create automated performance tracking systems that demonstrate your focus on business outcomes and results

Defining and Implementing Key Performance Indicators (KPIs)

Key Performance Indicators (**KPIs**) are the **critical metrics** that measure success. Whether you're tracking **business growth, employee productivity, or customer satisfaction**, KPIs serve as a **compass**, guiding organizations toward their strategic objectives. However, not all metrics are KPIs—**effective KPIs must be relevant, actionable, and aligned with business goals**.

Let's break down how to define and implement KPIs effectively using Excel.

1. What Makes a Good KPI?

A KPI isn't just a number—it's a **measurement tied to strategic success**. The best KPIs follow the **SMART criteria**:

- **Specific** – Clearly defined and focused (e.g., "Increase customer retention by 10%").
- **Measurable** – Quantifiable with available data (e.g., tracking churn rate monthly).
- **Achievable** – Realistic based on business conditions.
- **Relevant** – Directly linked to business goals.
- **Time-Bound** – Has a defined timeframe (e.g., "Reduce customer response time to under 24 hours within the next six months").

Example: KPIs in Different Business Areas

- **Sales:** Monthly revenue growth, lead conversion rate.
- **Customer Service:** Net promoter score (NPS), average response time.
- **Operations:** Order fulfillment accuracy, production downtime percentage.

2. Structuring KPIs in Excel

Once you've defined your KPIs, **Excel becomes the perfect tool for tracking them**. The key is structuring data so that it's **easy to analyze and visualize**.

- **List the KPIs** in the first column (e.g., "Customer Acquisition Cost").
- **Define the target value** in the second column (e.g., "$200 per customer").
- **Input actual performance data** in the third column (e.g., "$215 per customer").
- **Calculate variance** in the fourth column (e.g., `=C2-B2` to show over/underperformance).
- **Use Conditional Formatting** to highlight trends (e.g., red if under target, green if exceeding expectations).

KPI NAME	TARGET VALUE	ACTUAL VALUE	VARIANCE
Customer Retention Rate	85%	80%	-5%
Monthly Sales Growth	10%	12%	+2%
Response Time (Hours)	24	20	-4

3. Visualizing KPIs for Quick Insights

Raw numbers can be overwhelming. To **make data actionable**, use:

- **Gauge Charts** – Show performance against a target (ideal for financial metrics).
- **Progress Bars** – Indicate percentage completion of a KPI (e.g., sales quota progress).
- **Conditional Formatting** – Automatically highlight high or low performance.

4. Automating KPI Updates with Dynamic Formulas

Excel allows **automatic KPI tracking** using formulas like:

- **SUMIF / COUNTIF** – Calculate metrics based on conditions (e.g., only count completed sales).
- **AVERAGEIFS** – Find the average KPI score for a specific time period.
- **VLOOKUP / XLOOKUP** – Pull in KPI values dynamically from different sheets.

By defining meaningful KPIs and implementing **structured tracking and visualization techniques in Excel**, businesses can ensure they stay on track and make **data-driven decisions with confidence**.

Creating a System for Continuous Performance Monitoring

Tracking KPIs is not a one-time task—it requires a **systematic approach** to ensure continuous **performance monitoring, real-time insights, and proactive decision-making**. A well-designed **Excel-based performance monitoring system** can help businesses stay agile, identify trends, and make informed decisions before problems escalate.

1.   Designing a KPI Dashboard for Real-Time Tracking

An effective **KPI dashboard** acts as a **control center** for monitoring performance metrics. Instead of digging through spreadsheets, decision-makers should be able to glance at a **single dashboard** and instantly understand where the business stands.

Key Elements of a KPI Dashboard:

- **Live Metrics:** Automatically updated figures (e.g., monthly revenue, customer retention rate).
- **Visual Indicators:** Conditional formatting, color-coded cells, and icons to flag performance (e.g., green for on-target, red for underperformance).
- **Historical Trends:** Line charts showing KPI movement over time.
- **Filters & Slicers:** Allow users to drill down by region, time period, or department.

How to Set It Up in Excel:

- **Pivot Tables** to summarize large datasets dynamically.
- **Integrate Named Ranges** so formulas automatically update as data is added.
- **Apply Conditional Formatting** to highlight KPIs that exceed or miss targets.
- **Incorporate Charts & Graphs** to visualize performance trends.
- **Use Drop-Down Menus & Slicers** for interactive filtering.

2.   Automating KPI Updates with Excel Functions

Manual data entry is inefficient and prone to errors. To **keep KPI tracking effortless**, automation is key.

Essential Excel Functions for Automation:

- **SUMIFS & AVERAGEIFS** – Automatically calculate total or average performance based on set criteria.
- **VLOOKUP & XLOOKUP** – Fetch KPI data dynamically from a master table.
- **INDEX-MATCH** – Retrieve specific performance data for different time periods.
- **IF & IFERROR** – Create logical conditions to flag underperformance.

Example: Automating Monthly Sales Tracking

Instead of manually updating a report, use:

=SUMIFS(SalesData[Amount]; SalesData[Date]; ">="&StartDate; SalesData[Date]; "<="&EndDate)

This formula **automatically sums sales data within a defined period**, ensuring real-time tracking.

3. Setting Up Alerts for KPI Deviations

Performance monitoring isn't just about tracking numbers—it's about **catching issues before they become problems**.

How to Create Automatic Alerts in Excel:

- **Conditional Formatting:** Highlight KPIs in **red** when below target, **green** when on track.
- **Data Validation Rules:** Prevent incorrect or incomplete entries.
- **Excel Macros & VBA Scripts:** Send alerts when metrics fall outside acceptable thresholds.

Example: Flagging Underperforming Regions

Use a **conditional formula** to highlight areas needing attention:

=IF(A2<B2, "> Action Needed", "> On Track")

This way, executives can **instantly see where intervention is required**.

4. Ensuring Long-Term KPI Consistency

A performance monitoring system must be **scalable** and **repeatable**. Best practices include:

- **Standardized Data Entry:** Use **consistent formats** for dates, numbers, and text.
- **Automated Report Generation:** Set up **monthly/quarterly reporting templates**.
- **Regular Data Audits:** Periodically review KPI calculations for accuracy.

By building a **structured, automated, and visual performance tracking system**, businesses can **stay proactive** and make **data-driven decisions with confidence**.

CHAPTER 15

CONCLUSION: YOUR PATH
TO EXCEL MASTERY

Develop a personalized roadmap to showcase your new Excel
skills and position yourself for promotion within 60 days

Your Next Steps for Continued Growth

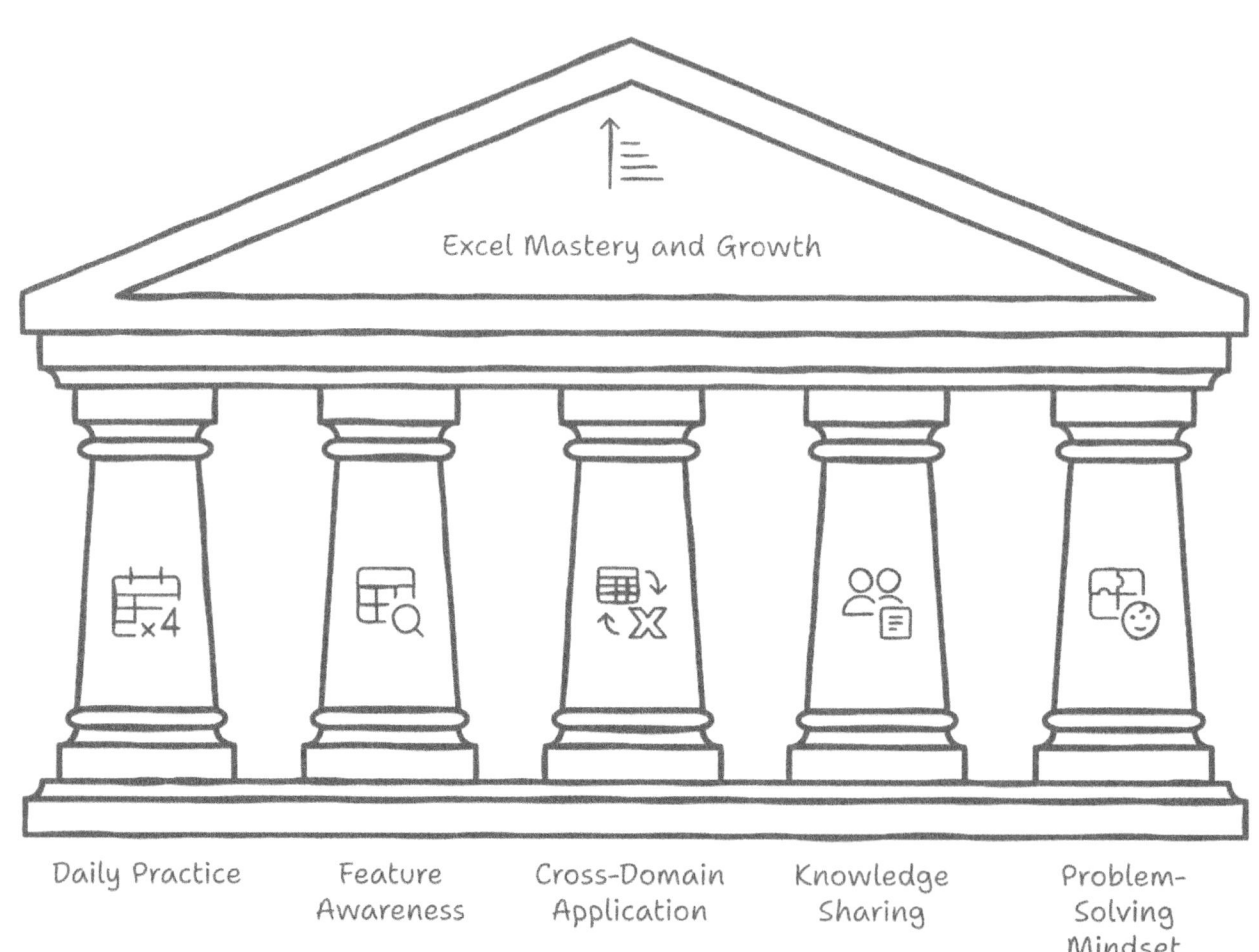

Excel Mastery and Growth

Daily Practice | Feature Awareness | Cross-Domain Application | Knowledge Sharing | Problem-Solving Mindset

Mastering Excel isn't just about learning formulas and shortcuts—it's about **building a long-term strategy for continuous improvement**. You've come a long way, but staying ahead in today's fast-moving workplace means **adopting a mindset of lifelong learning**. Now that you have a strong foundation, here's how to keep growing your Excel expertise and making yourself indispensable in your career.

1. Make Excel a Daily Habit

Skills fade if they're not used regularly. The best way to **solidify what you've learned** is through **consistent, hands-on practice**. Try these strategies to make Excel a **part of your daily workflow**:

- **Apply what you've learned immediately.** Find ways to **integrate formulas, pivot tables, or automation** into your current projects.
- **Set up a personal challenge.** Create a **mock business report** or **automate a repetitive task** using macros.
- **Reverse-engineer complex spreadsheets.** Study and deconstruct **existing Excel files** in your company to understand how advanced users structure data.

2. Stay Updated with New Excel Features

Excel is constantly evolving, with Microsoft introducing **new functions, AI-powered tools, and automation capabilities**. Staying current ensures you're **using the most efficient techniques available**.

- **Subscribe to official Excel blogs & updates.** Microsoft regularly releases updates that improve functionality.
- **Join Excel-focused communities.** Engage in online forums like **MrExcel, Reddit's r/excel, or LinkedIn Excel groups** to learn from experienced professionals.
- **Experiment with Power Query & Power BI.** These advanced tools take **data analysis and visualization to the next level**, and many companies expect professionals to know them.

3. Expand Your Excel Knowledge into Other Domains

Excel doesn't exist in a vacuum—it's **a tool that interacts with other platforms and programming languages**. If you want to boost your value in the job market, consider expanding your expertise into:

- **Power BI:** Learn to build **interactive dashboards** that provide deeper insights.
- **SQL:** A foundational database language that complements Excel's **data processing capabilities**.
- **Python for Data Analysis:** Many analysts and financial professionals use **Python and Pandas** alongside Excel.

4. Build an Excel Portfolio & Share Your Knowledge

One of the best ways to **reinforce what you've learned** is to teach it. Whether through blogging, video tutorials, or internal workshops at your company, **sharing your expertise** will make you a more confident Excel user and set you apart in the job market.

- **Create an Excel portfolio.** If you're looking to advance your career, build a collection of **sample reports, dashboards, and automation scripts** to showcase your skills.
- **Mentor colleagues.** Helping others solve Excel challenges will strengthen your **problem-solving abilities**.

- **Consider certification.** Earning a **Microsoft Excel Expert Certification** can add credibility to your resume and open doors to **higher-level roles**.

5. Adopt a Problem-Solving Mindset

Rather than memorizing formulas, **focus on Excel as a problem-solving tool**. When faced with a new challenge, ask:

- What's the **most efficient** way to solve this problem?
- Can I automate this process?
- How can I **visualize the data** to make the insight clearer?

By constantly **pushing your Excel abilities**, you'll continue evolving as a **data-driven professional**—one who doesn't just use Excel but **leverages it for smarter decision-making**.

How to Keep Improving and Staying Ahead in Your Career

Mastering Excel is an ongoing journey, not a final destination. The most successful professionals don't just **learn Excel**—they **evolve with it**, constantly refining their skills and adapting to new trends. If you want to stay ahead in your career and make Excel a powerful asset, here's how to keep improving and ensuring you remain a **valuable, in-demand expert**.

1. Develop a Proactive Learning Strategy

The workplace is evolving fast, and Excel is no exception. Staying ahead means **committing to continuous learning** and actively seeking out new knowledge.

- **Stay updated on new Excel features:** Microsoft frequently releases updates, new functions, and AI-powered tools. Follow **Microsoft's official Excel blog**, YouTube tutorials, and community forums to stay informed.
- **Join professional communities:** Engaging with others is one of the best ways to **discover hidden tricks and shortcuts**. Consider joining **LinkedIn Excel groups, Reddit's r/excel, or local meetup groups** to connect with other professionals.
- **Subscribe to Excel newsletters and online courses:** Platforms like **Coursera, Udemy, and LinkedIn Learning** offer courses to help you specialize in advanced areas like **Power Query, Power BI, and VBA automation**.

2. Apply Advanced Excel Skills to Real-World Problems

You don't just want to know Excel—you want to **use it to solve real business challenges**. Many professionals **plateau** because they stop applying what they learn. To avoid this, make Excel a **problem-solving tool** in your daily work.

- **Take initiative in your workplace.** Offer to **automate reports**, build **interactive dashboards**, or improve existing spreadsheets with **better formulas and logic**.

- **Challenge yourself with real projects.** Try **analyzing sales trends, automating an HR database, or forecasting business performance** using advanced Excel techniques.
- **Learn from real case studies.** Study how other professionals use Excel for **financial modeling, operations management, and business intelligence**.

3. Expand Your Skillset Beyond Excel

Excel is a **powerful tool**, but it doesn't operate in isolation. To remain a top-tier professional, **develop complementary skills** that extend your data-handling capabilities.

- **Power BI & Data Visualization:** Learning Power BI lets you **transform Excel data into interactive reports**, making your insights even more impactful.
- **SQL for Database Management:** Many companies **store large datasets in databases**, and knowing SQL helps you extract and manipulate data efficiently.
- **Python for Data Analysis:** Python is increasingly used for **data science, automation, and complex analysis**—and integrates well with Excel.

4. Build a Reputation as an Excel Expert

The best way to **stay relevant** in your career is to **make yourself known** as an Excel expert. Whether within your company or in the professional world, **sharing your knowledge helps solidify your expertise**.

- **Teach and mentor others.** Helping coworkers with Excel not only improves your skills but also enhances your leadership reputation.
- **Create an online presence.** Consider writing blog posts, recording YouTube tutorials, or contributing to Excel forums.
- **Earn industry-recognized certifications.** Becoming a **Microsoft Certified Excel Expert** adds credibility to your skillset and opens doors to advanced career opportunities.

5. Cultivate a Problem-Solving Mindset

Excel is not just about **knowing formulas**—it's about **thinking critically**. The best professionals don't just input numbers; they **ask questions, find trends, and develop insights**.

- Approach Excel with **curiosity**—ask, "How can I do this faster or better?"
- Keep looking for **automation opportunities**—repetitive tasks should never stay manual.
- Think like an **analyst**—interpret data in ways that influence **business decisions**.

By staying curious, proactive, and adaptable, you'll ensure that your **Excel skills never stagnate—and your career keeps advancing**.

Pathways to Professional Excellence

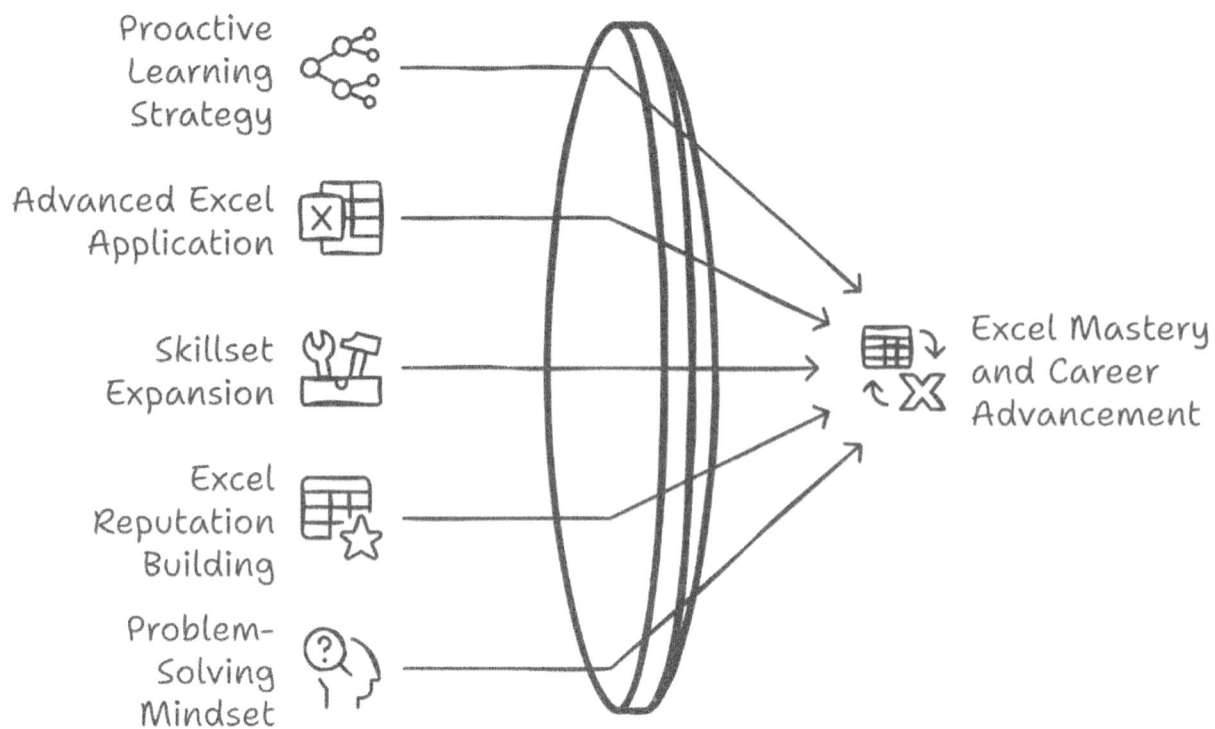

Proactive Learning Strategy

Advanced Excel Application

Skillset Expansion

Excel Reputation Building

Problem-Solving Mindset

Excel Mastery and Career Advancement

CHAPTER 16

QUICK REFERENCE TOOLKIT: YOUR EXCEL SURVIVAL KIT

Access a complete reference system that helps you solve any Excel challenge in under 5 minutes with total confidence

Formula Powerhouse

When it comes to Excel, **formulas are your ultimate superpower**. They transform raw data into meaningful insights, automate complex calculations, and eliminate repetitive manual work. Whether you're crunching numbers, analyzing trends, or cleaning up messy data, having a **solid command of essential formulas** will drastically improve your efficiency.

1. Essential Formulas You Must Know

Excel offers **hundreds of built-in formulas**, but mastering a **core set of powerful ones** will cover 90% of your needs. Let's break them down into categories:

- **Basic Arithmetic:**
- `SUM(range)`: Adds up numbers in a selected range.
- `AVERAGE(range)`: Finds the mean value of a range.
- `ROUND(value, num_digits)`: Rounds a number to the specified decimal places.
- **Logical & Conditional Formulas:**
- `IF(logical_test, value_if_true, value_if_false)`: Returns different results based on a condition.
- `AND(condition1, condition2)`: Checks if all conditions are TRUE.
- `OR(condition1, condition2)`: Returns TRUE if at least one condition is met.
- **Lookup & Reference Formulas:**
- `VLOOKUP(lookup_value, table_array, col_index, [range_lookup])`: Searches for a value in a column and returns a related value.
- `XLOOKUP(lookup_value, lookup_array, return_array, [if_not_found])`: The modern replacement for VLOOKUP, allowing flexible searches.
- `INDEX(array, row_num, [column_num])` + `MATCH(lookup_value, lookup_array, [match_type])`: A dynamic lookup combination for advanced users.
- **Text Manipulation:**
- `LEFT(text, num_chars)`: Extracts characters from the start of a string.

- `RIGHT(text, num_chars)`: Extracts characters from the end of a string.
- `LEN(text)`: Counts the number of characters in a text string.
- `CONCATENATE(text1, text2, …)` or `TEXTJOIN(delimiter, ignore_empty, text1, text2, …)`: Joins multiple pieces of text.

2. Automating Data Analysis with Powerful Functions

If you need **fast insights** from large datasets, these formulas **do the heavy lifting**:

- **Conditional Summing & Counting:**
- `SUMIF(range, criteria, [sum_range])`: Adds values that meet a condition.
- `COUNTIF(range, criteria)`: Counts how many times a condition is met.
- `SUMPRODUCT(array1, array2, …)`: Multiplies and sums values across arrays—a se**cret weapon f**or weighted calculations.
- **Date & Time Calculations:**
- `TODAY()`: Returns the current date.
- `NOW()`: Returns the current date and time.
- `DATEDIF(start_date, end_date, unit)`: Calculates the difference in years, months, or days.

3. Combining Formulas for Maximum Efficiency

Most professionals stick to **single-use formulas**, but true **Excel experts combine** multiple formulas for **unmatched efficiency**. Here's an example:

- **Finding the Most Recent Order Date per Customer:**

=MAXIFS(Order_Dates, Customer_Names, "John Doe")

This formula returns the **latest order date** for a specific customer—something that would otherwise take **manual filtering and sorting**.

- **Creating a Dynamic Report Title Based on Data:**

="Sales Report for "&TEXT(TODAY(),"mmmm yyyy")

This dynamically updates a report title **each month** without manual changes.

4. Pro Tips for Using Formulas Efficiently

- **Use Named Ranges:** Instead of writing `A1:A100`, assign a name (`SalesData`) to make formulas more readable.
- **Apply Array Formulas:** Modern Excel supports **dynamic arrays**, allowing formulas to spill results into multiple cells automatically.
- **Minimize Volatile Functions:** Formulas like `NOW()`, `TODAY()`, and `RAND()` **recalculate constantly**, which can slow down large workbooks.

By **mastering and combining** these formulas, you'll be able to **tackle any data challenge with confidence**—turning Excel into your **most powerful productivity tool**.

Speed-Boost Command Center

Excel isn't just about getting the right results—it's about getting them **fast**. The difference between a casual user and an Excel power user often comes down to **speed and efficiency**. Whether you're navigating spreadsheets, formatting data, or automating repetitive tasks, a few **key commands and shortcuts** can **shave hours off your workflow**.

1. The Must-Know Keyboard Shortcuts for Instant Speed

Using the mouse is **slow**. Every time you reach for it, you're wasting precious seconds. The best Excel users rely on **keyboard shortcuts** to fly through their tasks. Here are some that will **instantly boost your speed**:

- **Navigation & Selection:**
- `Ctrl + Arrow Keys` – Jump to the ed**ges o**f data ranges.
- `Shift + Space` – Select an en**tire row.**
- `Ctrl + Space` – Select an en**tire column.**
- `Ctrl + A` – Select al**l data i**n a worksheet.
- **Data Entry & Editing:**
- `F2` – Edit the active cell without using the mouse.
- `Ctrl + Enter` – Fill se**lected cells w**ith the same entry.
- `Alt + Enter` – Insert a li**ne break i**nside a cell.
- **Formatting & Clean-Up:**
- `Ctrl + 1` – Open the Fo**rmat Cells m**enu instantly.
- `Alt + H + O + I` – Auto-adjust column width to fit content.
- `Ctrl + Shift + L` – Toggle fi**lters o**n and off.
- **Formula & Calculation Shortcuts:**
- `Ctrl + Shift + +` – Insert a new row or column.
- `Ctrl + Shift + -` – Delete a selected row or column.
- `F9` – Recalculate all formulas in the workbook.

Mastering these shortcuts alone can **double your Excel speed**—but why stop there?

2. Quick Access Toolbar: Your Personal Control Panel

The **Quick Access Toolbar (QAT)** is a **hidden gem** that lets you keep your most-used commands **one click away**—no more digging through menus.

How to customize the QAT:

- Click the **down arrow** in the upper-left corner of Excel.
- Select **More Commands**.
- Choose from a list of **popular or advanced functions** (or add macros).
- Reorder them based on your workflow priorities.

Some **game-changing commands** to add to your QAT:

- **Format as Table** – Instantly convert messy data into a structured table.
- **AutoSum** – One-click access to quick totals.
- **Remove Duplicates** – Clean up data with **zero effort**.
- **Paste Values** – Strip away formulas while keeping the results.
- **Freeze Panes** – Lock headers in place for easier scrolling.

3. Ribbon Customization: Cut Through the Clutter

Excel's Ribbon is packed with features—but let's be honest, you **probably only use a handful of them**. Instead of clicking through multiple tabs, **why not build your own Ribbon section** with **only the commands you use daily?**

Steps to create a custom Ribbon tab:

- Right-click anywhere on the Ribbon and select **Customize the Ribbon**.
- Click **New Tab**, then rename it (e.g., "My Tools").
- Add commands that match your workflow (like Pivot Tables, Macros, or Charts).
- Save and enjoy **one-click access** to your most-used tools.

4. Automate Repetitive Actions with Macros

If you find yourself **repeating the same steps over and over**, **Macros** are your best friend. Even if you don't know VBA coding, you can **record a Macro** in minutes.

Example: Automating Report Formatting

- Go to **Developer › Record Macro**.
- Perform the formatting actions you want (bold headers, auto-fit columns, apply color).
- Stop recording and assign the Macro to a button or keyboard shortcut.
- Run it **instantly** whenever needed.

This alone can **save hours** each week if you work with recurring reports.

5. Excel's Hidden Productivity Boosters

- **Flash Fill (Ctrl + E):** Let Excel **predict patterns** and fill data for you.
- **Power Query:** Automate **data cleaning** from different sources.
- **Dynamic Arrays:** Use formulas like `SORT()`, `FILTER()`, and `UNIQUE()` to **eliminate manual sorting and filtering**.

By setting up your **Speed-Boost Command Center**, you'll **outpace 90% of Excel users**—turning every spreadsheet into a **seamless, efficient, and time-saving machine**.

Chapter 17 – Quick Reference Toolkit: Your Excel Survival Kit

The Perfection Checklist

Creating an Excel file that is **error-free, visually clean, and easy to navigate** isn't just a luxury—it's a necessity. Whether you're preparing reports for executives, analyzing business performance, or sharing a collaborative spreadsheet, the smallest mistake can **cost time, money, and credibility**. That's where **The Perfection Checklist** comes in—a structured **quality control system** for ensuring every Excel file is **flawless before it's shared or used** for critical decisions.

1. Data Integrity: Accuracy First

Mistakes in data lead to incorrect conclusions, wasted efforts, and bad decisions. Before finalizing any spreadsheet, **verify** its accuracy with these steps:

- **Check for errors:** Use `Ctrl + ~` to quickly inspect formulas instead of values.
- **Validate references:** Ensure formulas reference the **correct cells and ranges**—no accidental links to unrelated data.
- **Spot duplicates:** Use `Conditional Formatting > Highlight Duplicates` or `Remove Duplicates` to clean up redundant data.
- **Run error checks:** `Formulas > Error Checking` helps catch #VALUE!, #DIV/0!, and other common formula mistakes.

2. Formatting for Clarity and Readability

Excel files should be **visually intuitive** so users can immediately understand **what matters most**. A well-formatted spreadsheet is **self-explanatory, easy to scan, and free of clutter**.

- **Freeze panes for navigation:** Use `View > Freeze Panes` to keep headers visible when scrolling.
- **Apply consistent number formatting:** Avoid mixing **currency, percentages, and decimal places** in the same column.
- **Use cell styles sparingly:** Stick to one or two highlight colors—**over-formatting confuses the eye**.
- **AutoFit columns and rows:** Use `Alt + H + O + I` to prevent truncated data.

3. Formula Reliability: No Hidden Surprises

Formulas are Excel's **superpower**, but even a minor **miscalculation** can lead to major consequences.

- **Avoid hardcoded numbers:** If a formula contains a fixed number instead of referencing a cell, it's a red flag.
- **Test with dummy data:** Plug in unexpected values to see if the formula **handles edge cases correctly**.
- **Use `IFERROR` wisely:** Don't hide mistakes—use `IFERROR(value, "Check Input")` instead of just `" "` or `0`.

- **Audit formulas with Trace Precedents/Dependents:** (`Formulas > Trace Precedents`) helps **track relationships between cells**.

4. Security and Protection: Locking Down What Matters

If your file contains **sensitive data**, **important calculations**, or **shared inputs**, you don't want someone accidentally deleting or modifying **critical elements**.

- **Protect key worksheets:** Use `Review > Protect Sheet` to prevent **accidental edits** to locked cells.
- **Restrict user access:** Define who can edit, comment, or view using **Excel's permissions** (`File > Info > Protect Workbook`).
- **Use Data Validation:** Prevent incorrect inputs by **restricting** users to a pre-defined list or numerical range.

5. Final Review: Is Your File Executive-Ready?

Before saving or sharing, run this **last-minute checklist** to ensure **your Excel file looks professional and polished**:

- **Spell Check (`F7`):** Even in Excel, typos **ruin credibility**.
- **Check for hidden sheets:** Unhide (`Right-click > Unhide`) any sheet that **should be visible**.
- **File size optimization:** Remove excess formatting, unused sheets, and volatile functions (`File > Check for Issues`).
- **Test on another computer:** Open the file on a **different screen or Excel version**—does it still look good?

With this **Perfection Checklist**, your Excel files will always be **error-free, structured for clarity, and optimized for efficiency**.

Chapter 17 – Quick Reference Toolkit: Your Excel Survival Kit

Excel Glossary

Excel is packed with functions, formulas, and tools that can transform raw data into actionable insights. But let's be honest—sometimes the **terminology alone** can feel like a foreign language. Whether you're a beginner or an advanced user, understanding key Excel terms **at a glance** will save you time and frustration. Below is a **quick-reference glossary** to help you decode Excel's most essential terms, ensuring you always have the right tool for the job.

1. Essential Excel Terms

Active Cell

The currently selected cell in an Excel worksheet, indicated by a bold border. Anything you type or paste will appear in this cell.

Cell Address (Cell Reference)

The unique identifier for a cell, consisting of a column letter and a row number (e.g., `B3` refers to column B, row 3).

Worksheet vs. Workbook

- **Worksheet** – A single spreadsheet within an Excel file.
- **Workbook** – The entire Excel file, which may contain multiple worksheets.

Formula vs. Function

- **Formula** – A custom equation you create (e.g., `=A1+B1`).
- **Function – A built-in Excel command for calculations (e.g., `=SUM(A1:A10)`).**

Absolute vs. Relative References

- **Absolute Reference** (`$A$1`) – Stays fixed when copied to other cells.
- **Relative Reference** (`A1`) – Adjusts based on the new location when copied.

2. Power Functions & Calculations

SUM, AVERAGE, COUNT

- **SUM (`=SUM(A1:A10)`)** – Adds a range of numbers.
- **AVERAGE (`=AVERAGE(A1:A10)`)** – Finds the mean of a range.
- **COUNT (`=COUNT(A1:A10)`)** – Counts numeric values in a range.

IF, AND, OR

- **IF (`=IF(A1>10, "High", "Low")`)** – Returns one value if a condition is met, another if not.
- **AND (`=AND(A1>10, B1<5)`)** – Returns TRUE if **both** conditions are met.
- **OR (`=OR(A1>10, B1<5)`)** – Returns TRUE if **at least one** condition is met.

VLOOKUP, HLOOKUP, and XLOOKUP

- **VLOOKUP (`=VLOOKUP(lookup_value, table, column_index, FALSE)`)** – Searches for a value **vertically** in a column.

- **HLOOKUP (`=HLOOKUP(lookup_value, table, row_index, FALSE)`)** – Searches for a value **horizontally** in a row.
- **XLOOKUP (`=XLOOKUP(lookup_value, lookup_array, return_array)`)** – A modern, flexible alternative to VLOOKUP.

3. Formatting & Data Visualization

Conditional Formatting

Automatically changes a cell's color, font, or style based on a set condition (e.g., highlight values **above $1,000** in green).

Pivot Table

A tool that allows you to **summarize, analyze, and rearrange large data sets** with simple drag-and-drop functionality.

Data Validation

Restricts what users can enter in a cell (e.g., forcing a dropdown list or limiting numbers to a specific range).

4. Automation & Speed-Boosters

Macro

A recorded sequence of actions that **automates** repetitive Excel tasks **without coding**.

Power Query

An advanced data transformation tool for **cleaning, shaping, and combining large data sets** before analysis.

CTRL Shortcuts

- **CTRL + C / V / X** – Copy, Paste, Cut
- **CTRL + Z / Y** – Undo, Redo
- **CTRL + Arrow Keys** – Jump to the next filled cell in a direction

This **Excel Glossary** is your **go-to reference** for decoding Excel's most powerful tools—so you can **spend less time searching for answers and more time getting results.**

EXCEL-LERATION PACK

Congratulations! Your Professional Transformation Has Begun (But It's Not Over Yet)

I know you've spent endless hours wrestling with formulas that wouldn't work and chasing impossible deadlines. I completely understand the frustration of holding in your hands a tool with so much potential—like Excel—yet not fully knowing how to harness it.

With this book, however, you've already taken a huge step forward: you've learned how to turn a simple spreadsheet into a genuine career ally. Now comes the most crucial part: **APPLYING** what you've learned and putting into practice the techniques that can make you a go-to figure in your company. Reading accounts for only 20% of the work; the remaining 80% is your daily implementation.

Why Taking Action Right Now Makes All the Difference

If you stop here, you risk:

- **Staying in the shadows**, while more proactive colleagues catch the eye of higher-ups.
- **Missing out on growth and promotion opportunities**, because tangible results carry more weight than a thousand words.
- **Continuing to waste hours** on outdated reports, without ever finding the time for more rewarding strategic projects.
- **Seeming like "just another face in the crowd"**, never truly standing out as a leader.

Is that the future you want? A career where your potential remains untapped, your ideas go unnoticed, and doors close before you can even open them?

Your 3-Phase Action Plan

Phase 1: Daily Practice (Days 1-14)

Spend 20–30 minutes a day strengthening the skills you've just discovered:

- Recreate a report using advanced formulas (Chapter 7).
- Automate a repetitive task (Chapter 8).
- Turn raw data into a Pivot Table (Chapter 9).

Don't aim for perfection: focus on **continuous progress** and train your mind to see Excel as a tool for **competitive advantage**.

Phase 2: Strategic Implementation (Days 15-30)

Choose a high-visibility project:

- A monthly report reviewed by the entire team.
- An analysis your manager requested.
- A lingering problem that's been unsolved for far too long.

Apply your most advanced techniques: **build interactive dashboards**, automate complex calculations, and make data easy to interpret.

Phase 3: Professional Positioning (Days 31-60)

Now that you know what to do and how to do it, it's time to showcase your value:

- Organize a brief internal presentation to highlight your new analyses.
- Propose new report templates that simplify your department's work.
- Document the benefits you've achieved (time saved, fewer errors, impact on decisions).

This is where Excel stops being just a tool and becomes your **secret weapon** to stand out and gain credibility.

The Big Question: How Can You Speed Things Up?

Top professionals **act quickly** and know how to use the right tools. That's why I created the **Excel-leration Pack Bonus**: a comprehensive system that **condenses** a 60-day path into just two weeks.

What's Inside the Excel-leration Pack?

- **Visual Impact Arsenal:** Advanced formatting tools that make your reports pop at first glance. How to transform raw data into visually striking reports that catch your boss's and your clients' attention. You'll learn to use advanced conditional formatting, dynamic pivot tables, and interactive charts to communicate even complex information clearly and effectively!

- **Automation Productivity Suite:** Templates and automation systems that free you from hours of manual work each week. Tired of spending hours on repetitive tasks? In this module, you'll learn how to automate reports, analyses, and data management with the help of professionally pre-configured templates. Save valuable time and focus on what really matters!

- **Strategic Planning Powerhouse:** Forecasting and analytical systems that turn data into winning strategic decisions. Discover how to create detailed project plans and reliable forecasts that will set you apart as a high-level Project Coordinator. Master Excel techniques for project management that will impress your superiors! But your Excel-leration doesn't end here. You'll also find an additional module that will completely shift your perspective:

- **Excel R.O.I. Multipliers:** Five exclusive bonuses designed to give you an extra edge and help you achieve extraordinary results in record time. Get ready to radically transform the way you work and gain a competitive advantage in your field!

- » **Leadership Communication Kit:** Communicate with Impact to Management: Executive presentation templates, persuasive email scripts, objection-handling strategies, and data storytelling techniques. Prepare your next presentation with confidence and earn the recognition you deserve.
- » **Career Evolution Map:** Plan Your Professional Growth: A guided workbook to document your Excel skills, track your progress, define career goals, and create a personalized action plan for success.
- » **Analysis Accelerator Pack:** Advanced Data Analysis Tools: Advanced statistical functions, regression analysis, sensitivity analysis, and simulations. Deepen your analytical skills and make strategic, data-driven decisions.
- » **Dashboard Success Kit:** Design Interactive, Engaging Dashboards: Best practices for data visualization, design methods for effective dashboards, and examples of interactive dashboards. Create dashboards that grab attention and clearly communicate key insights.
- » **Implementation Timeline:** A weekly/monthly plan to gradually integrate these skills into your everyday workflow.

Think you'll have to reinvent the wheel? Not at all. This pack is designed to save you time and deliver **tangible** results as quickly as possible.

Just Imagine What Could Happen as Soon as Tomorrow...

- An automated report that frees you from tedious formulas, showing you that just a few clicks can keep your data up-to-date.
- A dashboard that wows your superiors, instantly making you the go-to expert.
- A clear, impactful presentation that earns you trust and support for your initiatives.

Take Charge of Your Professional Future

The risk of "doing nothing" is huge: you may keep doing what everyone else does and remain stuck in a cycle of mediocrity, with little chance of advancing. Instead, with the Excel-leration Pack, you'll **turbocharge** everything you've learned so far, ensuring that your potential won't go to waste.

Every day you spend "thinking about it" is a day lost for demonstrating your true worth.

Your Final Move: Scan the QR Code

- Scan the QR Code shown here.

- Download your Excel-leration Pack Bonus.
- Elevate your projects to a higher level in record time.

You've put in time and effort to get this far. Now it's up to you to **capitalize** on it. Don't just stand by; **act** and prepare for a career leap that will surprise even you.

See you on the other side.

Good luck and here's to your professional transformation!

Alex

Printed in Dunstable, United Kingdom

68821374R10098